W9-BYT-125

Black and Mormon

Black and Mormon

Edited by
Newell G. Bringhurst
and Darron T. Smith

UNIVERSITY OF ILLINOIS PRESS
URBANA AND CHICAGO

© 2004 by the Board of Trustees
of the University of Illinois
All rights reserved
Manufactured in the United States of America
C 5 4 3 2 1

∞ This book is printed on acid-free paper.

Library of Congress Cataloging-in-Publication Data
Black and Mormon / edited by Newell G. Bringhurst
and Darron T. Smith.
p.   cm.
Includes bibliographical references and index.
ISBN 0-252-02947-X (cloth : alk. paper)
1. African American Mormons.
I. Bringhurst, Newell G.
II. Smith, Darron T., 1965–
BX8643.A35B57   2004
289.3'089'96073—dc22   2004003479

To Carolyn Smith
and to the memory of Alice Cooper Bringhurst,
our mothers,
who instilled in us a fundamental thirst
for knowledge and a desire to pursue basic truth

CONTENTS

ACKNOWLEDGMENTS

The coeditors wish to acknowledge a number of individuals whose help was invaluable in the preparation of this volume. Essential are the seven authors who have contributed essays, namely Alma Allred, Ronald G. Coleman, Darius A. Gray, Jessie L. Embry, Armand L. Mauss, Cardell K. Jacobson, and Ken Driggs. Armand Mauss, moreover, offered important suggestions in reading and critiquing several of the individual essays, allowing the coeditors to benefit from his extensive knowledge of Mormon-black race relations. Important insights were also provided by Wilfred D. Samuels, director of the Black Studies Department at the University of Utah; Audrey Thompson, William Smith, and Edward Buendia, professors in the Department of Education, Culture, and Society at the University of Utah; Cliff Mayes and Scott Ferrin, Department of Educational Leadership and Foundations, David O. McKay School of Education, Brigham Young University; and Margaret Blair Young, Department of English, Brigham Young University.

Liz Dulany, acquisitions editor at the University of Illinois Press, has been essential in facilitating the process of revision and editing. Her sagacious insights and suggestions have been useful in improving the scholarly content and literary quality of this volume.

Finally, most critical to making this volume a reality has been the encouragement and forbearance of our wives, Mary Ann and Joy, both of whom tolerated our numerous long-distance, long-winded telephone conversations as we struggled to hammer out the form and features of this work.

INTRODUCTION

NEWELL G. BRINGHURST AND DARRON T. SMITH

Friday, June 9, 1978, "the long promised day" when Latter-day Saints Church officials announced that "all worthy male members of the church [could] be ordained to the priesthood without regard for race or color," was like no other day in the history of the church. The historic policy change came through "revelation," according to the church's First Presidency announcement, after Spencer W. Kimball, the LDS president, spent "many hours in the upper room of the Temple supplicating the Lord for divine guidance."[1] This momentous day eliminating Mormonism's long-standing ban on black priesthood ordination was dubbed, with some irony, "Black Friday" by an Associated Press writer, David Briscoe, who speculated about its "blessed implications."[2]

Indeed, the implications were epic. Within Utah, the state's largest daily newspaper, the *Salt Lake Tribune,* editorialized that "a burden has been lifted from all Utahans, whether members of the LDS faith or of other beliefs." It characterized the just-lifted black priesthood ban as "an irritating barrier to better human relationships, in this state and wherever Utahns go."[3] Outside of Utah, the black priesthood revelation received extensive media coverage. "Nearly every major newspaper" in the United States carried the announcement "as front-page news."[4] The church's announcement was the lead story on the NBC network's widely watched *Nightly News.* It even elicited comment from the U.S. president, Jimmy Carter, who commended Kimball for his "compassionate prayerfulness and courage in receiving [this] new doctrine."[5]

Scholars both within and outside of the LDS Church also weighed in. One noted non-Mormon scholar, Mario S. De Pillis, a professor of history at the University of Massachusetts, Amherst, stated in a *New York Times* essay that "the new priesthood revelation [differed] in magnitude" from earlier revelations in that it reclassified "a whole segment of humanity."[6] Professor Jan Shipps of

Indiana University, also a non-Mormon academician and then the incoming president of the Mormon History Association, commented in the pages of the *Christian Century*. She characterized the now-defunct prohibition on black priesthood ordination as "a crucial obstacle which almost certainly would have prevented the LDS church from ever becoming a universal church."[7]

Speaking from within the LDS community, Sterling M. McMurrin, professor of philosophy at the University of Utah, a leading Mormon intellectual, the U.S. Commissioner of Education under President John F. Kennedy, and a long-time critic of the restrictive practice, characterized June 9, 1978, as "the most important day for the church in this century."[8] Later McMurrin went even further, commenting that Kimball "in one stroke . . . transformed a parochial religion into a universal religion." Underscoring the announcement's significance, he called it "the most important event in the church since its founding."[9] Dallin H. Oaks, a former president of the LDS Church–owned Brigham Young University and a member of the church's elite Quorum of the Twelve Apostles, echoed this view. Reflecting on this event in 1988, Oaks stated that "it is difficult to overstate [the] importance" of the black revelation "in the fulfillment of divine command that the gospel must go to every nation, kindred and people."[10]

Those individuals most directly affected—African American Latter-day Saints—also stressed the importance of this change. Monroe Fleming, a popular speaker at church functions and civic organizations, expressed the complex, varied feelings of those individuals when he confessed that he had "yearned for this day [and] prayed for this day," adding that being black and being Mormon is no longer "feeling you're a guest in your father's house."[11] He then predicted: "It will take some time for the Negro people to adjust themselves to [this] quick change. But eventually, it will attract a lot more black people to the church." Fleming called on his fellow Latter-day Saints to "join hands and move forward . . . [and] just forget about the past."[12]

Similarly, James Dawson, one of two black members of the famed Mormon Tabernacle Choir and an employee at the Mormon church headquarters, was "overjoyed . . . for the fact that blacks can now receive the priesthood" and that "this gives the gospel a much greater opportunity to be heard worldwide."[13] Ruffin Bridgeforth, president of the Genesis Group, an officially sanctioned organization of black Latter-day Saints, characterized Friday, June 9, as "the greatest day" of his life.[14] Bridgeforth went further in speculating on the millenarian implications of this change: "I think that we are getting close to the end of times because I think that we perhaps have reached a state of brotherhood or at least a partial state."[15]

Attracting the most widespread attention, at least in the short run, was a twenty-six-year-old African American Mormon, Joseph Freeman, a member of the Granger Fifteenth Ward in the Granger Utah North Stake in the Salt Lake Valley. On Sunday, June 10, 1978, Freeman was ordained an elder in the Melchizedek priesthood during what was reported to be a "simple and brief ceremony."[16] The semi-official *Deseret News* described Freeman as "the first black ordained to the priesthood of The Church of Jesus Christ of Latter-day Saints in this era."[17] Less than two weeks later, on June 23, Freeman and his wife, Toa, "were married in the Salt Lake Temple" and "sealed along" with their two young sons, three-year-old Alexander and two-year-old Zachariah.[18] The ordination of Joseph Freeman and the subsequent temple sealing of his family provided tangible proof of the church's newly affirmed commitment to accept blacks in full fellowship.

The momentous importance of the Mormon black revelation notwithstanding, Latter-day Saint leaders and official spokesmen were curiously low-keyed in their reaction to the revelation. Most striking was the *Deseret News,* which merely carried the text of the official First Presidency statement under the somewhat vague headline, "LDS Church Extends Priesthood to All Worthy Male Members."[19] There was nothing more. Paul Swenson, a journalist, explained this tactic: "Word came down from church authorities" to the editorial staff of the *Deseret News* "that the First Presidency statement was to stand on its own and that no additional story was necessary." William B. Smart, editor of the *Deseret News,* said that "further comment on the revelation seemed inappropriate" and would "be gilding the lily," given that Latter-day Saints "believed the announcement meant 'God had spoken.'"[20] As if to underscore this position, the official *Church News* supplement to the *Deseret News* did not feature the black revelation as its cover story for its issue published immediately after the black revelation.[21]

Most emphatic in maintaining a position of relative silence was none other than Spencer W. Kimball. According to the recollections of his son and chief biographer, Edward L. Kimball, the president "asked those involved not to publicize or argue or explain the new doctrine. 'Let it stand on its own,'" the elder Kimball stated. Edward Kimball added, "He wanted it to be what it was without interpretations and explanations." The Mormon leader "simply moved on to the next thing he was supposed to do."[22]

Such avoidance represented a double-edged sword. On the one hand, it allowed the church to move forward vigorously in accepting blacks in full fellowship without having to confront the unpleasant, negative historical and theological questions in justifying the now-defunct practice. But at the same time, the failure to discuss these issues allowed a pernicious racist folklore to persist, which, in turn, hindered long-range Latter-day Saint efforts at prose-lytizing among African Americans.

Also problematic was the way in which the church dealt with critical his-torical issues involving blacks in the early Mormon church. Their experiences and treatment were obscured and/or misrepresented in official church publi-cations, particularly in the immediate aftermath of the black revelation. The *Church News* for June 17, 1978, in an essay entitled "Prophets Tell of Promise to All Races," quoted two ambiguous statements by Joseph Smith and Brigham Young, asserting that each had "spoken of the day when the blessings of the priesthood would come to blacks." But, in fact, neither statement referred to the specific issue of priesthood ordination for black Mormon men. (Mormon women have never been ordained.) Two crucial historical facts were complete-ly left out of this essay: first, that Joseph Smith had allowed for the ordination of blacks as founder and leader of the LDS Church; and second, that Brigham Young, not Joseph Smith, initiated the practice of denying blacks the priest-hood. Young did so in the 1840s as leader of the church following Joseph Smith's death in 1844.[23]

A second article in the same issue of the *Church News,* entitled "Since Ear-ly Church Days, Blacks Have Set an Example," failed to inform its readers of the true status of Elijah Abel, whom it described as "one of the first black mem-bers . . . who joined the Church in September 1832." This article left out the fact that Abel had been ordained to the Melchizedek priesthood during the 1830s—first to the office of elder and then a Seventy.[24] It also omitted any mention of a second important early African American Latter-day Saint, Wal-ker Lewis, a barber in Lowell, Massachusetts, who was ordained an elder by William Smith, a younger brother of Joseph Smith. This incomplete histori-cal account misrepresented the true status of black Latter-day Saints in the early LDS Church. But perhaps more important, it deprived contemporary African Americans, both within Mormonism and in American society at large, of positive role models from the early Latter-day Saint movement.

Indeed, after 1978, church spokesmen considered any reference or "re-membrance of" Mormonism's "racial past . . . an embarrassment and a hin-drance to multiracial evangelism"—that is, to the church's efforts to preach the message of Mormonism "without regard for race or color." These are the acute observations of Richard N. Ostling and Joan K. Ostling.[25] The signifi-cance of the 1978 revelation was downplayed in the textbook distributed by the Church Education System and used in its high school seminary system.[26] This work contains just "ten words about the revelation" buried in a "laun-dry list" of other events during the Spencer W. Kimball administration, according to the Ostlings, who also point out that the textbook never mentioned "race or the long-standing [black priesthood] ban."[27]

The church's position on interracial marriage was also problematic at the time of the black revelation. Don LeFevre, a church spokesman, stated that "interracial marriages generally have been discouraged in the past and until the Prophet [President Spencer W. Kimball] further elaborates on the subject, that remains our position." Expanding on this point, LeFevre stated that the church "discourages [interracial marriage] by counseling its members to consider the potential negative impact of different backgrounds and cultures on marriages and on the posterity of the union." In quoting Kimball the statement continued, "marriage is a very difficult thing under any circumstances and the difficulty increases in interracial marriages." Yet, at the same time, LeFevre emphasized that "the Church does not prohibit, nor can it prohibit interracial marriages but it does discourage them."[28] The recently ordained and temple-sealed Joseph Freeman was immediately and directly affected by this position. His wife, Toa, was Samoan and had served a mission for the church prior to her marriage to Freeman.[29] Thus the church's policy relative to interracial marriage appeared confusing, contradictory, and ambiguous.

In contrast, Latter-day Saint leaders were very clear and concise concerning their position on women's admission to the priesthood, which remained one of adamant opposition. "The priesthood is something sacred," stated President Kimball, "and was established by the Lord for the men in his kingdom." Kimball further explained: "We pray to God to reveal his mind and we always will, but we don't expect any revelation regarding women and the priesthood." He said that "the Church . . . gives women just as much prominence and importance as men, but [it is] a different kind of prominence."[30] Kimball stated his opposition to female priesthood ordination even more emphatically in *Time* magazine in explaining Mormon opposition to the Equal Rights Amendment. The amendment had passed Congress and was making its way through state legislatures toward ratification, an effort that failed, at least in part, due to the LDS Church's vigorous and well-organized opposition. "Unlike blacks," the Mormon leader said, "it is impossible that women would ever attain the priesthood."[31] "The question of female ordination is not even an issue among Mormon women," *Newsweek* magazine asserted with some understatement, pointing out that their "religious obligation is to be good wives and mothers."[32]

Despite lingering ambivalence concerning interracial marriage and unresolved issues involving the historic status of blacks in early Mormonism, Latter-day Saint officials quickly reached out to African Americans in the immediate aftermath of the 1978 revelation. They did so with a twofold purpose: to improve relations with the African American community in general and, more important, to attract black converts to the faith. In fact, the total number of black Latter-day Saints was thought to be minuscule in 1978. According to *Newsweek*, "most estimates [ranged] between 1,000 and 5,000" out of a total LDS Church membership of 4.2 million.[33]

Almost immediately, Kimball called for the extension of Mormon missionary activity to "America's inner cities" as well as to predominately black sub-Saharan Africa.[34] In this same spirit, he urged "a doubling" of Mormonism's missionary force worldwide. "In view of recent revelations—the blacks holding the priesthood—we can use many more missionaries in the United States," the Mormon leader added, in order to reach more effectively the "great abundance of these people."[35]

The results of such Mormon missionary activity have proved mixed over the course of the years since the revelation. Most visibly, a handful of prominent, high-profile African Americans have joined the church. Among the first was Eldridge Cleaver, one-time radical Black Panther Party leader and 1968 presidential candidate for the Peace and Freedom Party, who was baptized in 1982 and ordained to the Aaronic priesthood shortly thereafter. Cleaver's conversion was widely noted in newspapers and magazines throughout the United States. Unfortunately, Cleaver's active involvement with the church was short lived, although he remained a member of record up until his death in May 1998.[36]

A second prominent African American, the rhythm-and-blues singer Gladys Knight, joined the church in August 1997. Widely known as the one-time lead singer for the performing group Gladys Knight and the Pips, Knight has continued to perform on her own before various audiences, both within and outside of the LDS community, thereby attracting widespread media attention.[37] Particularly noteworthy was her performance as a featured artist at "An Evening of Celebration" in honor of LDS President Gordon B. Hinckley's ninetieth birthday on June 23, 2000, held before an audience of twenty-one thousand in the LDS Conference Center in Salt Lake City.[38] Prominent among a number of African American athletes who have embraced Mormonism are the one-time Utah Jazz professional basketball player-turned-singer Thurl Bailey and two professional football players, Burgess Owens and Jamal Willis, who played for the Oakland Raiders and San Francisco 49ers, respectively.[39]

The number of less-prominent African Americans who joined the church after 1978 has not been as well publicized. By 1988 there were "an estimated 100,000 to 125,000 black members throughout the world," representing "at least fifty times as many as 10 years ago," according to the *Los Angeles Times* columnist Russell J. Chandler.[40] However, the overwhelming majority of this total resided in sub-Saharan Africa, Brazil, and throughout other parts of Latin America, where Mormonism had much greater appeal than among American blacks. A more modest figure of "several thousand" African American Latter-day Saints as of 1988 was offered as a "guesstimate" by Alan Cherry, an African American Latter-day Saint scholar.[41] He along with Jessie L. Embry, then director of the oral history program at BYU's Charles Redd Center of Western History, interviewed several hundred black Latter-day Saints as part of an extensive oral history project during the late 1980s. Some six years later Embry herself estimated that the number of African American Mormons had "grown to thousands."[42]

Since Embry made her estimate, however, the number of African American Latter-day Saints does not appear to have grown significantly. Worse still, among those blacks who have joined, the average attrition rate appears to be extremely high. One survey found that the attrition rate among African American converts was 60 to 90 percent in Columbia, South Carolina, and Greensboro, North Carolina. Commenting on this survey, Richard and Joan Ostling noted, "If these two towns are at all typical, there is a major, if unacknowledged problem."[43]

The reasons for Mormonism's limited appeal among African Americans are varied and complex, and this is a key issue considered in the essays in this volume. Arguably, the church has not done enough to rectify its racist past, which remains a major obstacle in its mission to teach, convert, fellowship, and retain African Americans. To change its image as a racist organization, the church needs to forthrightly confront its past history of racial exclusion and discrimination. Admittedly this constitutes a challenging undertaking given the pervasiveness and persistence of racism in American society at large, where it is evident in virtually all institutions and organizations including many religions.

To understand the problem of race in contemporary American society, it is essential to recognize that racism is commonly expressed in multiple and complex ways. Racism is often misunderstood as being limited to overt acts of individual aggression against others of a different race. Such a definition assumes that only individuals are involved in racist practices, overlooking the critical role of institutions in shaping people's attitudes, or discounting institutional involvement as rare or nonexistent in supporting racist outlooks. A narrow personalized notion of individual racism ignores and obfuscates the reality of institutional racism, in which individuals speak and act on behalf of a particular group or organization.

Complicating the problem of institutional racism is the fact that when racism is discussed, there is a tendency to distort the historical conditions that led to its evolution in the first place. Essential to the development of American racism were the successive institutions of slavery, sharecropping, and legalized segregation (Jim Crowism), as well as other, more subtle practices. These pernicious developments helped to form negative racial stereotypes of black Americans as the racialized "other." This in turn has influenced basic modes of interaction within contemporary social institutions, including the LDS Church. Indeed, most Americans, including Latter-day Saints, generally see themselves in relation to others through the prism of racial differences.

Racial differences promote ethnocentric language usage in which color is used to symbolize sharp moral differences. In white European cultural discourse, black or blackness symbolizes danger and evil. In moral contrast, white or whiteness symbolizes hope and virtue. The representational use of black stereotypes is pervasive in American cultural, political, and economic life and, among other things, reinforces white Americans' sense of moral superiority in relation to people of color. In the course of its development as an American religion, the LDS Church not only incorporated many of these highly negative cultural connotations associated with blackness into its own moral vocabulary, but also added an important religious element of theological and scriptural racist folklore to its institutional practices. In particular, Latter-day Saints came to believe that nonwhite races were cursed by God on the basis of melanin. For example, the LDS apostle Bruce R. McConkie, now deceased, affirmed that blacks were not to hold the priesthood because they were not equal with people of other races.[44] McConkie's assertion is, unfortunately, not unique. All too many Latter-day Saints, particularly among the rank-and-file church membership, continue to embrace similarly negative beliefs relative to people of African descent.

Latter-day Saints' moral expressions of blackness versus whiteness take on special significance, given various LDS scriptural writings, especially passages in the Book of Mormon and the Pearl of Great Price. The Book of Mormon is replete with racial code words affirming the inherent negativity of dark or black skin color. Blackness in the Book of Mormon is presented as a sign or punishment for not obeying God's law. In contrast, various populations in the Book of Mormon who kept the laws of God are described as "pure and wholesome" and/or "white and delightsome."[45] Negative Book of Mormon terminology traditionally has been used to explain the racialized experiences of people who fell out of favor with God. It is not uncommon for LDS Church members to speak of rescuing the so-called Lamanite population (the indigenous peoples of Latin and North America) from its own spiritual demise. Numerous references in the Book of Mormon maintain that "gentiles" (white people) are supposed to take the gospel to the Lamanites. Along with this scriptural injunction persists a racist folklore belief that a literal whitening of the skin will occur as these same dark-skinned Laminates accept the teachings of the LDS Church.[46]

The eight essays contained in this volume explore the varied issues affecting African Americans in the LDS Church, focusing on the period since 1978 and revolving around three fundamental issues: progress, continuing problems, and prospects for the future. Each essay explores a different aspect of that experience from the perspective of developments occurring over the past twenty-six years. The nine authors, each of whom has previously researched and written on this topic, bring their knowledge, expertise, and differing perspectives to their respective essays.

The book examines Mormon historical/scriptural perceptions of African Americans as they have evolved over the past quarter century. It analyzes the extent to which African Americans have been attracted to Mormonism, reports the differing experiences of African American Latter-day Saints following conversion, and discusses the varied reception given African American Mormons by nonblack, predominantly white Latter-day Saints on all levels—from the church hierarchy down to the "grass roots."

The first four essays consider these issues from a historical/scriptural perspective. Newell G. Bringhurst, in his essay "The 'Missouri Thesis' Revisited: Early Mormonism, Slavery, and the Status of Black People," critically reevaluates the so-called "Missouri Thesis." This was long considered by observers, both within and outside of Mormonism, as the basis for the denial of black priesthood. In the second essay, "The Traditions of Their Fathers: Myth vs. Reality in LDS Scriptural Writings," Alma Allred critically examines and deconstructs myths concerning the alleged ancestors of contemporary blacks as presented in LDS scriptural writings. The third essay, coauthored by Ronald G. Coleman and Darius A. Gray, is "Two Perspectives: The Religious Hopes of 'Worthy' African American Latter-day Saints before the 1978 Revelation." It provides a detailed examination of two African American Latter-day Saints whose experiences predate the 1978 revelation. Similarly, Jessie L. Embry, in her "Spanning the Priesthood Revelation: Two Multigenerational Case Studies," provides an additional historical dimension in chronicling the experiences of African American Latter-day Saints.

The final four essays focus on the contemporary situation of African American Latter-day Saints, examining what could be termed the "three P's": progress enjoyed thus far, problems that continue, and potential for African Americans that has yet to be realized within Mormonism. Armand L. Mauss provides a comprehensive overview of all these three issues in his "Casting Off the 'Curse of Cain': Extent and Limits of Progress since 1978." Cardell K. Jacobson documents through careful quantification these same issues in "African American Latter-day Saints: A Sociological Perspective." Ken Driggs emphasizes progress in "'How Do Things Look on the Ground?': The LDS African American Community in Atlanta, Georgia." Darron T. Smith is more critical in examining problems plaguing African American Latter-day Saints, in his "Unpacking Whiteness in Zion: Some Personal Reflections and General Observations."

The primary goal of this volume is to inform the reader about the current situation of African American Latter-day Saints as it has evolved over the past quarter century. But it is hoped that these essays will also stimulate continuing open discussion concerning persistent problems involving race and racism, along with prospects for future progress. Indeed, the ideal goal for African Americans relative to Mormonism is best articulated in the Book of Mormon passage 2 Nephi 26:33. "And he [Christ] inviteth them all to come unto him, black and white, bond and free, male and female; and he remembereth the heathen; and all are alike unto God, both Jew and Gentile."

Notes

1. "LDS Church Extends Priesthood to All Worthy Male Members," *Deseret News,* June 9, 1978. The statement was later printed as Official Declaration No. 2, dated June 8, 1978, in *The Doctrine and Covenants of the Church of Jesus Christ of Latter-day Saints* (Salt Lake City: Church of Jesus Christ of Latter-day Saints, 1981).

2. David Briscoe and George Buck, "Black Friday—Its Blessed Implications," *Utah Holiday,* July 1978, 38–40.

3. "A Burden Is Lifted" (editorial), *Salt Lake Tribune,* June 11, 1978.

4. "Reaction to Revelation Varies," *Church News* (weekly supplement in LDS Church-owned *Deseret News*), July 15, 1978, 4.

5. "Carter Praises LDS Church Action," *Deseret News,* June 10, 1978, A-1.

6. Mario S. De Pillis, "Mormons Get Revelations Often, But Not Like This," *New York Times,* June 11, 1978, E-10.

7. Jan Shipps, "The Mormons: Looking Forward and Outward," *Christian Century,* August 16–23, 1978, 761.

8. "Carter Praises LDS Church Action," A-1.

9. Quoted in Dawn House, "A Heretic? U. Professor Distrusts LDS Orthodoxy, Pursues Reason," *Salt Lake Tribune,* November 20, 1988, B-1.

10. Quoted in Kevin Stoker, "LDS Blacks Hoping to Become 'Generic' in Growing Church," *Church News,* June 18, 1988.

11. Charles J. Seldin, "Priesthood of LDS Opened to Blacks," *Salt Lake Tribune,* June 10, 1978, A-1; idem, "No Longer Guest in 'Father's Home,'" *Kokomo (Ind.) Tribune,* June 11, 1978 (Fleming quote).

12. Quoted in Seldin, "Priesthood of LDS Opened to Blacks," A-1.

13. "Priesthood News Evokes Joy," *Church News,* June 17, 1978, 2–3.

14. Quoted in "No Longer Guest in 'Father's Home.'"

15. Quoted in Seldin, "Priesthood of LDS Opened to Blacks," A-1.

16. Lance Gudmundsen, "Black Enters LDS Priesthood, Shatters Long-Time Practice," *Salt Lake Tribune,* June 12, 1978, B-1, B-4. See also Twila Van Leer, "Black LDS Priesthood Holder Says, 'It's a Beautiful Day,'" *Deseret News,* June 12, 1978, A-1. According to this second article, on the same day, a second African American Latter-day Saint, Charles Turner, a member of the Butler Twenty-second Ward, Butler Utah West Stake, also in Salt Lake Valley, was ordained to the office of priest in the Aaronic priesthood.

17. Van Leer, "Black LDS Priesthood Holder." Less definitive concerning Freeman's status as Mormonism's first ordained black was "Reaction to Revelation Varies," an article in *Church News* (July 15, 1978, 4), which states that Freeman is "believed to be the first black since the announcement to be ordained to the priesthood." Gudmundsen ("Black Enters LDS Priesthood," B-1) states that the ordination of Freeman "broke nearly a century and half practice" of prohibiting blacks from holding the Mormon priesthood, suggesting that Mormonism had never ordained blacks to the priesthood. Briscoe and Buck ("Black Friday," 38) are more accurate in noting that Joseph Freeman was "the first black Mormon elder of modern times" and that Joseph Smith had authorized the ordination of "at least one black, Elijah Abel."

18. Gudmundsen, "Black Enters LDS Priesthood," B-1 (quote); Van Leer, "Black LDS Priesthood Holder," B-1.

19. "LDS Church Extends Priesthood to All Worthy Male Members," *Deseret News,* June 9, 1978, A-1.

20. Paul Swenson, "Muting the Message," *Utah Holiday* 7 (July 1978): 18.

21. "Sound of a Trump, Ted Lewis, Victor Bowman and Jeffery Novak Lend LDS Note to U.S. Air Force Band," cover story, *Church News,* June 17, 1978.

22. Edward L. Kimball, quoting Spencer W. Kimball, in Heidi Swinton, "One More Lengthening Stride," *This People,* Summer 1988, 22.

23. "Prophets Tell of Promise to All Races," *Church News,* June 17, 1978, 4.

24. "Since Early Church Days, Blacks Have Set an Example," *Church News,* June 17, 1978, 6.

25. Richard N. Ostling and Joan K. Ostling, *Mormon America: The Power and the Promise* (New York: Harper San Francisco, 1999), 102.

26. The LDS seminary is a system of weekday religious instruction for high school students, usually conducted early in the morning or on a released-time basis.

27. Ostling and Ostling, *Mormon America,* 102.

28. "Mixed Marriages 'Discouraged,'" *Salt Lake Tribune,* June 18, 1978, C-2.

29. Van Leer, "Black LDS Priesthood Holder," A-1.

30. "Not for Women," *Deseret News,* June 13, 1978.

31. Quoted in "Mormonism Enters a New Era," *Time,* August 7, 1978, 56.

32. Kenneth L. Woodward, "Race Revelations," *Newsweek,* June 19, 1978, 67.

33. Ibid. In an article entitled "Revelation," *Time* (June 19, 1978, 55) provides a somewhat lower estimate of "fewer than 1,000" blacks in the entire Church. The difficulty of arriving at a precise total is compounded by the fact that the LDS Church, despite maintaining prodigious and complete membership records, does not specify race or ethnicity.

34. "Not for Women."

35. "President Kimball Wants Missionary Force Doubled," *Ensign,* August 1978, 79.

36. See the discussion in Newell G. Bringhurst, "Eldridge Cleaver's Passage through Mormonism," *Journal of Mormon History* 28 (Spring 2002): 80–110.

37. See Paul Swenson, "Gladys and Thurl: The Changing Face of Mormon Diversity," *Sunstone,* July 2001, 14–16; Anna Gabriel, "Gladys Knight Sings New Song since Her Conversion A Year Ago," *Church News,* October 31, 1998, 7; David Nathan, "Soulful Knight Heads down a Gospel Road," *Fresno Bee,* May 30, 1999, H-3. Knight's autobiography, *Between Each Line of Pain and Glory: My Life Story* (New York: Hyperion Books, 1997), discusses her activities before her LDS baptism.

38. "Happy Birthday, Pres. Hinckley—Artists Line Up," *Church News,* June 17, 2000; Sarah Jane Weaver, "An Evening of Celebration," *Church News,* July 1, 2000, 3, 6.

39. Swenson, "Gladys and Thurl," 14–16; R. Scott Lloyd, "Gospel Gives NBA Vet 'Foundation,'" *Church News,* October 2, 1999, 11; "Former Oakland Raiders Player Able to Take 'Big Step' on Faith," *Church News,* September 2, 1989, 10; Gordon Monson, "Willis Learns to Let It Be," *Salt Lake Tribune,* August 7, 2001, D-1, D-5.

40. Russell J. Chandler, "Mormonism: A Challenge for Blacks," *Los Angeles Times,* August 12, 1988, 4, 28–30.

41. Quoted in ibid.

42. Jessie L. Embry, *Black Saints in a White Church* (Salt Lake City, Utah: Signature Books, 1994), xiii.

43. Ostling and Ostling, *Mormon America,* 378.

44. According to Bruce R. McConkie, *Mormon Doctrine* (Salt Lake City: Deseret Book, 1957): "Negroes in this life are denied the priesthood; under no circumstances can they hold this delegation of authority from the Almighty. The gospel message of salvation is not carried affirmatively to them. . . . Negroes are not equal with other races where the receipts of certain spiritual blessings are concerned" (343). This is the first edition of *Mormon Doctrine.* The second edition of *Mormon Doctrine* (Salt Lake City: Bookcraft, 1966) uses the same language (527). This passage was deleted in post-1978 printings.

45. For example, the first (1830) edition of the Book of Mormon describes God's punishment upon the Lamanites for their unrighteousness: "Wherefore, as they were white, and exceedingly fair and delightsome, that they might not be enticing unto my people the Lord God did cause a skin of blackness to come upon them . . . that they shall be loathsome unto thy people [the Nephites]." However, if they repent, "many generations shall not pass away among them, save they shall be a white and a delightsome people" (72–73, 117). The first edition is not divided into chapters and verses. In 1981, when the current edition was prepared, the editors left the first passage unchanged (2 Ne. 5:21–22), but changed the second one to read: "save they shall be a pure and a delightsome people" (2 Ne. 30:6).

46. Significant in arguing this point is Thomas W. Murphy's essay "Lamanite Genesis, Genealogy, and Genetics," in *American Apocrypha,* ed. Dan Vogel and Brent Metcalfe (Salt Lake City: Signature Books, 2002), 47–48.

The "Missouri Thesis" Revisited:
Early Mormonism, Slavery, and the
Status of Black People

NEWELL G. BRINGHURST

The "Missouri thesis" was at one time seen as the key to understanding the origins of the ban on black priesthood ordination in the LDS Church.
The thesis developed within the context of the so-called new Mormon history, which emerged during the second half of the twentieth century. This new
scholarship was produced by writers both within and outside the Latter-day
Saint faith who sought to reexamine carefully the Mormon past in a scholarly and nonpolemical manner, utilizing the latest historical techniques. It differed from traditional Mormon history in that its practitioners sought objec-
tivity by avoiding "pro-" or "anti-" positions in interpreting events in the
Latter-day Saints past.[1]

The first person to articulate the Missouri thesis was Fawn McKay Brodie,
through her highly controversial *No Man Knows My History: The Life of Joseph
Smith,* published in 1945. According to Brodie, the origins of Mormon black
priesthood denial could be traced to conflicts between Mormons and non-
Mormons in the slave state of Missouri during the 1830s. Those Latter-day
Saints who had migrated to this slaveholding state from nonslave regions of
Ohio, New York, and New England were anxious to prevent further misunderstanding on the issues of race and slavery and therefore adopted a proslav-
ery and antiblack position, which included the denial of black priesthood.[2]

Brodie also saw a direct relationship between the Book of Abraham and the
implementation of black priesthood denial. She asserted that the Book of Abraham not only upheld a so-called curse that blacks, as the alleged descendants
of Ham, were doomed to be a "servant of servants" but that along "with this
curse went a denial of the right of priesthood." Thus the Book of Abraham expressed, in Brodie's words, Smith's "theorizing on the subject of race"; in the
same way that the "Book of Mormon had solved the problem of the origins of
the red man, so the Book of Abraham dispatched the problem of the origins

of the Negro." It "crystallized Joseph's hitherto vacillating position on the Negro problem." Brodie was not completely objective in expressing her moral outrage, proclaiming the Book of Abraham "the most unfortunate thing that Joseph ever wrote" and black priesthood denial "the ugliest thesis in existing Mormon theology." Moreover, Brodie suggested that Smith developed "a complicated justification of slavery that went even further than the curse of Ham" by linking the blacks' present condition to behavior during a premortal "war in heaven," in which "one third of the spirits had been neutral choosing neither side, but wanting to join the victors"—hence the black race.[3]

Following Brodie's lead, other scholars writing during the 1950s and 1960s utilized elements of the Missouri thesis. They included L. H. Kirkpatrick, Jan Shipps, Dennis L. Lythgoe, and Naomi Woodbury, all of whom viewed the Mormon Missouri experience as crucial in the development of Mormon black priesthood denial and related proslavery, antiblack practices and attitudes.[4]

The most thoroughly researched work linking black Mormon priesthood denial to church difficulties in Missouri was Stephen L. Taggart's widely circulated *Mormonism's Negro Policy: Social and Historical Origins.* First published in 1970, it went through three printings. The church, according to Taggart, "had no explicit doctrine regarding slavery when it entered Missouri" in 1831.[5] But during the following eight years, in response to the Mormon presence in this slave state, the church through its leaders and spokesmen abandoned its "abolitionist attitudes . . . moving toward an essentially pro-slavery position." This was done to "reduce the conflict" between the Latter-day Saints and their non-Mormon Missouri neighbors.[6]

But conflict intensified following the publication in July 1833 of a controversial article, "Free People of Color," in the church's semiofficial *Evening and the Morning Star,* edited by William Wines Phelps. "Free People of Color" outlined the restrictions and related procedures necessary for free blacks to emigrate into Missouri, noting: "Slaves are real estate in this and other states" and adding that "so long as we have no special rule in the church, as to people of color, let prudence guide." But then Phelps added the provocative observation: "In connection with the wonderful events of this age much is doing towards abolishing slavery, colonizing the blacks, in Africa."[7] Non-Mormon response to this article was immediate. Though a "Secret Constitution," anti-Missouri Mormons accused the Latter-day Saints of "tampering with our slaves, and endeavoring to sow dissensions [*sic*] and raise sedition among them" and of "inviting free negroes and mulattoes from other states to become 'Mormons'" and settle in Missouri. The "introduction of such a caste [of free blacks] amongst us would corrupt our blacks and instigate them to bloodshed."[8]

Phelps reacted with an "Extra" edition of the *Evening and the Morning Star* issued in the form of a handbill. It stated that the intent of his earlier article had been "misunderstood" and "that our intention was not only to stop free people of color from emigrating to this state, but to prevent them from being admitted as members of the Church." This "Extra" essay, in the words of Taggart, "illustrates the process by which social stress was the instrumental factor in causing the Missouri Mormons to abandon their northern attitudes in favor of an anti-Negro posture."[9]

This incident was soon followed by "the first hint of the emergence of the practice of excluding Negroes from the priesthood," as characterized by Taggart. This came following the expulsion of Latter-day Saints from Jackson County and the Zion's Camp expedition of 1834. Taggart cited as evidence of Joseph Smith's intentions the 1879 recollections of Zebedee Coltrin and Abraham O. Smoot, both of whom knew Smith. Coltrin recalled that, during the Zion's Camp expedition, he argued with a fellow Latter-day Saint, John P. Greene, whether "the Negro [had] a right to the priesthood. . . . I took up the side he had no right," while Greene argued that he did. To settle this dispute, Coltrin and Greene "immediately" consulted Joseph Smith. The Mormon leader, Coltrin remembered, "kind of dropped his head, and rested it on his hand for a minute, and then said, 'Brother Zebedee is right for the spirit of the Lord saith the Negro has no right nor cannot hold the Priesthood.' He made no reference to Scripture at all, but such was his decision."[10]

Smoot, according to Taggart, had confronted the issue of black ordination while doing missionary work "in the Southern States in 1835 and 1836." At the time, some blacks "made application for baptism. And the question arose with them whether Negroes were entitled to hold the Priesthood." A decision was postponed until Joseph Smith was consulted. His judgment, as Smoot understand it, was that black slaves "were not entitled to the Priesthood, nor yet to be baptized without the consent of their Masters." Smoot further recalled that upon becoming "acquainted with Joseph [Smith] myself in . . . Far West," Missouri, in 1838, he (Smoot) asked "what should be done with the Negro in the South?" He received from "Brother Joseph substantially the same instructions" that "I could baptize them by consent of their masters, but not to confer the Priesthood upon them."[11]

Such recollections, in the words of Taggart, indicated a lack of "general consensus or Church-wide policy covering the subject [of black priesthood ordination] as late as 1838." But at the same time, Joseph Smith, "concerned for the safety of the Southern membership, appears to have begun informally advising individuals in about 1834 not to ordain Negroes to the priesthood."[12] Taggart summarized: "As no supporting theology was initially invoked or developed, and in light of events subsequent to 1834, it appears that

Joseph Smith probably began to advise Negro priesthood denial without envisioning the initiation of a doctrine or even a Church-wide policy. His initial action was a precautionary expedient."[13]

Taggart also notes that during the 1830s, in reaction to their Missouri difficulties, the Mormons abandoned "their initial abolitionist tendencies," assuming a "proslavery posture." In August 1835 the church, according to Taggart, issued its "first official declaration of policy regarding Negroes," stating that the Latter-day Saints did "not believe it right to interfere with bond servants, neither preach the gospel to, nor baptize them contrary to the will or wish of their masters, nor to meddle with or influence them in the least to cause them to be dissatisfied with their situations in this life." A Mormon "proslavery theological argument" followed in April 1836. Joseph Smith led the way, quoting certain passages from the Bible . . . affirming "the holding of the sons of Ham in servitude," specifically Genesis 9:25–26: "'And he said cursed be Canaan; a servant of servants shall he be unto his brethren. And he said, Blessed be the Lord God of Shem; and Canaan shall be his servant.'" Smith then stated: "I can say, that the curse is not yet taken off the sons of Canaan, neither will be until it is affected by as great power as caused it to come; and the people who interfere the least with the decrees and purposes of God in this matter, will come under the least condemnation before him."[14]

Mormon proslavery tendencies were strengthened after Joseph Smith fled from Kirtland, Ohio, to Far West, Missouri, in March 1838, thus making Missouri "the center of Mormonism." In the words of Taggart, "This shift in the Church's center of gravity meant that the tone of normative Mormonism was now being set in Missouri—where the membership was directly exposed to the conflicts forcing the Church away from abolitionism."[15]

Meanwhile, the "expedient of denying the Negro the priesthood remained a practice without a theological underpinning," although, in Taggart's words, Joseph Smith "contemplated the development of a theological justification for the practice of denying the priesthood to Negroes" by the mid-1835s.[16] Serving as a basis was a crucial section of the Book of Abraham—a work that Joseph Smith began "translating" from a set of ancient Egyptian papyrus rolls in his possession during July 1835.[17] The crucial passages focused on Pharaoh and the Egyptians, identified as ancestors of Ham. Pharaoh was described as "a descendant from the loins of Ham and . . . a partaker of the blood of the Canaanites by birth." According to Taggart, the Book of Abraham "suggests that Noah's son Ham perpetuated the seed of Cain through his wife Egyptus, who was of Canaanite descent, and that consequently Ham's descendants were forbidden to hold the priesthood."[18]

This passage from the Book of Abraham built on "the curse of Canaan argument" that was used to justify black slavery, as recently embraced by Joseph Smith, as well as on the "informal [Mormon] practice of denying the priesthood to blacks."[19] "With the publication of The Book of Abraham [in 1842] all the elements for the Church's policy of denying the priesthood were present," Taggart wrote, although he conceded that the "ordination of Negroes continued within the Church until as late as 1841."[20]

In essence, Taggart's 1970 work was designed as an argument for lifting the ban on Mormon black priesthood ordination, which he characterized "a historical anachronism—an unfortunate and embarrassing survival of a once expedient institutional practice . . . founded, indeed, on an inadequate premise. . . . Mormonism's practices regarding Negroes," he added, "should be viewed as matters of policy rather than points of doctrine."[21]

Taggart's book Mormonism's Negro Policy was subjected to close scrutiny by a fellow Mormon scholar, Lester E. Bush Jr., who was deeply immersed in his own study on the Mormon black issue. Bush questioned both the facts and the basic validity of Taggart's Missouri thesis in two influential essays published in Dialogue: A Journal of Mormon Thought. The first, "A Commentary on Stephen G. Taggart's Mormonism's Negro Policy: Social and Historical Origins," appeared in early 1970, shortly after the publication of Taggart's book.[22]

Bush concedes that Taggart's study "appear[s] more comprehensive than previous treatments, and . . . cites some uncommon, though seemingly very relevant references." Thus it gave the "impression that a very good case is being made." But despite its "generally accurate and well-documented rehearsal of the Jackson County period," Bush found that it was marred "by an increasing incidence of speculative statements and secondary sources, and a sprinkling of factual errors. . . . More disturbingly . . . a number of relevant points [were] omitted from" Taggart's treatment of "Mormon history and doctrine and the general setting in which they arose."[23]

Bush challenged Taggart's undocumented assertion "that the early Mormons, were, in fact, abolitionists." Bush also questioned Taggart's effort to place the origins of Mormon black priesthood denial in the 1830s and found unconvincing the 1879 testimonies of Coltrin and Smoot. Coltrin's testimony was "an artifact . . . recorded forty-five years after the fact" and therefore "it would be unwise to accept its details without question." Also, Bush believed that Coltrin's account "reflect[ed] prejudice to the subject" and was undermined by the fact that Coltrin himself had ordained Elijah Abel, an early African American Mormon, to the priesthood office of Seventy in December 1836, two years after the date that Coltrin claimed was when Smith inaugurated a policy of denying blacks the priesthood. Smoot's testimony is also suspect, according to Bush, because Smoot, a Southerner, was not only descended "from a line of slaveholders" but also owned at least two black slaves, whom he apparently acquired after settling in Utah in 1848.[24]

More seriously, Bush questioned Taggart's assertion that Joseph Smith intended the Book of Abraham as a "theological justification" for black priesthood denial. Bush pointed to Taggart's own admission that the Book of Abraham was "vague and cannot by itself be said to justify denying the priesthood to Negroes." Bush also noted the "lack of evidence that Joseph Smith ever used the book of Abraham to justify priesthood denial (nor apparently did any other Church leader, until the Utah period)."[25] In fact, according to Bush, the earliest or "first known documentation of the policy of priesthood denial" came in 1849, five years after Joseph Smith's death. "There remains no period source to support the contention that Joseph Smith was the author of [Mormon black priesthood denial]." Bush conceded that "Joseph Smith did express the then-prevalent opinion that Negroes were descendants of Canaan and Cain; yet he did not relate this to the priesthood in any account now available."[26]

Three years after his thorough review of Taggart's book, Lester Bush "offered his own reconstruction of the history of church teaching on blacks" in a second *Dialogue* essay, "Mormonism's Negro Doctrine: An Historical Overview," published in 1973.[27] While continuing to refute the essence of the Missouri thesis, Bush's essay provided additional information and insights concerning Mormon affairs in this slave state. In discussing the violent response of Missouri non-Mormons to "Free People of Color," as published in the *Evening and Morning Star,* Bush noted that "free Negroes were rare in Missouri," adding that "Jackson Country had none."[28] Bush conceded that "the Jackson County experience demonstrated the need for a clear statement of Church policy on slavery," most evident in "the 'official' Church position on slavery . . . adopted in August 1835" and incorporated into the Doctrine and Covenants.[29]

But at the same time, Bush suggested that certain proslavery statements made by Joseph Smith, Oliver Cowdery, and Warren Parrish during the mid-1830s were not simply responses to events in Missouri, but were also direct reactions against increased abolitionist activities in various northern communities, especially in Kirtland, Ohio, the site of the Mormons' first completed temple and, until 1838, the home of the Mormon headquarters. Here a local chapter of the American Anti-Slavery Society was established in April 1836 with eighty-six members.[30] Bush, moreover, tended to discount the significance of slavery and race as factors in the escalating violence between Latter-day Saints and their non-Mormon neighbors, culminating in the 1838 Mormon War. In Bush's words, "After 1836 the Mormons . . . largely ignored the subject of slavery for nearly six years. During this time they periodically reaffirmed that they were not abolitionists, but the charge was no longer common in Missouri nor elsewhere in the South."[31]

As for the specific issue of blacks and the priesthood, Bush affirmed that "in spite of the many discussions of blacks and slavery that had been published by 1836, no reference had been made to the priesthood." Bush did concede the possibility of a "policy . . . in effect denying the priesthood to slaves or isolated free southern Negroes . . . notwithstanding the lack of contemporary documentation." Such "a de facto restriction is demonstrable in the South, and empirical justification for [such a] policy is not difficult to imagine." All this notwithstanding, Bush found "the earliest record of a Church decision to deny the priesthood to" blacks to be a statement made by Brigham Young on February 13, 1849, in response to a question concerning what "chance of redemption there was for the Africans." The Mormon leader insisted that "the curse remained upon them because Cain cut off the lives of Abel. . . . The Lord had cursed Cain's seed with blackness and prohibited them the Priesthood."[32] Bush's assertion that Brigham Young, not Joseph Smith, had inaugurated black priesthood denial refuted the central tenet of the Missouri thesis.

Still, the Missouri thesis continued to be accepted by certain respected scholars and writers of Mormon studies. Among the most prominent was the non-Mormon sociologist Thomas F. O'Dea. O'Dea's widely praised 1957 book *The Mormons* did not deal at all with the issues of slavery, race, and blacks within Mormonism.[33] But O'Dea's later essay "Sources of Strain in Mormon History Reconsidered," published in 1972 in a book-length anthology, *Mormonism and American Culture,* confronted the race issue and the changing place of blacks as central themes. In the words of O'Dea, the Latter-day Saints during the 1830s "made what has been called their own 'Missouri Mormon Compromise' in an attempt to clear themselves in the eyes of Missourians, many of whom seemed to regard them as Yankee abolitionists." The "Missouri experience . . . gave a racist cast to Mormon thinking."[34] Likewise, a second non-Mormon writer, the anthropologist Mark Leone, characterized "the doctrine" of black priesthood denial as "a holdover from the days when the church in Missouri had to compromise on the slave issue for survival."[35]

Two noted Latter-day Saint scholars also embraced the Missouri thesis as plausible. The first was the award-winning historian Dean L. May, in an important 1980 entry on Mormon ethnicity in the *Harvard Encyclopedia of American Ethnic Groups.* Black priesthood denial, noted May, "apparently arose as a reaction to criticism of Mormon opposition to slavery in the 1830s."[36]

A second Mormon historian, Klaus J. Hansen, subscribed to certain aspects of the Missouri thesis, albeit in a more circumscribed fashion, in his 1981 *Mormonism and the American Experience.* On the one hand, Hansen praised

Lester Bush's "seminal essay" as "the most ambitious and brilliant attempt to divorce Joseph [Smith's] authority from the 'Negro doctrine'" but then asserted that Bush had gone too far in discounting the Mormon Missouri experience. According to Hansen, the Saints, in the wake of their 1833 expulsion from Jackson County, "seemed to have learned their lesson and from then on discouraged missionary activities among blacks." These same Saints, moreover, "hardened their racial position" at least in part "as a result of [such] persecution."[37]

Hansen also disagreed with Bush concerning the Book of Abraham and its significance. Assuming that Joseph Smith "believed there was . . . a link between Ham and the modern Negro . . . the Book of Abraham is indeed the linchpin in the Negro doctrine." Hansen carefully added: "The fact that neither Joseph nor Brigham Young apparently felt it necessary to use the Book of Abraham as proof text does not negate my point. I am reminded of Jacob Burckhardt's comment that 'everywhere in the past we encounter things which remain unexplained only because they were completely self-understood in their time.'" Hansen concluded: "If Joseph [Smith] was the author of the Negro doctrine, there are plausible historical reasons why he should have been."[38]

Also questioning Bush, but at the same time moving beyond the Missouri Thesis, was Ronald K. Esplin, a Latter-day Saint historian and the second director of the Joseph Fielding Smith Institute for Latter-day Saint History at Brigham Young University. In 1979 he published "Brigham Young and Priesthood Denial to the Blacks: An Alternative View." Esplin revived the argument that Joseph Smith rather than Brigham Young initiated the "doctrine" of black priesthood denial. But Esplin did not look back to the 1830s or Mormon difficulties in Missouri. Instead, he based his arguments on events in Nauvoo during the 1840s. Black priesthood denial, Esplin argued, emerged in 1842–43 in relationship to and concurrent with Joseph Smith's introduction of the more advanced temple rituals developed at this time.

Esplin acknowledged that the earliest known recorded Mormon statement affirming black priesthood denial came about three years after Smith's death from Apostle Parley P. Pratt on April 25, 1847, following the departure from Nauvoo of those Saints following Brigham Young. According to Esplin, it "offhandedly referred to priesthood denial to the Blacks"—specifically prompted by the unauthorized practice of polygamy at Winter Quarters by one William McCary, a black Indian whom Pratt characterized as a "black man with the blood of Ham in him which lineage was cursed as regards to the priesthood." According to Esplin, "Pratt, a long-time intimate of meetings of the Twelve, understood the policy [of black priesthood denial] clearly."[39]

As for Brigham Young, Esplin asserted that the Utah Mormon leader "throughout his lifetime . . . but especially during [the] early period" of his leadership "saw himself charged by Joseph [Smith] to carry out" the Mormon Prophet's "specific program." In particular "the early brethren were concerned about priesthood lineage and about who would have access to temple ordinances." According to Esplin: "Even if Joseph did not raise the question, himself, it is not difficult to envision someone asking about the Blacks and Joseph providing the answer. It is my feeling that the doctrine was introduced in Nauvoo and consistently applied in practice at least by 1843, although it would require additional documentation to raise the possibility from the realm of the probable to the certain." Esplin conceded that "the problem in attributing the priesthood policy to Joseph Smith remains: so far as presently known documentation is concerned, one cannot point to a specific date or place where Joseph Smith taught the doctrine." In further discounting the role of Brigham Young, Esplin notes that the Utah Mormon leader "went to great lengths to deny in the most unequivocal language that he was not the author of the practice of priesthood denial to the Blacks and to assert that the Lord was."[40]

The "Esplin thesis" prompted a response from Lester E. Bush in a 1984 essay, "Whence the Negro Doctrine? A Review of Ten Years of Answers," updating the most recent scholarship concerned with this issue. Bush found "merit" in Esplin's efforts to link "black policies" with the development of certain "new temple rituals" in Nauvoo; but at the same time, he found Esplin's essay lacking in "contemporary documentation." Thus, Bush rejected Esplin's central argument, restating his own assertion that it was "difficult to believe . . . that a concrete policy of priesthood denial dated much before spring 1847 . . . given the apparent chronology of the actual practice."[41]

Bush did, however, find some validity in Esplin's argument that the Book of Abraham provided an earlier scriptural basis for black priesthood denial, albeit following Joseph Smith's death. Thus, Bush conceded that "the wording of Parley Pratt's 1847 characterization of McCary as having the 'blood of Ham in him which lineage was cursed as regards the priesthood'—whether descriptive or proscriptive—unmistakably derived in part from the book of Abraham." Bush, in fact, acknowledged the possibility that Joseph Smith "contemplated denying blacks the priesthood at the time that the earliest book of Abraham texts were in preparation," specifically the 1830s, "or at least considered that a rational implication of the text." But at the same time, "it is highly relevant to note that he never publicly espoused this potential application of his scripture."[42] Bush concluded his assessment of Joseph Smith's role:

In a very real sense, Joseph Smith . . . provided a context which, in his absence, inevitably led to a policy of priesthood denial to blacks. Whether this would have occurred had Joseph not been killed is debatable. He apparently had not felt it necessary to implement such a policy despite the precedents provided while he lived, but later developments may have changed his mind. It seems very unlikely that Brigham and his colleagues perceived themselves as moving away from Joseph's lead, but they may well have felt they were carrying it forward to its logical conclusion.[43]

Other writers moved beyond the Missouri thesis by focusing on Mormon ethnicity. Klaus J. Hansen in his *Mormonism and the American Experience* was one of the first scholars to link a growing sense of Latter-day Saint lineage self-consciousness to "the implementation of black priesthood denial." Hansen, vague as to precise dating, asserted that over time, early Latter-day Saints identified themselves as literal descendants of the House of Israel. Joseph Smith believed himself to be a literal descendant of Ephraim, divinely chosen to gather all of the descendants of Ephraim, predominantly found among white Europeans. "God had singled out the seed of Abraham for special blessings," according to Mormon belief. Other ethnic groups were less favored, except for the American Indians, who, according to the Book of Mormon, were also descendants of Manasseh, one of the sons of Joseph, and hence, also of the house of Israel. Like descendants of Ephraim, they were to be converted and gathered. In contrast, black Americans of African descent were viewed as literal descendants of Cain, Ham, and Canaan, and thus were the least favored in terms of blessings and status within Mormonism, including the priesthood.[44]

Rex Eugene Cooper was another scholar who elaborated on the role of Mormon ethnic identity on evolving Latter-day Saint racial practices and attitudes. In an important but often overlooked 1990 book, *Promises Made to the Fathers: Mormon Covenant Organization,* Cooper dated certain crucial developments from the 1830s. By the time of the 1838–39 Mormon expulsion from Missouri, "a code of conduct evident in the behavioral qualification associated with the baptismal covenant, and substance or blood (as manifested in the concept of Abrahamic descent) had clearly emerged as conceptual bases . . . for solidarity within the Mormon group."[45]

While such "concepts of Abrahamic descent and the baptismal covenant were incorporated into the [Mormon patriarchal] order" during the 1830s, a "more complex understanding of Mormon identity" emerged during the 1840s, according to Cooper. This involved the development within "Mormon thought" of a system of descent dividing "the world's population" into three basic groups, namely, "Israelites, Gentiles, and Blacks, based on the blessings and cursings [that] Noah pronounced on [his three sons] Shem, Ham, and Japheth. Israelites were the descendants of Shem, [the] Gentiles were the descendants of Japheth, and Blacks were the descendants of Ham." Generations later, "the Israelites were subdivided into tribes, based roughly on the twelve sons of Jacob." Three of these "had particular significance for Mormon covenant organization, specifically Ephraim and Manasseh (the two sons of Joseph), and Judah." All Israelites as descendants of Jacob were "heirs to the Abrahamic covenant." The "descendants of Ephraim," with whom most Latter-day Saints identified, were "singled out for special distinction." On the opposite extreme were blacks, whom Latter-day Saints "believed to be the descendants of Cain through Ham's wife [and] subject to the curse that God pronounced on Cain," which included denial of the priesthood.[46]

Cooper also asserted that the Book of Abraham established a clear link between Mormon ethnicity or lineage and priesthood authority: "Publication of the Book of Abraham [in 1842] further established the concept that Abraham's priesthood, received from 'the fathers' back to Adam, could be traced to his seed after him. . . . As Abraham's 'literal seed' through his favored son Isaac and grandson Jacob, Israelites were lawful heirs to the priesthood. This, of course, included Mormons who were regarded as Israelites."[47]

But at the same time, "The Book of Abraham provided much of the mythological justification" for denying blacks the priesthood, in Cooper's words, even though he agreed with Bush that "there is no conclusive evidence that such an exclusionary policy existed before the abandonment of Nauvoo in 1846."[48]

Cooper also took note of a "master-servant relationship" officially endorsed by the church that directly affected at least one black member. Such a relationship was given scriptural sanction through a portion of Joseph Smith's 1843 revelation on eternal marriage. In addition to polygamy, this revelation stressed the importance of matrimonial sealing for "time and eternity" through Mormon temple rites—deemed essential for full salvation. But a section of this revelation, in turn, dealt with "those individuals not so sealed but who are otherwise worthy of admittance to the celestial kingdom." Such individuals would receive a degree of salvation even though they would remain unmarried in the hereafter. This would come through their appointment as "ministering servants, to minister for those who are worthy of a far more, and an exceedingly, and eternal weight of glory." Thus they would be "saved but single," in the words of Cooper. Some nineteenth-century Latter-day Saints "believed that those exalted in the celestial kingdom would have personal servants."[49]

The church sanctioned such a relationship for Jane Elizabeth Manning James, a free African American, who had joined the Latter-day Saints in the 1830s and worked as a maid in Joseph and Emma Smith's Nauvoo home. Following Joseph Smith's death and after migrating to Utah, James petitioned church leaders to receive her endowments and be sealed to her husband and children. She failed, despite repeated efforts. Finally, in 1894 the LDS Church's First Presidency permitted Jane James "to be adopted to the Prophet as his servant." Through this process "she was declared to be eternally a servant to Joseph Smith and his household."[50]

A third scholar, Robert Ben Madison, also emphasized the importance of Mormon ethnicity as a link to restrictive policies affecting blacks. In his 1992 essay "'Heirs According to the Promise': Observations on Ethnicity, Race, and Identity in Two Factions of Nineteenth-Century Mormonism," Madison noted that "the appearance of 'ethnic' Mormonism [was] closely related to the severe persecutions suffered by the Mormons in the 1830s and 1840s." This condition ultimately led to the development of a "literal Abrahamic relationship." This Mormon sense of "Hebraic genealogical lineage" assumed doctrinal legitimacy thanks to the introduction during the 1830s of the patriarchal blessing which became an integral part of Mormonism. Through such blessings, church members were identified as descendants "of the particular portion of Abraham's family, the particular tribe, to which they belong[ed]."[51]

Madison's study was unique in that it considered evolving Mormon ethnicity from a comparative perspective, arguing that "the forces which led to Mormon ethnicity did not impact all segments of the Mormon community alike." Madison contrasted relevant developments within the Utah Mormon church with those occurring in the Reorganized Church of Jesus Christ of Latter Day Saints (RLDS, known as the Community of Christ since its name change in April 2001). "Utah Mormons saw themselves as heirs to the Old Testament," whereby they emphasized and reinforced their earlier established identity as "a literal 'restored Israel' of (White European or Anglo-Saxon) Abrahamic blood." In contrast, Latter Day Saints who did not go west and who formed the basis of the Reorganized Church viewed themselves not as an "ethnic group" per se, but simply "as heirs to the New Testament."[52]

The RLDS, in the words of Madison, viewed "ethnic considerations [as] sublimated to those of the promise by which Gentiles (whites and blacks) were figuratively 'adopted' and entitled to Abraham's blessings by virtue of their accepting the lordship of the God of Israel." In this spirit, in early 1865, Joseph Smith III, recently sustained as RLDS president and prophet, seer, and revelator, declared that "the prejudice of race, color, and caste would soon be done away with among the Saints." Then through revelation, Smith declared: "It is expedient in me that you ordain priests unto me, of every race who receive the teachings of my law, and become heirs according to the promise."[53] The inclusive RLDS approach stood in sharp contrast to more restrictive concepts and related practices within the early Utah Mormon community, which clearly and specifically excluded blacks based on their "less favored" lineage or ethnicity.

Armand L. Mauss moved even further away from the Missouri thesis in discussing Mormon ethnicity in his exhaustively researched and carefully written 1999 essay "In Search of Ephraim: Traditional Mormon Conceptions of Lineage and Race"—later incorporated as a crucial section in his *All Abraham's Children: Changing Mormon Conceptions of Race and Lineage.* Mauss argues "that the full-fledged racialist framework of Mormonism" did not emerge until after the migration of the Saints to Utah. "Mormon racialism," moreover, took a century to fully evolve.[54] According to Mauss, the fundamental basis of this "racialist framework" was rooted in concepts of "British Israelism" and "Anglo-Saxon triumphalism." "British Israelism" involved the belief that "most of the British were literally Israelites"—a concept widely held in Great Britain and the United States, with roots long antedating the birth of Mormonism. "Anglo-Saxon triumphalism," on the other hand, was the "secular counterpart" to "British Israelism," which affirmed that the peoples of Great Britain and northern Europe had established dominion over other peoples and nations because of "inherent racial superiority." So-called "elite clergy of the mid-nineteenth century were especially influential in synthesizing and propagating [these] two philosophical streams."[55]

"British Israelism" and "Anglo-Saxon triumphalism" were a prevalent "part of Joseph Smith's environment," according to Mauss, and "contemporaneous with the rise of Mormonism on both sides of the Atlantic." Joseph Smith's own related teachings "had much in common" with such ideas, even if they were not actually "influenced" or "stimulated by" them.[56]

Mauss's discussion of the impact of such ideas on Joseph Smith and Mormonism during the 1830s is somewhat ambiguous. On the one hand, he argues that Joseph Smith "clearly [identified] the Church with the tribe of Ephraim" as early as November 1831. But such identification at the early date was more symbolic than literal, he admits. He also concedes that "literal Ephraimite lineage" was mentioned in "an unscientific sampling of several hundred . . . early patriarchal blessings"—specifically "about a third of the time through 1836 and then about half the time through 1844." Also "by 1835, a genealogical link between the Smith families and Joseph and Ephraim of old was well established and long attributed to many other families" within the church. Yet "as late as 1835 Sidney Rigdon cited Ephesians 1:4 in support of the doctrine that all people, of whatever lineage, would be blessed like the 'seed of Abraham' through Christ having been 'chosen to be sons of God in Christ' in accordance with 'what God had purposed in Himself before the foundation of the world.'"[57]

In his discussion of events following Joseph Smith's death, Mauss is much less tentative in outlining the church's movement to a more exclusivist position. By January 1846, at least one LDS spokesman, through the semi-official *Times and Seasons,* argued that "'the blood of Israel' had special, even exclusive rights to the priesthood." As for specific developments adversely affecting the position of blacks within the church, Mauss sees these as occurring only after Joseph Smith's martyrdom, thereby rejecting the Missouri thesis.[58]

D. Michael Quinn and John L. Brooke, in two important but controversial studies, have undermined the Missouri thesis from yet another perspective. In his *Early Mormonism and the Magic World View,* Quinn notes Joseph Smith's practice of associating sorcery, black magic, Satan, and "secret combinations" with certain biblical counterfigures, specifically Cain and Ham—both considered direct ancestors of contemporary blacks. According to Quinn, these ideas were evident in Joseph Smith's initial scriptural writings, the Book of Mormon and Book of Moses, both completed in 1830. "Long before 1830," asserts Quinn, "there was a well-established tradition that sorcery originated with Cain, was passed from father to son, particularly by the angels who married the daughters of man, and was perpetuated after the flood by Noah's son Ham."[59]

Quinn also states that Smith, in developing early Mormon concepts of priesthood authority, evident in his September 1832 revelation, was influenced more by "traditional views of magic . . . than Judeo-Christian theology." Smith proclaimed that such priesthood authority was held by principal biblical figures in Genesis, beginning with Adam, and was passed down "through the lineage of their fathers." In this, Smith was clearly influenced by the "occult tradition [which] claimed that priesthood ceremony, or knowledge had been passed from father to son by biblical patriarchs." Smith also embraced the negative side concerning those lacking priesthood authority. According to Quinn, Smith and others subscribed to the concept that "Cain having murdered his brother Abel, his priesthood descended to Seth."[60]

But at the same time, Quinn maintained, Smith was ambivalent concerning the symbolism of blackness and the color black. On the one hand, "contemporary evidence" suggests that Smith, influenced by the occult, "used the color black to help obtain the gold plates in 1827." According to contemporary accounts cited by Quinn, Smith on this occasion was "dressed in black clothes, and riding a black horse." He also smeared lampblack on his palm, and "black was also the color of Smith's birth sign of Capricorn."[61] Yet within the Book of Mormon itself, blackness assumed clearly negative connotations, particularly in its association with the consequences of unrighteous behavior by the Lamanites in pre-Columbian America.

Emphasizing similar elements was John L. Brooke in his *The Refiner's Fire: The Making of Mormon Cosmology, 1644–1844,* published in 1994. Like Quinn, Brooke saw Joseph Smith as influenced by the occult in developing certain doctrines and beliefs. In particular Smith embraced hermeticism, involving the experimental practice of alchemy, whereby humanity could regain the divine powers held by Adam prior to the Fall. Smith was influenced by related, long-established concepts of "good vs. evil." These involved the idea of "'two seeds' . . . the good seed of the 'blessed Israelites' . . . the product of the union of Adam and Eve, and the bad seed of the 'cursed Canaanites' [which] was the product of Eve's seduction by the devil. Descending among the separate peoples of Adam and Cain, the two seeds had been mixed by the intermarriage of these two lineages, and caused good and evil behavior in humanity."[62] The "two seeds" concept of "descent from Adam and Cain" had, in the words of Brooke, "an echo in the saga of the Nephites and the Lamanites in the Book of Mormon."[63]

Smith also subscribed to what Brooke characterized as a "Masonic mythology," which involved a basic belief that "from Adam's sons Seth and Cain descended two races of men, good and evil, carrying pure and spurious versions of Masonic knowledge."[64] Brooke saw clear parallels with the Book of Mormon:

> Not unlike Smith's Nephites in the Book of Mormon, the virtuous Sethites suffered declension and merged with the Cainites, mixing together pure and spurious Masonry. The pure Masonic tradition was preserved from the Flood by Enoch, who buried the mysteries in his arched vault before being taken bodily up to heaven, and by Noah, who alone with his family was saved from the Flood. But once again there was declension and schism, and Noah's son, Ham, became the new progenitor of spurious, Cainite Masonry, which became even more deeply entrenched after the dispersion at the Tower of Babel.[65]

The Book of Mormon, according to Brooke, could be "read in terms of a contest between hermetic purity and danger, between diviners and counterfeiters, and between pure, 'primitive' Freemasons and corrupt 'spurious' Freemasons."[66]

Moving beyond the Book of Mormon, this same "two seed" tradition played "a significant role in Joseph Smith's later thinking," specifically in Smith's "revision of Genesis, his Book of Moses," wherein "Adam's 'pure and undefiled' language and 'Priesthood' were passed to Seth and his progeny" after Cain had murdered Abel. The unfavorable position of Cain was further underscored by the fact that Satan, and then Cain, was made "the father of all lies."[67]

Both the Book of Mormon and the Book of Moses, moreover, reinforced the fact that "Mormon society was structured by hierarchies of race and sex." In this, Mormonism was not unique, merely "reflecting its Jacksonian environment." Specifically, the Book of Mormon "made the white race morally superior to the red, and the Book of Abraham subordinated blacks" to whites, while "polygamous celestial marriage was merely an amplification of Mormon patriarchy subordinating women."[68]

The Book of Abraham, which was destined to have negative connotations for blacks, in the words of Brooke represented "another revision of Genesis, expanding on points made in the Book of Moses." But its exclusion of "blacks and Egyptians as the descendants of Ham from the 'right of Priesthood' . . . stood as the basis of Mormon racism."[69]

The later publication of the Book of Abraham notwithstanding, the critical period for Joseph Smith in constructing a Mormon cosmology was prior to 1830, according to Brooke:

> In the 1820s Joseph Smith combined contemporary images of hermetic danger—counterfeiting gangs and spurious Masonry—in composing his picture of the Gadianton Bands and the Lamanites in the Book of Mormon, counterposed to the hermetic purity of the Nephites. Divining and counterfeiting, prophecy and sorcery, pure Masonry and spurious Masonry, Nephites and Lamanites—Gadiantons, the seed of Adam and the seed of Cain, God and Satan: These were the elements of a dichotomous system of truth and falsity upon which Smith built a Mormon cosmology.[70]

In conclusion, what is the significance of all of these varied scholarly examinations? It is evident that both Fawn M. Brodie and Stephen L. Taggart overstated their cases relative to the Mormon Missouri experience. What about the contradictory, sometimes conflicting findings of John L. Brooke, D. Michael Quinn, Armand L. Mauss, Robert Ben Madison, Rex E. Cooper, Klaus Hansen, and Lester E. Bush? What do they tell us about the LDS presence in Missouri relative to evolving Mormon attitudes on race and the place of blacks?

In a sense, one is left with more questions than answers. But what is clear is that the Mormon sojourn in Missouri left a mixed legacy—both negative and positive. On the negative side, the Mormon presence in Missouri caused Joseph Smith and other church spokesmen to express tolerance for black slavery, which was most evident in the church's official 1835 statement in which the Latter-day Saints pledged not to "interfere with bond servants" or "influence them to become dissatisfied with their situations." This statement was eventually incorporated as Section 134:12 in the Doctrine and Covenants and thus accepted as Mormon church canon. Also adversely affecting the place of blacks within Mormonism was an evolving sense of ethnic self-awareness or identity among Latter-day Saints, also evident during the Missouri period. Specifically, an emerging sense of Mormon "whiteness" was underscored by a basic belief that Mormons of white European ancestry were the literal descendants of the house of Israel.

Conversely, African Americans were viewed as descended from the much less favored lineage of Cain, Ham, and Canaan, who were regarded in a highly negative light as biblical counterfigures. Such negative views were reinforced by two scriptural writings brought forth by Joseph Smith during this period, specifically the Book of Moses and Book of Abraham. The latter work would, in fact, ultimately provide a scriptural proof text for black priesthood denial, although there is no creditable evidence that it was intended, let alone used, for that purpose during Joseph Smith's lifetime.

As for black slavery, Mormon tolerance for that peculiar institution during the 1830s would provide a basis for the legalization of black slavery in the Utah Territory through the 1852 Act in Relation to Service—a measure vigorously promoted by Brigham Young. This statute remained in force until 1862 when it was repealed through federal statute. At the same time, Latter-day Saints still embraced a strong sense of ethnic self-identity in which Saints of European descent, through their "whiteness," considered themselves the literal seed of the house of Israel. Concurrently, these same Mormons persisted in relegating blacks to an inferior status as literal descendants of Cain, Ham, and Canaan, thereby providing a powerful rationale that was ultimately used to deny African American Latter-day Saints the priesthood. Indeed, Latter-day Saint "whiteness" became increasingly manifest during the course of the nineteenth and early twentieth centuries.

In contrast, on the positive side is the fact that Mormon black priesthood denial did *not* emerge during the 1830s, despite the negative developments outlined above, all of which occurred as the Latter-day Saints struggled to establish their Missouri Zion. Thus, the central tenet of the Missouri thesis lacks historical credibility. In fact, the practice of Mormon black priesthood denial was not implemented until 1847, three years after the death of Joseph Smith. Moreover, at least two African American Latter-day Saints received their priesthood ordinations during the Mormon prophet's lifetime—the most noteworthy being Elijah Abel.

This fundamental historical fact was at long last officially acknowledged by the LDS Church itself, through the actions of a high church official, M. Russell Ballard of the Council of the Twelve Apostles. Ballard was the featured speaker at the dedication on September 28, 2002, of a monument honoring Elijah Abel. This early African American Mormon was described in the LDS Church–owned *Deseret News* as "one of the few black members to receive the priesthood in the early Church." In stating that "black members were not allowed to hold the priesthood from 1852 to 1978," Ballard conceded, "We don't know all the reasons why the Lord does what he does. . . . It's difficult to know why all things happen."[71]

Making the situation of Elijah Abel even more ambiguous is that this black priesthood holder served three missions for the Mormon church, the last one in 1883, shortly before his death on December 25, 1884. Even more paradoxical is the fact that Elijah Abel's son, Enoch, also a Latter-day Saint, was ordained an elder on November 10, 1900, even though Mormon black priesthood denial had been enforced as a widely accepted practice since 1852. Still later, Abel's grandson, Elijah Abel Jr., was ordained a priest on July 5, 1934, and an elder on September 29, 1935. Such historical information is acknowledged on the monument erected for Elijah Abel and dedicated by Elder Ballard.[72] Thus, the epic tale of Elijah Abel, along with the stories of various other African American Mormons, is full of ambiguities, contradictions, and paradoxes.

Notes

1. A series of articles discussing this development are included in D. Michael Quinn, ed., *The New Mormon History: Revisionist Essays on the Past* (Salt Lake City, Utah: Signature Books, 1992).

2. Fawn M. Brodie, *No Man Knows My History: The Life of Joseph Smith* (New York City: Alfred A. Knopf, 1945), 131–33.

3. Ibid., 172–74.

4. See L. H. Kirkpatrick, "The Negro and the L.D.S. Church," *Pen* (1954), 113, 29; Jan Shipps, "Second Class Saints," *Colorado Quarterly* 11 (1962–63): 183–90; Dennis L. Lythgoe, "Negro Slavery and Mormon Doctrine," *Western Humanities Review* 21 (1967): 327–38; and Naomi Woodbury, "A Legacy of Intolerance: Nineteenth Century Pro-Slavery Propaganda and the Mormon Church Today" (M.A. thesis, University of California, Los Angeles, 1966).

5. Stephen G. Taggart, *Mormonism's Negro Policy: Social and Historical Origins* (Salt Lake City: University of Utah Press, 1970), 13.

6. Ibid., 13–14, 15.

7. Quoted in ibid., 22–25.

8. Ibid., 26.

9. Ibid., 29.

10. Quoted in ibid., 34–35.

11. Quoted in ibid., 43.

12. Ibid., 41–44.

13. Ibid., 15.

14. Ibid., 44, 47. This statement was initially adopted as a resolution by a "General Assembly" of the church in August 1835 and subsequently published in the *Latter Day Saints' Messenger and Advocate,* which replaced the *Evening and Morning Star* as the church's major organ. It became church law by virtue of its incorporation in the Doctrine and Covenants—a work primarily made up of the revelations of Joseph Smith—as Section 134:12.

15. Ibid., 56, 46–47.

16. Ibid., 48.

17. Ibid., 60–61.

18. Ibid., 58–59.

19. Ibid., 59.

20. Ibid., 62.

21. Ibid., 77, 81.

22. Lester E. Bush Jr., "A Commentary on Stephen G. Taggart's *Mormonism's Negro Policy: Social and Historical Origins*," *Dialogue: A Journal of Mormon Thought* 4 (Winter 1969): 86–103, reprint, *Neither White nor Black: Mormon Scholars Confront the Race Issue in a Universal Church,* ed. Lester E. Bush Jr. and Armand L. Mauss (Midvale, Utah: Signature Books, 1984), 31–52. Because *Dialogue* was behind in its own publication schedule, this issue appeared in 1970 (despite its 1969 date).

23. Bush, "A Commentary," 32.

24. Ibid., 33–34.

25. Ibid., 36.

26. Ibid., 38, 40–41.

27. Introduction to the reprint of Lester E. Bush Jr., "Mormonism's Negro Doctrine: An Historical Overview," originally published in *Dialogue: A Journal of Mormon Thought* 8 (Spring 1973): 11–68, reprint, Bush and Mauss, *Neither White nor Black,* 53–129.

28. Ibid., 54.

29. Ibid., 56–58.

30. Ibid., 56.

31. Ibid., 61.

32. Ibid., 60–61, 70.

33. See Thomas F. O'Dea, *The Mormons* (Chicago: University of Chicago Press, 1957).

34. Thomas F. O'Dea, "Sources of Strain in Mormon History Reconsidered," in *Mormonism and American Culture,* ed. Marvin S. Hill and James B. Allen (New York: Harper and Row, 1972), 158, 160.

35. Mark Leone, *Roots of Modern Mormonism* (Cambridge, Mass.: Harvard University Press, 1979), 224.

36. Dean L. May, "Mormons," in *Harvard Encyclopedia of American Ethnic Groups,* ed. Stephen Thernstrom (Cambridge, Mass.: Harvard University Press, 1980), 730.

37. Klaus J. Hansen, *Mormonism and the American Experience* (Chicago: University of Chicago Press, 1981), 185, 187–88.

38. Ibid., 186–87.

39. Ronald K. Esplin, "Brigham Young and Priesthood Denial to the Blacks: An Alternative View," *Brigham Young University Studies* 19 (Spring 1979): 395.

40. Ibid., 397, 399, 400.

41. Lester E. Bush Jr., "Whence the Negro Doctrine? A Review of Ten Years of Answers," in Bush and Mauss, *Neither White nor Black,* 201, 205.

42. Ibid., 207, 205.

43. Ibid., 208.

44. Hansen, *Mormonism and the American Experience,* 190–98. Shortly thereafter, I elaborated on the crucial link between a growing sense of ethnic self-awareness and black priesthood denial; see my *Saints, Slaves, and Blacks: The Changing Place of Black People within Mormonism* (Westport, Conn.: Greenwood, 1981), esp. 84–108.

45. Rex Eugene Cooper, *Promises Made to the Fathers: Mormon Covenant Organization* (Salt Lake City: University of Utah Press, 1990), 77.

46. Ibid., 116–17.

47. Ibid., 119. Cooper's discussion of the Book of Abraham and its role in the evolution of Mormon priesthood authority appears to build on earlier suggestions of Lester E. Bush Jr. According to Bush, writing in 1984, "What was distinctively new in the Book of Abraham was a creation account which accommodated a more fully developed Mormon theology and an extensive 'midrash' concerned with the developing Mormon notion of priesthood authority. It was this latter textual expansion that included references later central to the rationale for priesthood denial to blacks." Bush continues: "The story of Pharaoh's priesthood limitation was more particularly a vehicle for a message about authentic priesthood authority than a message about priesthood exclusion based on race per se. It clearly could have been both—and ultimately it was understood to be—but there is no necessary reason to assume this was originally the case or intent or that if it were so in 1837, it still was so viewed in 1842" (Bush, "Whence the Negro Doctrine?" 204–5).

48. Cooper, *Promises Made to the Fathers,* 120.

49. Ibid., 127–28.

50. Ibid., 128–29.

51. Robert Ben Madison, "'Heirs According to the Promise': Observations on Ethnicity, Race, and Identity in Two Factions of Nineteenth-Century Mormonism," *John Whitmer Historical Association Journal* 12 (1992): 69, 71, 73. Madison quotes Jan Shipps, *Mormonism: The Story of a New Religious Tradition* (Urbana: University of Illinois Press, 1985), esp. 83.

52. Madison, "'Heirs According to the Promise,'" 74–76.

53. Ibid., 80. Madison also discusses the Book of Abraham, which by the 1880s was utilized as a proof text by Utah Mormon leaders in affirming scriptural justification for black priesthood denial. The Book of Abraham was never canonized as scripture by the RLDS Church, in contrast to the LDS Church. In the words of Madison, this work "was never officially accepted as more than speculation by the Reorganized Church (although some early RLDS affirmed their belief in it)." Moreover, Joseph Smith "never claimed divine assistance in the work's production, nor did he ever call it scripture . . . unlike his earlier work on the Book of Mormon" (77).

54. Armand L. Mauss, "In Search of Ephraim: Traditional Mormon Conceptions of Lineage and Race," *Journal of Mormon History* 25 (Spring 1999): 133. Mauss used "racialist" rather than "racist" because "racialist . . . emphasizes the salient, or even determinative, role played by race in human nature and destiny," while "racist refers to explicit, invidious distinctions, prejudice, and discrimination based on attributions of race or racial characteristics."

55. Ibid., 134–43.

56. Ibid., 143.

57. Ibid., 145, 146, 153.

58. Ibid., 148, 155.

59. D. Michael Quinn, *Early Mormonism and the Magic World View* (Salt Lake City, Utah: Signature Books, 1987), 167. This statement in the first edition is not contained in the second and enlarged edition published in 1998.

60. Quinn, *Early Mormonism,* 1987 ed., 177, 179; Quinn, *Early Mormonism,* 1998 ed., 221, 222.

61. Quinn, *Early Mormonism,* 1987 ed., 141–42; Quinn, *Early Mormonism,* 1998 ed., 166.

62. John L. Brooke, *The Refiner's Fire: The Making of Mormon Cosmology, 1644–1844* (New York: Cambridge University Press, 1994), 24–25.

63. Ibid., 28.

64. Ibid., 165.

65. Ibid.

66. Ibid., 164–65.

67. Ibid., 166, 229.

68. Ibid., 216.

69. Ibid., 211.

70. Ibid., 226.

71. Quoted in Lynn Arave, "Monument in S.L. Erected in Honor of Black Pioneer," *Deseret News,* September 29, 2002, B-3.

72. Ibid.

ALMA ALLRED

I recently read a comment by a well-meaning Latter-day Saint whom I shall not identify. She was trying to defend the Church of Jesus Christ of Latter-day Saints against criticisms of racism. I cringed when I read what she thought was an official, doctrinal explanation for the fact that blacks of African descent were not ordained to the priesthood between 1847 and 1978: "There is scriptural support for withholding the priesthood from the Negro. They were a race set apart, descendants of Cain. And the black skin was the curse put upon Cain's descendants, this is according to Latter-day scripture." It is hard to imagine more folklore packed into fewer words, and it reminded me of an experience I once had. As a good friend and I discussed the three sons of Noah, he leaned over to me and asked, "How could Ham be such a righteous man and still marry a descendant of Cain?" Similar circumstances have been replayed thousands of times in Sunday school classes throughout the church.

These two devoted and active Latter-day Saints, along with perhaps millions of others, have elevated extracanonical theories to the status of church doctrine. Strictly speaking, there is no *doctrine* in the church that blacks are descendants of Cain. Neither is there a *doctrine* that Ham married a descendant of Cain. These and similar concepts persist in the church notwithstanding the silence of current church leaders on the subject and even though these concepts conflict with straightforward applications of LDS scripture.

Although some people might wish for a rapid change of perception among church members or an official explanation for the pre-1978 restriction, such developments are unlikely for several reasons. People tend to cling to their perceptions, and the church rarely offers official explanations for policies or doctrines. In 1844, Joseph Smith lamented the difficulty of teaching people something that was contrary to their traditions:

But there has been a great difficulty in getting anything into the heads of this generation. It has been like splitting hemlock knots with a corn-dodger for a wedge, and a pumpkin for a beetle [maul]. Even the Saints are slow to understand.

I have tried for a number of years to get the minds of the Saints prepared to receive the things of God; but we frequently see some of them, after suffering all they have for the work of God, will fly to pieces like glass as soon as anything comes that is contrary to their traditions: they cannot stand the fire at all.[1]

As might be obvious to the casual observer, things haven't changed much over the intervening one hundred sixty years. We still read and interpret scripture with a priori assumptions that may or may not be valid. We are not much different today than we were back then and we are just as likely to go to pieces if we have to abandon a tradition.

Other obstacles stand in the way of any rapid change in this arena. The LDS Church almost never offers official interpretations of its scriptures. People may look in vain for an authorized commentary of the Bible, the Book of Mormon, or any other scriptures. Even the footnotes in our scriptures carry no doctrinal weight. The church provides the scriptures, ordinances, and temple worship largely without explanation and always without apology.

While this practice gives the members of the church a great deal of latitude to believe as they wish, it also allows people to get bogged down in believing traditions that may very well be wrong. This is especially true with regard to ideas about blacks and the priesthood, because for many years church elders offered unofficial explanations that very often were perceived as official declarations of doctrine. In order to understand the doctrinal ramifications connected to this subject, it is important to understand first what constitutes doctrine in the LDS faith and how that differs from policies that may come and go.

Strictly speaking, LDS doctrine is embodied in the four books of scripture considered by the LDS Church as its canon, including the Bible, the Book of Mormon, Doctrine and Covenants, and the Pearl of Great Price. Joseph Fielding Smith, who became the tenth president of the church, taught as an apostle that every man's teachings need to be judged by the standard of the scriptures:

It makes no difference what is written or what anyone has said, if what has been said is in conflict with what the Lord has revealed, we can set it aside. My words, and the teaching of any other member of the Church, high or low, if they do not square with the revelations, we need not accept them. Let us have this matter clear. We have accepted the four standard works as the measuring yardsticks, or balances, by which we measure every man's doctrine.

You cannot accept the books written by the authorities of the Church as standards in doctrine, only in so far as they accord with the revealed word in the standard works.[2]

Joseph Fielding Smith's successor as church president, Harold B. Lee, emphasized the same idea when he explained how the church acquires additional doctrine:

> If anyone, regardless of his position in the Church, were to advance a doctrine that is not substantiated by the standard Church works, meaning the Bible, the Book of Mormon, the Doctrine and Covenants, and the Pearl of Great Price, you may know that his statement is merely his private opinion. The only one authorized to bring forth any new doctrine is the President of the Church, who, when he does, will declare it as revelation from God, and it will be so accepted by the Council of the Twelve and sustained by the body of the Church. And if any man speak a doctrine which contradicts what is in the standard Church works, you may know by that same token that it is false and you are not bound to accept it as truth.[3]

While doctrine may be considered a principle of truth that does not change, policies, in contrast, may be adopted or dropped as circumstances require. An example of such a policy would be the implementation of the Word of Wisdom in the church. The scripture outlining prohibitions against the use of alcohol, tobacco, and other substances states that it is "not by commandment," but Brigham Young, second church president, elevated it to a commandment during his administration, and Heber J. Grant, the seventh church president, made it a condition for full fellowship in the church.[4] In a similar circumstance of policy rather than doctrine, Brigham Young allowed young boys to be ordained to the Aaronic priesthood at various ages. Before that, priesthood holders were generally adults. Today, church policy has codified ordination in the Aaronic priesthood so that boys are ordained when twelve years old and become eligible for missions at nineteen. This doesn't represent a doctrine; rather it is indicative of a practice—a practice that could be changed.

Some policies have influenced doctrines and ordinances. For example, the administration of the sacrament incorporates both doctrine and policies. The LDS scriptures stipulate that priests administer the sacrament—which is interpreted to mean pronouncing the benedictions upon the emblems of the sacrament. Although many church members believe that only priesthood holders may pass the sacrament, church policy has always allowed women and unordained children to pass the trays down the rows. At one point in church history, Brigham Young withdrew the right to administer the sacrament from the whole church, not allowing it to occur for several months. The distinction between doctrine and policy can also be seen in the church's discontinuance of the practice of plural marriage while still retaining the doctrine in its canon.

Similarly, priesthood denial—first to slaves and then to all blacks of African descent—existed as a policy rather than a doctrine—as David O. McKay explained in a letter to Sterling McMurrin. As later reported by McMurrin, President McKay insisted that there was no doctrine of any kind pertaining to blacks: "There is not now, and there never has been, a doctrine in this Church that the negroes are under a divine curse. We believe that we have scriptural precedent for withholding the priesthood from the Negro. It is a practice, not a doctrine, and the practice will some day be changed. And that's all there is to it."[5]

Some time after the Mormons left Nauvoo, Illinois, church leaders in Utah implemented the policy that restricted blacks of African descent from being ordained to the priesthood. This practice had a devastating impact upon black members then and upon countless others since that time—leaving many to wonder how such a practice could be justified. Over the years, church leaders wrote and spoke on the subject in an effort to explain why one race of people was excluded from the priesthood. They offered several possible reasons for the prohibition. Brigham Young suggested that since Cain was the first murderer, none of his children could hold the priesthood.[6] Others proposed the idea that some spirits in the war in heaven were less valiant than others and consequently entered into mortality under restrictions—sort of a double probationary estate.[7] Over the process of time, the absence of a specific revelation on the subject resulted in the conclusion that these speculative theories were actually doctrinal statements officially promulgated by the hierarchy of the church. However, when such an explanation surfaced as in a 1939 discourse by George F. Richards, he hedged by noting, "We have no definite knowledge concerning this."[8]

At this point, I think it is important to provide a personal explanation. I have long been troubled by the theology that arose as an explanation for priesthood denial. At one point, it was easy to believe that it was a mistake—a result of racism among the prophets that was rectified by revelation. After more thought, however, I rejected that idea, just as I reject the theology that defended the practice. I don't believe that LDS scripture allows for a restriction against blacks' holding the priesthood. Nor do I think that LDS theology can reasonably maintain that today's blacks are descendants of Cain or that ancient intermarriage with Canaanites perpetuated any racial curse. Too many scriptures collide with those ideas for them to be valid.

The reasons I reject the Canaanite connections to priesthood restrictions lie in the fact that this church policy, and the proposed reasons behind the policy, conflict with basic concepts of LDS theology, good logic, scripture, and history. These elements combine to demonstrate that ideas connecting Cain and Canaanites belong to folklore and myth rather than to faith and truth. The second LDS Article of Faith states that "men will be punished for their own sins, and not for Adam's transgression." How surprising that thousands upon thousands of Latter-day Saint children could memorize that verse and not be struck with the obvious dichotomy that we were claiming at the same time that Cain's children were punished for his transgression. As elementary as that discrepancy now strikes us, the other suggested reasons suffer from the same deficiencies.

The implementation of the policy forbidding the ordination of blacks to the priesthood undoubtedly came about as several circumstances converged in American history. During the lifetime of Joseph Smith, there was at least one black priesthood holder. Elijah Abel was a member of the Third Quorum of Seventy and was called on three full-time missions—two during the administration of Joseph Smith and one under John Taylor. Joseph Smith Sr. mentioned Abel's ordination to the priesthood in his patriarchal blessing, and Abel's status as a black and an elder was known to the Prophet Joseph Smith.[9] Abel had a ministerial license issued by the church that was renewed several times during Smith's lifetime, for the last time in Nauvoo in 1841.

After Abel's death, some men claimed that Joseph Smith had announced that Abel could not hold the priesthood. The sources of these statements were Zebedee Coltrin and Abraham Smoot. Coltrin's testimony is not consistent with documentary evidence because he claimed that Joseph Smith informed him of the priesthood ban in 1834; yet it was Coltrin who ordained Elijah Abel in 1836.[10] Abraham Smoot's recollection faces similar obstacles. Evidence suggests that Smoot harbored racial prejudices that may have been amplified by a basic misunderstanding of church policy. When Joseph Smith announced his candidacy for the presidency of the United States, missionaries automatically became campaign representatives for their prophet. Smoot took a dim view of campaigning for Joseph Smith because his campaign included a plan for the cessation of slavery. Consequently, Smoot refused to distribute literature produced by Joseph Smith that was critical of slavery. Smoot was also a slave owner after his arrival in Utah. These circumstances indicate that Smoot's racial prejudices influenced his religious perspective—even to the extent that those prejudices helped influence LDS folklore and official policies. For example, Abraham Smoot is the source of a story regarding an early apostle named David W. Patten. According to the legend, Patten encountered the biblical figure Cain in his missionary travels. According to the description provided by Smoot, Cain was very large, had dark skin, wore no clothing, and was covered with hair. The impact of this bit of folklore cannot be underestimated. Even though few LDS leaders have commented on it,[11] many Mormons are familiar with the story and it lies in the subconscious, forming a racial link—however unjustified—between Cain and blacks.

Before the Mormons moved west, the church had already specified that slaves were not to be ordained to the priesthood. In a hierarchical church, the possibility of slaves' presiding over others—particularly their masters—would have been a terrible circumstance. Consequently, it makes sense that slaves would have been restricted from holding the priesthood. However, Smoot may have concluded that slaves could not be ordained because they were black rather than because they were slaves. This seems to have been a reasonable conclusion based upon the culture in which Smoot lived. For centuries, slave owners and slave traders sought to legitimize slavery by tying Cain, Ham, and their descendants to black Africans. They claimed that slavery was not only acceptable to God but ordained by him. Unfortunately, LDS writers adopted and adapted the rhetoric of slavery in order to explain the LDS position of priesthood denial to blacks. While Christians used passages in Genesis to justify physical bondage for blacks by Christians, Mormon writers later concluded that these passages still applied—but in a spiritual sense.

Those spiritual restrictions relied upon essential but practically impossible conditions: racial purity and a commandment against intermarriage with Canaanites. That is, if any of your ancestors were related to Canaanites, you were excluded from the priesthood. Historically, proving such racial separateness is improbable if not impossible. Scriptural evidence of interracial marriage also makes such a premise of racial separation untenable.

Intermarriage between blacks and whites has occurred for thousands of years. Frank Snowden, a classics scholar, noted that intermarriage between the races is a historical fact documented by several ancient authors:

> No laws in the Greco-Roman world prohibited unions of blacks and whites. Ethiopian blood was interfused with that of Greeks and Romans. No Greek or Roman author condemned such racial mixture. Martial and Juvenal condemned adultery when a mulatto child was evidence of illicit relations but said nothing of "racial purity." The scientists Aristotle and Pliny, like Plutarch, commented as scientists on the physical appearance of those born of black-white racial mixture but included nothing resembling certain modern strictures on miscegenation.[12]

Artwork from Greece, Italy, and Egypt chronicles the presence of black Africans as soldiers, merchants, servants, and statesmen throughout Mediterranean culture, where intermarriage was common and mixed-race progeny were a natural consequence.[13] Later in history, the Moors from the African continent moved north into Europe where they conquered portions of the

Iberian peninsula. When they were finally driven out of Spain, many moved to other areas of Europe where they were assimilated. Holland's Christmas mythology includes an African child, Zwarte Piet (Black Peter), who came from Spain with Sinterklaas (Santa Claus) to punish or reward children who were naughty or nice.

The slave trade carried out by the Portuguese brought thousands of black Africans to Portugal where they too eventually blended with their captors. Queen Charlotte, the wife of Britain's King George III and grandmother of Queen Victoria, was a descendant of Portuguese slaves who married into European nobility. Additionally, Alessandro de Medici, the illegitimate son of Giulio de Medici and a black servant, eventually was appointed Duke of Penna, and his descendants married into the Austrian Hapsburg line.[14]

Secondly, even though the terms *Canaanite* and *Negro* have been used interchangeably in the LDS Church, Canaanites weren't black and they certainly weren't African. Biblically, Canaanites descended from Canaan, the fourth son of Ham. African blacks are generally believed to be descendants of Cush, the first son of Ham. This is important because the Canaanites were those who have been referred to as the "cursed" lineage while practically nothing is said about Ham's other children. It was Canaan who was cursed by Noah—not specifically Ham and not Ham's other children. According to Genesis, Noah cursed Canaan after Ham saw his father naked and drunk and ridiculed his father to his other brothers (Gen. 9:21–25). Before this time, Ham had been righteous: "And Noah and his sons hearkened unto the Lord, and gave heed and they were called the sons of God" (Moses 8:13). This scripture appears in the Pearl of Great Price, which also contains this statement: "And thus Noah found grace in the eyes of the Lord; for Noah was a just man, and perfect in his generation; and he walked with God, *as did also his three sons, Shem, Ham, and Japheth* (Moses 8:27; italics mine).

These verses are particularly important because Mormon folklore contains the common belief that Ham wrongly married a descendant of Cain, bringing a curse upon himself and his descendants. If such a commandment forbidding marriage into Cain's lineage existed, how could Ham have contracted such a marriage and still have been considered righteous enough to get passage on the ark? The answer has always been that Cain's genes needed to be preserved; but this argument does not address the fact that Ham was righteous and "walked with God" after his marriage—a circumstance that, according to tradition, was impossible.

Although Canaan was not born until after the flood, there is a land of Canaan referred to in Moses 7:7 before the flood. There is also a land of Cainan. It is likely that both are variant spellings of the same word and refer to the same land. This is because the Book of Moses was dictated by Joseph Smith and the two terms are homophones. The decision to spell the antediluvian land "Cainan" was entirely editorial. Enoch came from the land of Cainan and called it "a land of righteousness unto this day" (Moses 6:42). In Moses 7:4–8, Enoch sees a vision of the world "for the space of many generations." He describes how the people of Canaan (Cainan?) destroy the people of Shum. After this, we are told that the land is cursed with heat and that a blackness comes upon all the children of Canaan—it was not inherited from Cain.[15]

These events seen by Enoch all took place before the flood. By the time of the flood, the whole earth had become corrupt, including the land of Cainan. Enoch's land of righteousness deteriorated along with the rest of the world. Immediately after the vision, Enoch saw several lands and people, and God commanded him to preach to them. Enoch called upon all the people to repent except the people of Canaan. Was that because the people of Canaan (Cainan) were righteous as stated in Moses 6:42 or because God did not care if they perished? According to the New Testament, God is not willing that any should perish (2 Pet. 3:9).

Bruce R. McConkie, a prominent LDS apostle of the 1970s and 1980s, refers to the fact that Enoch did not preach to the Canaanites as the reason why Mormons did not actively proselytize blacks.[16] Passages from the Book of Mormon and biblical history, however, differ with this interpretation, indicating that the message of salvation was actively carried to Canaanite cities. Nimrod, the "mighty hunter before the Lord," was a grandson of Ham through Cush:

> And Cush begat Nimrod: he began to be a mighty one in the earth. He was a mighty hunter before the Lord: . . .
> And the beginning of his kingdom was Babel, and Erech, and Accad, and Calneh, in the land of Shinar.
> Out of that land went forth Asshur, and builded Nineveh. (Gen. 10:9–11)

Nimrod and his descendants thus established two significant cities: Nineveh and Babel. Jonah preached to the city of Nineveh, and the brother of Jared (from the Book of Mormon) and his family came from Babel.[17] The Book of Mormon prophet Nephi claims that God sent prophets to preach to the Canaanite cities of the promised land and said they could have been as blessed as the Israelites had they only kept the commandments: "Behold, the Lord esteemeth all flesh in one; he that is righteous is favored of God. But behold, this people had rejected every word of God, and they were ripe in iniquity" (1 Ne. 17:35).

With regard to specific LDS doctrine, a few items should be mentioned concerning the idea that the priesthood was withheld from one specific race. Noah's curse upon Canaan rather than Ham seems to be contrary to certain aspects of LDS theology. Why curse Canaan for his father's actions? The ten commandments say that God visits the iniquities of the fathers upon the children:

> for I the Lord thy God am a jealous God, visiting the iniquity of the fathers upon the children unto the third and fourth generation of them that hate me;
> And shewing mercy unto thousands of them that love me, and keep my commandments. (Exod. 20:5-6)

In contrast, LDS theology affirms that children who repent are not punished for their ancestors' faults. The curse of Canaan, according to tradition, operated irrespective of the actions of his descendants. This alleged curse modifies the concept that "men will be punished for their own sins and not for Adam's transgression," as stipulated in the second LDS Article of Faith. Adam's sin, though entirely unique, is not answered upon the heads of his children. Cain's sin, which is relatively common, brought condemnation upon all his descendants, regardless of their willingness to repent. Ham's sin, though far short of murder, reaps the same penalty as Cain's. If the priesthood was withheld from Africans because their ancestor was a murderer, why were King David's descendants allowed the priesthood, for he too was a murderer? Why are not the white sons of murderers kept from the priesthood?

The Book of Abraham states that a descendant of Canaan discovered the land of Egypt and that all the Egyptians are descended from Canaan:

> Now this king of Egypt was a descendant from the loins of Ham, and was a partaker of the blood of the Canaanites by birth.
> From this descent sprang all the Egyptians, and thus the blood of the Canaanites was preserved in the land. (Abraham 1:21-22)

The problem that is immediately apparent is the fact that Abraham and Joseph each married an Egyptian woman. One response offered to counter that damaging evidence has been that the Egyptians at the time of these marriages were Semitic Hyksos who had conquered Egypt and so were not really Canaanites. This explanation contradicts Abraham 1:21-22. It also contradicts history. The Hyksos held power in Egypt for a maximum of only one hundred fifty years. If they were the Egyptians during Abraham's lifetime, it is not possible for them to still have been in power in Joseph's day.[18]

While it is true that the Hyksos were primarily Semitic, historians agree that they were a mixture of Semitic and Canaanite people. A respected encyclopedia of biblical archaeology describes the Hyksos as "largely Semitic of Canaanite and Amorite descent."[19]

Hugh Nibley, an LDS scholar, comments that Joseph's wife, Asenath, "was the daughter of the high priest of Heliopolis and hence of the pure line of Ham; she was also the wife of Joseph and the mother of our own vaunted ancestor Ephraim."[20] Ephraim, son of a Canaanite mother, acquired the birthright by blessing from his grandfather Jacob. According to LDS theology, the impact of this blessing cannot be underestimated. The birthright was the right to preside in the priesthood, as will be explained later.

The Bible contains other instances of intermarriage between Canaanites and descendants of Abraham. Esau, the son of Isaac and brother of Jacob, married several Canaanite women:

> And Esau was forty years old when he took to wife Judith the daughter of Beeri the Hittite, and Bashemath the daughter of Elon the Hittite:
> Which were a grief of mind unto Isaac and to Rebekah. (Gen. 26:34–35)

> Now these are the generations of Esau, who is Edom. (Gen. 36:1; see also Gen. 36:2–8)

Judah and Simeon each married Canaanite women and sired sons. The genealogy of Judah's Canaanite children is found in 1 Chronicles 4:21–22 where they are all given inheritances in the house of Israel. Simeon's Canaanite children also appear as part of the house of Israel (Gen. 46:10; Num. 26:12–14; 1 Chr. 4:24–27).

There is no doubt that there was a prohibition against intermarriage with some of the Canaanites. However, there were instances where Israelites married outside that rule, apparently without divine displeasure. When the Canaanite city of Jericho was under siege, Rahab hid the Israelite spies in return for a promise that she and her family would be spared. This Canaanite woman married Salmon and they were the parents of Boaz, a progenitor of Jesus Christ: "And Salmon begat Booz of Rachab; and Booz begat Obed of Ruth; and Obed begat Jesse" (Matt. 1:5). Marriages between Israelites and several nationalities were forbidden:

> When the Lord thy God shall bring thee into the land whither thou goest to possess it, and hath cast out many nations before thee, the Hittites, and the Girgashites, and the Amorites, and the Canaanites, and the Perizzites, and the Hivites, and the Jebusites, seven nations greater and mightier than thou;
> And when the Lord thy God shall deliver them before thee; thou shalt smite them, and utterly destroy them; thou shalt make no covenant with them, nor shew mercy unto them:
> Neither shalt thou make marriages with them; thy daughter thou shalt not give unto his son, nor his daughter shalt thou take unto thy son. (Deut. 7:1–3)

However, at the same time Moses gave this prohibition, God explained the reason behind the restriction: "For they will turn away thy son from following me, that they may serve other gods: so will the anger of the Lord be kindled against you, and destroy thee suddenly" (Deut. 7:4). Surely, if a curse accompanied marriage with these races, it would have been specified. Instead, we see that the reason behind the prohibition dealt with righteousness rather than priesthood eligibility.

Restrictions against others in the land—not Canaanites—were even stricter: "An Ammonite or Moabite shall not enter into the congregation of the Lord; even to their tenth generation shall they not enter into the congregation of the Lord for ever" (Deut. 23:3). Interestingly, even though Ruth the Moabitess and Rahab came from these prohibited nations, and Rahab's genealogy would have disqualified her descendants (according to tradition) from holding the priesthood, both women were ancestors of Jesus: the "Apostle and High Priest of our profession" (Heb. 3:1).

No provision allowed for Moabites or Ammonites (descendants of Lot) to be accepted into the congregation of Israel, but there was explicit provision for both Egyptians and Edomites—Canaanites—to enter into the congregation of Israel:

> Thou shalt not abhor an Edomite; for he is thy brother: thou shalt not abhor an Egyptian; because thou wast a stranger in his land.
> The children that are begotten of them shall enter into the congregation of the Lord in their third generation. (Deut. 23:7–8)

Assimilation into accepted status occurred with only one generation between Canaanites and Israelites. The genealogy of Nathan the prophet is important in this regard because, according to the Doctrine and Covenants, Nathan held the priesthood: "David's wives and concubines were given unto him of me, by the hand of Nathan, my servant, and others of the prophets who had the keys of this power" (Doctrines and Covenants [hereafter D&C] 132:39). Nathan held the keys of the sealing power and his grandfather was an Egyptian:

> Now Sheshan had no sons, but daughters. And Sheshan had a servant, an Egyptian, whose name was Jarha.
> And Sheshan gave his daughter to Jarha his servant to wife; and she bare him Attai.
> And Attai begat *Nathan,* and Nathan begat Zabad. (1 Chron. 2:34–37; italics mine)[21]

These instances demonstrate that descendants of Canaan married into the lineage of Shem and did so without any hint of impropriety. Josephus states that Moses married an Ethiopian woman while he held the status of a prince of Pharaoh.[22] Mormons holding to tradition might claim that Moses did not know any better because he had been raised as an Egyptian, but the apostle Paul makes it clear that Moses was well aware of God's statutes and forsook Egypt in large part because of his faith. The fact that Moses married a Cushite woman is additional evidence that there was no divine injunction against such marriages:

> By faith Moses, when he was come to years, refused to be called the son of Pharaoh's daughter;
> Choosing rather to suffer afflictions with the people of God, than to enjoy the pleasures of sin for a season;
> Esteeming the reproach of Christ greater riches than the treasures in Egypt: for he had respect unto the recompense of the reward. (Heb. 11:24–26)

Little doubt remains that intermarriage between Canaanites and Israelites destroyed any chance for a pure, non-Canaanite race among the chosen seed. One third of the house of Judah is Canaanite with an unknown portion among the other tribes. What then can we make of the curse pronounced by Noah and of Abraham's comments that Pharaoh's lineage could not have the "right of priesthood"? (Abr. 1:27). It may be that Mormons have simply misinterpreted those passages of scripture.

In the Book of Abraham, Abraham explains that he sought the blessings of the fathers and the right to be ordained to administer those blessings. He says that he became an heir holding the right belonging to the fathers. According to LDS theology, the right to administer the ordinances is held by the presiding priesthood authority on the earth. In the days of Abraham, that right was held by the presiding patriarch. It started with Adam and came in due course to Abraham. Abraham 1:3–4 stipulates that the appointment came by lineage. The right to preside was the birthright which went to Abraham, Isaac, Jacob, Joseph, and finally to Ephraim.

According to these LDS scriptures, even though the priesthood did not remain exclusively with Ephraim, the right to preside did. Moses presided over Israel even though he was of the tribe of Levi. Joseph Smith, however, claimed to be a "lawful heir" because he was the house of Ephraim (D&C 86:8–11). Since this authority was passed from father to only one son, when Noah gave it to Shem, Ham could not be the heir. Ham and Japheth, together with their descendants, did not have the right to administer the priesthood because it was given to Shem. Esau lost the right to Jacob. Reuben lost the right to Joseph. Manasseh lost that right when Jacob conferred it upon Ephraim. Each man who lost the birthright did not lose the right to be ordained to the priesthood;

rather, he lost the right to preside as *the* presiding high priest in a patriarchal order. The scripture does not say that Pharaoh could not hold the priesthood; it says that he could not have the "right of priesthood" (Abr. 1:27). This right had been given to Shem, who in turn gave it to his successor in the patriarchal office.

Years after the right of priesthood had been passed to Abraham, the Pharaohs were feigning a claim to it from Noah. They did not merely claim priesthood; they claimed the right to preside over the priesthood. Pharaoh, the son of Egyptus, established a patriarchal government in Egypt; but he was of that lineage by which he could not have the "right of priesthood" or "the right of the firstborn," which belonged to Shem and his posterity. In response to the Pharaoh's claims, Abraham states: "But the records of the fathers, even the patriarchs, concerning *the right of priesthood,* the Lord my God preserved in mine own hands" (Abr. 1:31; italics mine). In other words, Abraham retained the right to preside over the priesthood.

The words *right, priesthood,* and *lineage* all prominently figure in Abraham's history; and Joseph Smith used the same words to describe the appointment of his father, Joseph Smith Sr., as church patriarch:

> Blessed of the Lord is my father, for he [Joseph Smith Sr.] shall stand in the midst of his posterity and shall be comforted by their blessings when he is old and bowed down with years, and shall be called a prince over them, and shall be numbered among those who hold *the right of Patriarchal Priesthood,* even the keys of that ministry.[23]

Joseph Smith used the same words to later appoint his elder brother Hyrum as church patriarch after their father's death:

> And again, verily I say unto you, let my servant William be appointed, ordained, and anointed, as counselor unto my servant Joseph, in the room of my servant Hyrum, that my servant Hyrum may take the *office of Priesthood* and Patriarch, which was appointed unto him by his father, by blessing and *also by right;* (D&C 124:91; italics mine)

> This order of priesthood was confirmed to be handed down from father to son, and *rightly* belongs to the literal descendants of the chosen seed, to whom the promises were made. (D&C 107:40; italics mine)

Still, we should consider the curse pronounced upon Canaan. It parallels Jacob's blessing pronounced by Isaac and, conversely, Esau's curse. A side-by-side comparison of the two illustrates that Esau received the same curse as Canaan (table 2.1).

Noah's curse upon Canaan directly parallels Isaac's promise concerning

Table 2.1

Noah to Canaan	Isaac to Jacob
Cursed be Canaan; a servant of servants shall he be unto his brethren. And he said, Blessed be the Lord God of Shem; and Canaan shall be his servant (Gen. 9:25–26).	Let people serve thee, and nations bow down to thee: be lord over thy brethren, and let they mother's sons bow down to thee (Gen. 27:29).

Esau. They both promised lordship to one son and servitude to the other. The ability to hold the priesthood was not the issue; it was the ability to preside in a patriarchal order that allowed only one lineage.

The revelation of 1978 announced by President Spencer W. Kimball giving all worthy men the privilege of holding the priesthood is consistent with the principles of LDS theology and essential to a consistent interpretation of its scripture. As recorded in the Doctrine and Covenants, Joseph Smith claimed that at some future day, high priests will be ordained out of "every nation, kindred, tongue and people" (D&C 77:13). It is impossible to have high priests from every nation while excluding Africans. Joseph Smith stated that, if the work progressed, we would see people of every color, including the African "Hottentots," worship in the house of the Lord:

> If the work rolls forth with the same rapidity it has heretofore done, we may soon expect to see flocking to this place, people from every land and from every nation; the polished European, the degraded Hottentot, and the shivering Laplander; persons of every tongue, and *of every color,* who shall worship the Lord of Hosts in His holy temple and offer up their orisons in His sanctuary.[24]

Temple worship in LDS theology requires priesthood ordination for men. Consequently, Joseph Smith's idea that "Hottentots" would soon worship in the temple is a de facto promise of priesthood ordination. Brigham Young got on the same bandwagon when he claimed in 1860 that the restriction would be lifted within one generation: "Children are now born who will live until every son of Adam will have the privilege of receiving the principles of eternal life."[25] There can be no doubt that this meant priesthood ordination to every male descendant of Adam, regardless of race.

The above statements seem to coincide with Isaiah 19, in which God calls Egypt "my people" (v. 25) and says they shall have altars, "do sacrifice and oblation," and "vow unto the Lord, and perform it" (vv. 19, 21). In LDS thought, that can occur only if Egyptians participate fully as ordained priests.

From about 1847 until the 1970s, LDS authors wrestled with the task of finding out what it was that blacks did to merit being denied the priesthood. Clearly they were looking at the problem from a mistaken perspective. Rather than looking at blacks to assign blame, white church members might have looked at themselves to see if we were the primary hindrance.

Notes

1. Joseph Fielding Smith, comp. and ed., *Teachings of the Prophet Joseph Smith* (Salt Lake City: Bookcraft, 1976), 331.

2. Joseph Fielding Smith, *Doctrines of Salvation,* 3 vols. (Salt Lake City: Bookcraft, 1954), 3:203.

3. Harold B. Lee, Address, *The First Area General Conference for Germany, Austria, Holland, Italy, Switzerland, France, Belgium, and Spain of the Church of Jesus Christ of Latter-day Saints, held in Munich Germany, August 24–26, 1973, with Reports and Discourses,* Area Conference Proceedings, 1971–80, Archives, Family and Church History Department, Church of Jesus Christ of Latter-day Saints, Salt Lake City, Utah (hereafter LDS Church Archives).

4. Doctrine and Covenants 89:1–2: "A Word of Wisdom, for the benefit of the council of high priests, assembled in Kirtland, and the church, and also the saints in Zion—To be sent greeting; *not by commandment or constraint,* but by revelation and the word of wisdom" (italics mine); "Minutes of the General Conference," *Millennial Star* 14 (February 1, 1852): 35; Thomas G. Alexander, *Mormonism in Transition: A History of the Latter-day Saints, 1890–1930* (Urbana: University of Illinois Press, 1986), 265.

5. Quoted in Lester E. Bush Jr., "A Commentary on Stephen G. Taggart's *Mormonism's Negro Policy: Social and Historical Origins,*" in *Neither White nor Black: Mormon Scholars Confront the Race Issue in a Universal Church,* ed. Lester E. Bush Jr. and Armand Mauss (Midvale, Utah: Signature Books, 1984), 39.

6. Elden J. Watson, comp. and ed., *Brigham Young Addresses,* 6 vols. (Salt Lake City: privately published, 1979–84), 2:unpaginated. Young gave this address on June 29, 1851.

7. Bruce R. McConkie, *Mormon Doctrine* (Salt Lake City: Bookcraft, 1958), 477, entry titled "Negroes." Editions of this book published after the 1978 revelation eliminated this article and replaced it with another reporting the effect of President Spencer W. Kimball's announcement without any reference to spiritual valiance.

8. George F. Richards, *Report of the Semi-Annual Conference of the Church of Jesus Christ of Latter-day Saints,* April 6, 1939 (Salt Lake City: Church of Jesus Christ of Latter-day Saints, semi-annual), 59.

9. First Council of Seventy, Records, 1835–85, entry of June 1, 1839, extracted by staff, LDS Church Archives. Lester Bush observes, "This reference suggests that Abel was out of favor with a number of the brethren in the quorum 'because of some of his teachings.' It is of interest that Abel was clearly in possession of his priesthood, a fact obviously known to Joseph Smith, who was at this meeting. Yet Smith is not recorded as having made any comment" ("A Commentary," 43n15).

10. First Council of Seventy, Records, December 20, 1836.

11. Spencer W. Kimball referred to this account in his *The Miracle of Forgiveness* (Salt Lake City: Bookcraft, 1991), 127–28.

12. Frank M. Snowden Jr., *Blacks in Antiquity: Ethiopians in the Greco-Roman Experience* (Cambridge, Mass.: Harvard University Press, 1970), 195.

13. See Frank M. Snowden Jr., *Before Color Prejudice: The Ancient View of Blacks* (Cambridge, Mass.: Harvard University Press, 1983).

14. Research by Mario de Valdes y Cocom, a historian of the African Diaspora, reported in "Blurred Racial Lines," *Frontline* Web site: <www.pbs.org/wgbh/pages/frontline/shows/secret/famous>, accessed May 2003.

15. It is possible that those who followed Cain in his wicked practices were referred to as the "seed of Cain" in the same manner that the Jews were called the children of the devil (John 8:44).

16. McConkie, *Mormon Doctrine*, 1976 ed., 527.

17. Parley P. Pratt referred to the possible Hamitic lineage of the Jaredites when he made mistaken comments about the Kinderhook plates, claiming they provided "the genealogy of one of the ancient Jaredites back to Ham the son of Noah." Quoted in Stanley B. Kimball, "Kinderhook Plates Brought to Joseph Smith Appear to Be a Nineteenth-Century Hoax," *Ensign*, August 1981, 73. While the account of the translation of the Kinderhook plates is unreliable and was constructed from secondary and tertiary sources, the point of Pratt's statement is that he believed Ham was the progenitor of Jaredite prophets, who clearly would have held priesthood.

18. Abraham's wife Hagar bore Ishmael when Abraham was eighty-six. Isaac was born fourteen years later and Jacob sixty years after that. When Jacob came into Egypt, he told Pharoah that he was one hundred thirty years old. When Joseph brought his children to Jacob to receive his blessing, they were evidently little boys. They were born nearly two hundred years after Ishmael was born.

19. Charles F. Pfeiffer, *The Biblical World: A Dictionary of Biblical Archaeology* (New York: Bonanza Books, 1966), 298–99.

20. Hugh Nibley, *Abraham in Egypt* (Salt Lake City: Deseret Book, 1981), 215.

21. There is little doubt that the Nathan referred to is the prophet Nathan. Those at Solomon's court are listed in 1 Kings 4:2–6. Most of the advisors were also advisors to King David. Nathan the prophet is notably missing although two of his sons are among the courtiers.

22. Flavius Josephus, *The Antiquities of the Jews*, Book 2, chap. 10 in *Josephus: Complete Works*, trans. William Whiston (Grand Rapids, Mich.: Kregel Publications, 1978).

23. Smith, *Teachings of the Prophet*, 38; italics mine.

24. Joseph Smith Jr. et al., *History of the Church of Jesus Christ of Latter-day Saints*, ed. B. H. Roberts, 7 vols. (1902–12, 1932; reprint, Salt Lake City: Deseret Book, 1976), 4:216.

25. Brigham Young, July 8, 1860, *Journal of Discourses*, 26 vols. (London and Liverpool: LDS Book Depot, 1855–86), 8:116.

3   Two Perspectives: The Religious Hopes of
     "Worthy" African American Latter-day Saints
     before the 1978 Revelation

RONALD G. COLEMAN AND DARIUS A. GRAY

On June 8, 1978, the First Presidency of the Church of Jesus Christ of Latter-day Saints issued a statement that reversed the long-standing practice of denying the priesthood to men of African lineage. The statement said in part: "all worthy male members of the Church may be ordained to the priesthood without regard for race or color."[1] In the years since the priesthood was opened to "worthy" black males, women and men of African descent who are "worthy" members of the Church of Jesus Christ of Latter-day Saints have been permitted to participate in temple work and receive ordinances available to all "worthy" members of the faith. The number of persons of African descent converting to the Mormon religion has increased dramatically during this time, most notably in Latin America and Africa. Greater numbers of African Americans have also converted to the LDS Church. The singer Gladys Knight and the former National Basketball Association player Thurl Bailey are two of the increased number of black American converts to the church.[2]

In 1988, ten years after the priesthood pronouncement, a panel discussion titled "Blacks and the Mormon Church" was part of the program at the annual meeting of the Mormon History Association. A plenary session was also held in the LDS tabernacle in Logan, Utah. Alan Cherry, an African American member of the Church of Jesus Christ of Latter-day Saints, emphasized the responsibilities associated with the priesthood as the major theme in his remarks. Cherry overlooked the historical importance of the topic to African American Saints who had converted to the LDS faith in its formative years and in the decades before June 1978.[3] These black Mormons, secure in their beliefs and faith in the gospel as expressed in the writings and teachings of the Church of Jesus Christ of Latter-day Saints, patiently waited for the day when they would be able to participate fully in the church they had embraced spiritually and intellectually.

The remainder of this chapter provides some insights into the minds and hopes of two Mormon African Americans whose membership spanned the years when the denial of the priesthood to blacks was in full force. Although priesthood denial applied specifically to men of African lineage, it also imposed restrictions on black women. Jane Elizabeth Manning James was an African American woman who converted to the LDS church in 1842. Len Hope Sr. was a black man who converted to Mormonism in 1919. It is hoped that the accounts of the religious trials and tribulations of these early black Saints will give readers a greater understanding of the possibilities for people of African descent within the Church of Jesus Christ of Latter-day Saints in the first decades of the twenty-first century.

Jane Elizabeth Manning James

One of five children of Isaac and Phillis Manning, a free African American couple, Jane Elizabeth Manning was born in southwestern Connecticut sometime between 1813 and 1822. She converted and was baptized into the Church of Jesus Christ of Latter-day Saints in 1842 after hearing the message of Charles Wesley Wandell, an LDS missionary traveling through the area. Several other members of Jane Elizabeth's family also accepted the message of Wandell and became members of the Mormon church. These black Saints decided to join other converts from their area in relocating to Nauvoo, Illinois, then the headquarters for the Church of Jesus Christ of Latter-day Saints. Following their arrival in Buffalo, New York, the black Saints discovered they did not have enough money to continue their journey by boat and therefore walked the remaining eight hundred miles to Nauvoo. The only time they had to confront the issue of whether they were free or slave was when they arrived in Peoria, Illinois. Upon convincing local authorities that they were not fugitive slaves, the group was allowed to continue onward to Nauvoo.[4]

The long, arduous trip was completed in November 1843. After arriving in Nauvoo, they were directed to the home of Joseph Smith Jr., the founder of the LDS Church, and his wife, Emma. Shortly thereafter Jane began residing and working in the Smith household. The experiences within the household had a profound impact on Jane that lasted throughout her life. She unquestionably believed that Joseph Smith was a prophet, and she took great pleasure over the years in recalling the special relationship she had with the Mormon prophet and his wife. Jane was genuinely grieved upon learning of the slaying of Joseph and his brother Hyrum by a mob in nearby Carthage, Illinois, in 1844.[5]

In Nauvoo, Jane met Isaac James, a free black LDS convert from New Jersey. The couple subsequently married; and when the decision was made by the LDS leadership to seek a new refuge in the West, Isaac and Jane, along with their two sons, journeyed to Utah as part of one of the pioneer companies of Saints. Arriving in Salt Lake Valley in the fall of 1847, the James family joined their Mormon compatriots in transforming the mountain river valley into a burgeoning community of Saints desiring to create a new "gathering place" for their people.[6]

Over the course of two decades, more children were born to Jane and Isaac. The family was able to carve out an economically stable existence based upon subsistence farming and Isaac's employment as a laborer and occasional coachman for Brigham Young, Joseph Smith's successor. Jane Elizabeth spun cloth and made clothing for the family.

Disharmony between Isaac and Jane led to divorce in 1869 or 1870. The breakup wrecked the family's financial stability. Jane resumed employment as a domestic and also made and sold soap. The family income was augmented by two of her sons who worked as laborers. The deaths of three of her children were an especially heavy burden for Jane James. In 1890, after an absence of nearly twenty years, Isaac, Jane's former husband, returned to Salt Lake. He had his church membership reactivated; and when he died one year later, the funeral service was held in Jane's house. Two other children died within three years of their father.[7]

Through all of her personal turmoil, Jane Elizabeth remained resolute in her faith in the writings and teachings of the gospel as adhered to by members of the Church of Jesus Christ of Latter-day Saints. Jane used some of her meager resources to contribute to the building of LDS temples and was a member of the women's Relief Society.[8]

She was in her mind an exemplary model of what a good Latter-day Saint should be. The deaths of a former husband, children, and church leaders such as Brigham Young led Jane Elizabeth James to think about her own death and, more important, her place in the afterlife. She was acutely aware of the Bible-based LDS theological teachings that were used as rationales for prohibiting Mormon women and Mormon men of African descent from holding the priesthood, participating in temple work, or receiving endowments. Jane was also aware that these ordinances were prerequisites of eligibility for entering the highest level of the tripartite heaven as envisioned by the LDS church: the telestial, the terrestrial, and the celestial kingdoms. According to Mormon theology, individuals are assigned to one level of this multitiered kingdom in the afterlife.[9]

Beginning in late 1884, Jane Elizabeth James began periodically contacting LDS leaders in an effort to persuade them to grant her requests that, if approved, would provide her with the permission to receive the endowments and be sealed. Those ordinances were key to her attaining exaltation in the celestial kingdom in the afterlife. Following a visit to the home of John Taylor, president of the LDS Church, Jane dictated a letter to him in which she acknowledged her acceptance of the LDS theological beliefs that were utilized to explain the proscriptions against black Mormons.[10] Ironically, Jane made known her awareness and belief in the passage in the Pearl of Great Price, one of four books accepted as part of the LDS canon, that records a conversation between God and Abraham, in which God promised Abraham that in his seed "shall be all the families of the earth be blessed, even with the blessings of the Gospel, which are salvation, even of life eternal." Accordingly, Jane believed that God had kept his promise to Abraham and that she was of Abraham's seed, thereby holding membership in "the families of the earth" (Abr. 2:11).

In her letter, Jane told Taylor of Emma Smith's earlier invitation for her to be adopted into the Smith family as a child, an offer Jane had declined because of not comprehending the meaning of the invitation. Forty years later Jane saw the invitation as a means that could lead to her receiving her endowments, and she asked the LDS leader to speak with his advisors and grant her request to be adopted into the Smith family as a child.[11] Church leaders did not comply with Jane's request. In January 1888 Jane received a letter from Angus M. Cannon, president of Salt Lake Stake. He enclosed a signed recommend that authorized Jane to enter the temple and to be baptized for her deceased kindred. She was told to "be content with this privilege, awaiting further instructions from the Lord to his servants."[12] Unwilling to wait on the Lord, in February 1890, Jane dictated a letter to Joseph F. Smith, nephew of the late Prophet Joseph Smith and counselor to Wilford Woodruff, John Taylor's successor as LDS president. Once again Jane asked to be adopted into Joseph Smith's family as a child. She also noted that she and Isaac James had been divorced more than two decades and asked if it was possible for her to be sealed to Walker Lewis, an African American LDS convert who had been dead for thirty-five years or more. She believed that Walker held the priesthood and that if she were sealed to him, she would be able to obtain her endowments.[13]

In 1894 Jane met with Woodruff and raised the issue of obtaining her endowments. He praised Jane for her faithfulness but denied her request, saying: "I would not do it as it was against the Law of God . . . and that the seed of Cain would have to wait for redemption until all the seed that Abel would have had that may come through other men can be redeemed."[14] Undaunted by the rejection of her requests, Jane persisted and was not pacified when LDS leaders authorized her adoption into the Joseph Smith family as a servant in a special ceremony in 1902.[15] On April 16, 1908, Jane Elizabeth Manning died at the age of ninety-five. The LDS president, Joseph F. Smith, said that Jane Elizabeth James "would in the resurrection attain the longings of her soul."[16]

In 1979 a group of "special friends," black and white Latter-day Saints, conducted a ceremony in the Salt Lake City Temple in which the long sought-after endowment was bestowed upon Jane James by proxy.[17] The life of Jane Elizabeth Manning James has an important place in the hearts and minds of African American Mormons, especially those who were LDS before June 1978. Jane's difficult journey to Nauvoo, the personal relationship to Joseph and Emma Smith, and the trek to Utah in 1847 illustrates an African American presence early in the history of the faith. Jane's unswerving devotion to the Church of Jesus Christ of Latter-day Saints in difficult times is inspiring regardless of one's religious beliefs.

Jane Elizabeth Manning James's story is becoming better known to all segments of the LDS membership and to non-Mormon Utah residents as well. The 1997 Days of Forty-Seven Parade, celebrating the sesquicentennial of the arrival of Mormon pioneers in Utah, included a float sponsored by the Genesis Group, a unit of the LDS Church designated to support black Saints. The float featured a historical presentation of Jane Elizabeth James and Elijah Abel, also an early African American Mormon convert who relocated to Utah in the pioneer period. One hundred years earlier, Jane, proud of her Mormon pioneer heritage, joined her fellow Saints in celebrating the fiftieth anniversary of their arrival in Utah. The Genesis Group has also sponsored a number of performances of Margaret Blair Young's *I Am Jane,* a play based upon the life of Jane James. In 1999 Genesis placed a special monument in tribute to Jane Manning James at her grave site in the Salt Lake City cemetery. Funding was provided by a cross-section of the community.

By her words and actions Jane James made it clear that she understood the role her race and gender played in preventing her from obtaining full participation in the Church of Jesus Christ of Latter-day Saints during her life. She refused to acquiesce to repeated denials of her requests and was ever vigilant in trying to obtain what she legitimately believed she was entitled to as a devout member of the LDS faith.

Len Hope Sr.

Len Hope was born in 1892 in Magnolia, Alabama.[18] As an adolescent, Len pondered the meaning of religion and wondered what expectations he should look forward to upon finding religion. Len sought the counsel of older members of the Baptist congregation that he was attending. They advised the young man to pray and wait for visionary experiences and "peculiar dreams" such as seeing "yourself crossing Hell on a spider web."[19] Over the course of two to three years, Len Hope followed the counsel of the elders and sought religion through regular prayer, both in and outside the church setting. Disappointed that his prayers had not been answered and that his dreams were not peculiar, Hope nonetheless promised to abide by the rules of the Baptist Church and to follow the commandments of Jesus Christ. He was baptized and became a member of the local Baptist church.

Shortly thereafter Len had a dream in which the Lord told him that he must be baptized again because he was not in the right church. Perplexed, Len embarked upon an intensive examination of the scriptures, hoping to discover the identity of the right church. His studies led him to ask several ministers about the gift of the Holy Ghost. Their answers varied, and Len decided to follow the suggestion of the preacher who told him that prayer was the key to obtaining the gift of the Holy Ghost. Hope went to an isolated abandoned home whose roof was in such a state of disrepair that one could view the stars and moon in the sky from within the house. Following two to three days of prayer and fasting, he still had not received the gift he desired.[20]

According to Hope, it was somewhere around 1913 that he first heard of the Church of Jesus Christ of Latter-day Saints. LDS missionaries came to the Hope family's rural home. They left a pamphlet with Len's sister, who in turn gave it to Len when he arrived later. He read the pamphlet and was surprised to learn that LDS missionaries believed they had a special calling to preach the gospel and that through the laying of hands upon a person that individual could receive the gift of the Holy Ghost. Len Hope said, "I was convinced right there and then."[21] He went to the LDS chapel and requested an application for baptism. The missionaries were favorable to his inquiry but suggested that Len read additional materials before they proceeded with his request. He agreed and waited for the arrival of the Book of Mormon, Doctrine and Covenants, Pearl of Great Price, and other LDS writings. Len Hope's initial impressions of the Church of Jesus Christ of Latter-day Saints were confirmed, and he was determined to be baptized into the LDS faith. That desire was postponed as Len was drafted into the U.S. Army and sent to Europe to fight in World War I. Hope believed the Lord was protecting him during his time overseas, and upon returning to Alabama, he applied for baptism.[22] On June 22, 1919, Len Hope Sr. was baptized and confirmed as a member of the Mormon church. Approximately six months later, he married Mary Lee Pugh, a native of Lamison, Alabama, who, like her husband, became a convert to the LDS Church in 1925.

Apparently Len believed that he had received the Holy Ghost as a result of his new religious affiliation for he said he felt great joy and felt like jumping.[23] The LDS elders told him that rather than looking for an emotional sensation, he should follow the teachings of the LDS doctrine and he would experience "a small voice telling you to feel as wise as a serpent, harmless as a dove, bold as a lion and humble as a lamb."[24] Years later Hope noted: "From that day to this, I haven't had any doubt in my heart that the Church of Jesus Christ of Latter-day Saints was the only true Church on this earth."[25]

Some white residents of the area did not approve of Len Hope's membership in a predominately white church. Shortly after baptism, his life was threatened if he did not withdraw from his new faith community. Upon conferring with the LDS elders in the area, Len was told they could remove his name from the local record of membership but he would remain on the official membership rolls in Salt Lake City.[26]

Like many members of southern African American families, Len and Mary decided that opportunities would be better in the North. The family moved to Cincinnati, Ohio, during the post–World War I period. Initially the Hopes attended religious services at the local LDS branch in the city. Some of the white members of the local branch were uncomfortable attending church services with the black Hope family. Although it is unclear as to how the Hopes were advised not to attend church services, they no longer participated weekly in the Cincinnati branch of the LDS Church. Marion D. Hanks, an LDS general authority, recalled: "It was just understood. It had been made known to them that they were not to be there."[27] Embarrassed over the matter, the LDS branch president offered to bring the sacrament and meet once a month in the Hope home. In these monthly gatherings, there would be a testimony meeting in which all of the members of the Hope family would bear their testimony followed by a period of instruction. Following the services, the Hopes served a meal to all of those in attendance, including a steady stream of young missionaries in the area. During the years of fellowship denial, Len Hope faithfully paid his tithing. His wife's facial expressions often showed her disappointment that they could not attend regular services. According to Mary Hope's last bishop, "They would have loved to have been Latter-day Saints in a full sense."[28]

Following World War II, the Hope family visited, then subsequently relocated to, Salt Lake City. They became members of the Millcreek Ward in southeast Salt Lake City. Mary attended Relief Society meetings and Len attended high-priest group meetings although he could not fully participate. Not having the priesthood was extraordinarily painful to this faithful Saint.[29] One LDS member recalled that Len Hope cried when he talked about the priesthood and that he said "he'd be willing to be stripped of his skin if only he could hold that priesthood."[30] Len Hope died in Salt Lake City's Veteran's Hospital in September 1952.

During a June 1978 meeting in the Salt Lake LDS Temple, Elder Hanks described Len Hope in the most endearing terms, using words such as "heroic," "beautiful," "pure," and "patriotic." He closed his remarks by saying Len Hope "was ready to give his life rather than surrender his membership."[31]

Jane Manning James and Len Hope Sr. were members of the LDS Church for sixty-six and thirty-three years, respectively. At the time they converted to the religion, they were both dissatisfied with their respective church affiliations. By their own words, they remained spiritually unfulfilled. The vacuums in their religious lives were filled after they heard the proselytizing messages of LDS missionaries. They and other persons of African descent converted and embraced the LDS Church even though they knew that beliefs about their race prevented them from complete participation.

Historically, a number of African American Mormons, especially converts who reside in Utah, have privileged their identity as Latter-day Saints over racial identity. Their social and cultural lives are primarily church oriented. In part, this can be attributed to the fact that, although African Americans have never comprised more than 1 percent of Utah's population, for most of the twentieth century the small black population was primarily non-LDS. There may have been some concerns as to how black converts would interface with non-Mormons in the African American community, especially before 1978. Utah black Mormons whose membership was based upon their parents' religious affiliation do not appear to have experienced many anxieties, as they often had family members who had religious affiliations outside of the LDS Church, and family ties outweighed religious differences.

Nonmembers of the Church of Jesus Christ of Latter-day Saints may wonder how a person of African descent could maintain his or her faith in the LDS Church, given the obstacles that precluded participation in many aspects of the religion before the 1978 revelation. That steadfastness appears rooted in the depths of each individual's personal religious convictions. These dark-skinned followers of Christ in a predominantly white church needed unusual strength to withstand questions raised both inside and outside of their chosen faith. They persevered because of their religious convictions, and not until that is understood can outside observers make sense of their participation.

Notes

1. Charles J. Seldin, "Priesthood of LDS Opened to Blacks," *Salt Lake Tribune,* June 10, 1978, A-1.

2. In the years following the 1978 revelation, the LDS Church expanded its proselytizing efforts among people of African descent as part of its goal of being a universal church.

3. Ronald Coleman attended the plenary session and heard Cherry's remarks.

4. Henry J. Wolfinger, "A Test of Faith: Jane Elizabeth James and the Origins of the Utah Black Community," in *Social Accommodation in Utah,* ed. Clark Knowlton (Salt Lake City: American West Center, University of Utah, 1975). See also "Autobiography of Jane E. Manning James," Archives, Family and Church History Department, Church of Jesus Christ of Latter-day Saints, Salt Lake City, Utah.

5. "Autobiography of Jane E. Manning James," 6.

6. Wolfinger, "Test of Faith," 130, 158.

7. Ibid., 132–33, 138–39, 160–61.

8. Ibid., 135.

9. For information on the historical development of LDS black priesthood practice, see Newell G. Bringhurst, *Saints, Slaves, and Blacks: The Changing Place of Black People within Mormonism* (Westport, Conn: Greenwood Press, 1981), and Lester E. Bush Jr., "Mormonism's Negro Doctrine: An Historical Overview," *Dialogue: A Journal of Mormon Thought* 8 (Spring 1973): 11–68. Also see Lester E. Bush Jr. and Armand L. Mauss, eds., *Neither White nor Black: Mormon Scholars Confront the Race Issues in a Universal Church* (Midvale, Utah: Signature Books, 1984); Jane E. James to President Taylor, December 27, 1884, reproduced in Wolfinger, "Test of Faith," Document No. 1, 147–48. For information on LDS temple endowments and other ceremonies, see David John Buerger, *The Mysteries of Godliness: A History of Mormon Temple Worship* (San Francisco: Smith Research Associates, 1994;) see also Bruce R. McConkie, *Mormon Doctrine,* 2d ed. (Salt Lake City: Bookcraft, 1966), 226–28.

10. *Gospel Principles* (Salt Lake City: Church of Jesus Christ of Latter-day Saints, 1992), 301–5; Wolfinger, "Test of Faith," 147–48.

11. Wolfinger, "Test of Faith," 147–48.

12. Angus M. Cannon, president of Salt Lake Stake, to Jane E. James, June 16, 1888, reproduced in Wolfinger, "Test of Faith," Document No. 2, 147–48.

13. Jane E. James to Joseph F. Smith, February 1890, reproduced in Wolfinger, "Test of Faith," Document No. 3, 149.

14. Wilford Woodruff, Journal, October 16, 1894, reproduced in Wolfinger, "Test of Faith," Document No. 5, 150.

15. "Minutes of a Meeting of the Council of Twelve Apostles, January 2, 1902," reproduced in Wolfinger, "Test of Faith," Document No. 7, 151.

16. "Death of Jane Manning James," *Deseret News,* April 16, 1908, 1.

17. Linda King Newell and Susan Easton Black did the temple work. Other participants included Mary Lucille Perkins Bankhead, Lowell Bennion, Ruffin Bridgeforth, and L. Jackson Newell.

18. Jessie L. Embry, *Black Saints in a White Church: Contemporary African America Mormons* (Salt Lake City: Signature Books, 1994), 43–44.

19. Len Hope Sr., address to LDS audience; title, date, and place unknown; audiocassette in possession of Darius Gray.

20. Ibid.

21. Ibid.

22. Ibid.

23. Embry, *Black Saints in a White Church,* 44.

24. Hope, address, audiocassette.

25. Ibid.

26. Ibid.

27. Quoted in Embry, *Black Saints in a White Church,* 44.

28. Ibid., 45.

29. Ibid., 44–45.

30. Margaret Blair Young heard this anecdote from Elder Marion D. Hanks in a telephone interview, May 21, 2002, and related it to Darius Gray. Young and Gray are co-authors of *Standing on the Promises,* a trilogy about African Americans in the LDS Church, all published in Salt Lake City by Bookcraft: *Book 1: One More River to Cross* (2000), *Book 2: Bound for Canaan* (2002), and *Book 3: The Last Mile of the Way* (2003).

31. Quoted in Embry, *Black Saints in a White Church,* 47.

JESSIE L. EMBRY

My scholarly and professional interest in African Americans and their experience in the Church of Jesus Christ of Latter-day Saints is situated in my personal experience.[1] I am typical of many Utah-born Latter-day Saints who first welcomed black members to their congregations before and especially after President Spencer W. Kimball's revelation of June 1978, which allowed black men to be ordained to the Mormon priesthood and permitted black men and women to participate in temple blessings.

Although this essay, a qualitative analysis of two case studies, is not about my own changing perceptions, I disclose my own attitudes in two ways. First, I present them as a backdrop against which to appraise my analysis of two African American families whose experience in Mormonism spanned June 1978. Second, I consider them as a proxy for the attitudes of white Mormons that most African American converts to Mormonism would have found waiting for them in LDS congregations. Although this essay focuses only on the social reality of the black experience, both whites and blacks in Mormon congregations experienced a deconstruction of their received attitudes and a reconstruction on the basis of new experience and knowledge. For some black converts—and no doubt for some white members as well—the reshaping of that social reality was too complex and costly, leading to either psychological or actual disaffiliation. This essay focuses on two successful experiences but acknowledges other, less positive, outcomes.

I spent most of my childhood and teenage years in North Logan, Utah, a small community in northern Utah, where I met no black children and where the only African Americans I saw played for the Utah State University basketball team. When I was in the eighth grade, in 1966, my family lived in Columbia, Missouri, where blacks experienced a mixture of integration and discrimination. An African American was the star basketball player and student body president of my junior high school. But the black students in my home room all sat in the back row while the whites sat in alphabetical order. I admired the student leader from afar but ignored the blacks in my home room. When I went to Brigham Young University in the early 1970s, Alan Cherry, an African American Mormon, was in my black history class, but I never spoke to him.

Without the corrective of real experience with real African Americans, my knowledge of and attitudes toward blacks were a virtual compendium of stereotypes drawn from American and Mormon culture: blacks were great athletes but poor scholars. Slavery was bad, and the civil rights movement was good. Still, blacks had been "less valiant" in a pre-earth life, so they were born to descendants of Cain, the first murderer, who had been cursed with a dark skin as a consequence of his crime. As a result, black men were unique among all races on earth in that they could not be ordained to the LDS priesthood, although someday they would receive that privilege. In the meanwhile, it was unfair for black protesters to target BYU or the LDS Church. Civil rights was one thing; the Mormon church's internal policies were something else—not the business of outsiders. None of these opinions was unusual among Latter-day Saints of the time.

Then in the early 1980s through mutual friends, I finally met Alan Cherry, a New Yorker who had converted to Mormonism in 1968. Alan, who was in his thirties when we met, had just returned from an LDS mission. As one of very few African American converts in the 1960s and 1970s, he received a constant stream of invitations to "tell his story." In addition to numerous speaking engagements, he also wrote of his experience in a slim autobiography, *It's You and Me, Lord.* Ten years later, an African American convert to Mormonism named Mary Sturlaugson produced her own autobiography, *A Soul So Rebellious.* A vivid and energetic writer, she was candid about her early negative opinions about whites. After explaining her treatment of the one white student in her high school in Tennessee and her negative reaction to the all-white college in North Dakota to which she had received a scholarship, she bluntly wrote, "Whites were my enemies."[2]

In one of our numerous conversations, Alan told me that those who had read both his and Sturlaugson's autobiographies frequently asked him whether all blacks had such negative reactions to whites as Sturlaugson. While not denying the validity of Sturlaugson's feelings, Cherry stressed that all blacks are not the same and that to generalize from one experience to the whole group easily leads to stereotyping. He suggested that someone needed to record the experiences of other African American Mormons to show the variety of experiences. At that time, I was the director of the Oral History Program of the Charles Redd Center for Western Studies at BYU. My major responsibility was to collect oral histories.[3] Consequently, the center funded the LDS African American Oral History Project from 1984 to 1988, with Cherry as the interviewer. The finished project numbers 226 oral histories, collected from LDS African Americans in the Northeast, the Midwest, the Deep South, the intermountain West, the Southwest, northern and southern California, and Hawaii. I supplemented these interviews with a questionnaire administered in 1988. The survey was mailed to all the interviewees, and I used a "snowball" sample (a technique wherein the initial subjects refer researchers to additional subjects) to collect demographic data and reactions to some social/ecclesiastical situations they may have encountered during interactions with other Latter-day Saints.[4] Of the 500 mailed, only 201, or 40 percent, returned the survey. Because the sample, by its nature, could not be a random one, it overrepresents African Americans who found reasons to remain affiliated with Mormonism, despite problems, rather than those who found the social and personal costs of affiliation onerous.

Official LDS Church membership records do not include race and are, in any case, not available to researchers. Hence, it is impossible to determine how many African Americans are Mormons, their conversion rates, and/or the degree to which they participate fully, which, in a Mormon context, means attending weekly worship services, accepting "callings" (or assignments from congregational ecclesiastical leaders to serve as a teacher, staff, or executive in one of the local programs), paying tithing, and maintaining worthiness— determined by both ward and stake officers through interviews—to enter the faith's most sacred structures, its temples.[5] My sense, based on anecdotal reports and observations, is that relatively few blacks in the United States have become Mormon and that the LDS Church still has the reputation of being a racist organization. No systematic data are available that sample attitudes of white Mormons toward African Americans. Again, anecdotal evidence leaves an impression that there is some deliberate bigotry among white Mormons but also that there exists a more widely spread ignorance, acceptance of stereotypes, and insensitivity among them.

Even though the oral history project overrepresents African American Mormons who have chosen to remain affiliated, some interviewees and survey respondents recalled instances of discrimination, suggesting that they must deal at least some of the time with some level of socially uncomfortable situations. These feelings were not related to their views of priesthood restriction, though, since about three-fifths accepted the LDS Church's policy as "the Lord's will." Of the rest, 29.4 percent were "concerned" about the policy's implications, while 7.1 percent were "appalled."[6]

There are three primary reasons that suggest why they accepted priesthood restriction and remained members of an organization where they felt
discrimination.

1. They had a high level of tolerance for ambiguity, manifest as a willingness to suspend demands for explanations on racial matters.
2. They placed an emphasis on meeting spiritual needs, rather than social
   needs, through engagement with Mormonism.
3. They had a sense of personal peace that, however phrased, derives from
   faith that God has guided them to Mormonism and approves their individual choice to remain Mormon. This final reason is by far the most important, even though, because of its transcendent nature, it is not susceptible to quantification.[7]

These three reasons will be explored in greater detail through two extended
case reports. For now we might say that, as these case studies will show, African Americans who believe that the Church of Jesus Christ of Latter-day Saints
is the "true church" and the key to their eternal salvation have a resilience that
enables them to overlook nonaffirming behavior of other Mormons.[8]

In an example drawn from another interview—one that does not come
from the two families of interest in this chapter—a woman of black and Native American parentage was baptized LDS as a college sophomore in 1977.
When she enthusiastically volunteered to serve a mission, her local church
leader told her she could not because blacks could not receive temple blessings. Her reaction was anger. "I just told [him] I felt the Church was prejudiced,
and I didn't want anything to do with it. I was not [coming] back." When the
leader suggested that she pray, she retorted that she would not pray to a God
who was also prejudiced, even though answers to prayers had been an important part of her decision to become a Mormon. "I went home that Sunday
resolving not to pray. I didn't for two or three days. It seemed like it was on a
Wednesday when all of a sudden I found myself on my knees praying and
saying, 'Why can't blacks hold the priesthood?' A comforting feeling came
over me, saying, 'I have not given a reason why, but eventually blacks will hold
the priesthood with all the blessings.'" She concluded, "That calmed me
down."[9] Although this "answer" did not provide a logical explanation to her
question, it enabled her to accept a policy that treated her differently from
other Mormon women because of her skin color. A year later, in June 1978, she
felt this promise was fulfilled.

The two case studies I consider here, chosen because they are both multigenerational, illustrate the extent to which faith drives action. The first is that
of the Sargent-Keys family in Virginia and New York, covering the century be-

tween 1895 and 1986, and the second focuses on the extended Brown-Wright family in Louisiana, between the 1960s and 1986.[10] While factors such as family ties, personal contact with LDS members, and acceptance by white Mormons were important, the Sargent-Keyes' faith and their communication with God were most important. In both cases, these converts to the LDS Church, which denied them the same privileges enjoyed by nonblacks, accepted baptism before the 1978 revelation and maintained their affiliations afterward because they believed that it represented God's will for them. This faith was strong enough to overcome unanswered questions about the priesthood ban and less than Christian behavior toward them by some white Mormons.

The Sargent-Keys Family

The story of the Sargent family's conversion is, in many ways, typical of late nineteenth- and early twentieth-century proselytizing. Mormon missionaries frequently traveled throughout rural areas without funds, following the New Testament model of the apostles preaching without "purse or scrip." They relied on the hospitality of the local people for food and shelter, and usually received it, whether or not these individuals were willing to consider the Mormon message or read the Book of Mormon. Often LDS members were sprinkled throughout a large geographical area without enough of a concentration to form a congregation who could meet together regularly. In contrast to the contemporary system of teaching via six sharply focused missionary discussions leading directly to baptism, nineteenth-century teaching often moved discursively through a series of doctrinal lessons or, more informally, scripture study, questions and answers, and so forth. Conversion was often a lengthy process.[11]

In 1895 Nellie Payton Sargent, a white woman, and her husband, John Sargent, a black man, were living in Caroline County, Virginia, midway between Fredericksburg and Richmond. According to their daughter Novella, Mormon missionaries called on a neighboring family and then came to "Mama's house." For the next decade, Nellie welcomed various teams of missionaries. She "would feed them, she would put soles on their shoes, and she would take their clothes to the creek and wash them." In August 1906, Nellie, six daughters, and one son were baptized. John "liked the Mormons, but he was never baptized."[12]

The other six or seven Mormon families in the area, all white, eventually moved to Utah. The Sargents inhabited an uncomfortable social no-man's-land in Virginia, excluded from weddings and other social events. In their white neighbors' eyes, they were black because of John's race. Yet their African American neighbors regarded them as "white niggers"—"trying to be white because we joined a white church." Once the family visited a "colored church" where a preacher "rebuked" a storm but "wished the lightning would strike us." Novella affirmed, "It didn't make a difference. We had seen the power of the holy priesthood. We knew what we could do and we knew that the Church was true. We didn't bother with what they were saying."

The restriction on priesthood was not an issue in the family because there was no Mormon congregation in the area, which would have made the limitations on Novella's baptized brother conspicuous. Her brother was old enough that he could have been ordained, but the family did not question why he had not. In fact, Novella could not remember whether the missionaries had explained the ban on priesthood ordination but added that she might have missed the explanation because she was "younger and didn't pay that much attention." It was not "until thirty years or more" that she learned about the exclusion.

In 1908, two years after becoming a Mormon, sixteen-year-old Novella moved to Washington, D.C., to find work. In 1910 she talked to some people and found out about Mormon meetings in a rented hall on I Street. She attended these meetings and learned that the "crowd of people [sitting] all along a big porch," whom she had frequently noticed on Sundays as she took the streetcar to work, was the Mormon congregation meeting at the home of Senator Reed Smoot of Utah. Smoot himself "asked me why didn't I come to his home. I told him I didn't even know that the Mormons were here in Washington. I didn't know they were holding meetings at his house."

She began attending the meetings, and although she was the only black in attendance, she always felt welcomed by Smoot. "Senator Smoot was a wonderful person. You would never know that he was a senator by the way he acted. He was just plain." In contrast, one memory still pricked after sixty years or more. One conference was so crowded that the only empty seat was next to her. A stranger entered near Novella but, rather than taking the seat, stood against the wall. "He just stood there," Novella described. "It was very noticeable. Everyone was bound to see it. Sister [Alpha Mae Eldredge] Smoot got up from her seat and came back and sat by me. He went there and sat in her seat." Novella quickly acknowledged that she did not know whether the man was a Mormon; but another time, someone who was a Latter-day Saint refused to pass her the sacrament. Novella remembered but shrugged off these incidents: "Those things didn't hurt me. Just pray for them."

Novella married Joseph Milton Gibson in Washington, D.C., on June 18, 1913. Joseph was not a Mormon, but he encouraged her church activity. It is unclear from the interview with Novella whether she raised their children as

Mormons, but as adults, they became bitter toward the LDS Church. One niece feared that when Novella died her children would not respect their mother's wishes to have a Mormon funeral. Fortunately, they did.[13] Despite all these problems, according to another niece, Novella "was such a dutiful worker in the Church."[14] After the priesthood revelation, she attended the Washington, D.C., Temple. She died in May 1986, aged ninety-four, unfortunately mere months before Cherry's interview schedule brought him to the Washington area.

Novella's six Mormon siblings also married non-Mormons but, unlike Novella, could not attend LDS meetings and saw missionaries only at infrequent intervals. Their degree of attachment to Mormonism varied. Cherry was able to interview some of Novella's nieces in the mid-1980s. One of them described to Cherry the piety of Novella's sister, Mary Virginia Sargent Keys. She "never stopped" telling her twelve children "about the Mormons and the Mormon Church." She observed the monthly Mormon fast day, even though she cooked meals for the family on that day. She also scrupulously observed the Word of Wisdom and had great faith in the Mormon missionaries and their priesthood. At one point in the 1920s, she was so ill that "they were not expecting her to live." She asked for the Mormon elders, even though they had not visited for years. While Mary's husband, Julius Keys, went for the doctor, the Mormon missionaries arrived, seemingly out of nowhere, and announced: "We are here to administer to the sick if you wish us to." By the time Julius returned, Mary was "sitting up in the bed . . . and preaching." As a result, Julius listened to the missionaries and was baptized.[15]

The Keys lacked transportation to attend the nearest Mormon branch in Fredericksburg and most often attended a Baptist church in Beaver Dam, Virginia, when they were able. A daughter felt that Julius "kind of strayed from the Church some. But the night before he died, he asked for the elders" and received a blessing from them.[16]

Only three of the devoted Mary's twelve children affiliated with Mormonism: Ethel, Virginia, and Raymond. Ethel, who moved to Washington, D.C., in 1940 to attend high school, married James Kelley while she was still in her teens. The couple then moved to New York City where, as a young mother, she decided she wanted to know more about the Mormon church, whose teachings she remembered from her youth. She also recalled that her mother, Mary, had a Book of Mormon that "was very precious" to her. All of the children were "taught to be careful not to damage this book." Ethel telephoned Aunt Novella, complaining that there were no Mormons in New York City and saying she wanted a Book of Mormon. Aunt Novella assured her that there *were* Mormons in New York and sent her niece a Book of Mormon.[17]

Ethel reports that she "became so engrossed in this book until I didn't want to put the book down." When her reading interfered with getting meals on the table promptly, "there was a little tension" with her husband. He asked accusingly, "What do you expect to gain from this? Do you expect to become white?" Ethel told him, "Not white in color, but I expect to become as pure as white with the truth because I know it is true." Perhaps recalling the missionaries who materialized when her mother was so ill, Ethel expected the Mormon missionaries to appear at her door. When they did not, she called Aunt Novella for advice and, following her instructions, looked up the Mormon church's number in the telephone book and invited the missionaries to come teach her. She was baptized in July 1961, "the happiest day of my life."[18]

Her husband, James, did not join the LDS Church and used his nonmembership as a reason not to attend services with her. He was reluctant to have their son, James Jr., attend Mormon services; but when Ethel encouraged him to take young James to another church, he did not act on that suggestion. Instead, he drove Ethel and James Jr. to their Mormon meetings, even though he grumbled that "all this is of the devil." James Jr., after studying independently with the missionaries, was baptized in November 1963 at age sixteen, two years after his father died.[19]

Ethel and James Jr. were the only black members of their Mormon congregation, and Ethel, interviewed two decades later, remembered how difficult the social isolation could be. Every Sunday she questioned if anyone would miss her if she did not go, but she plucked up her courage with the reminder that the meeting place was a "House of the Lord and he is our father and we are his children. I have as much right as the next one to go." She was sensitive to those who seemed reluctant to shake hands or speak to her but insisted that she "like[d] the Church and Saints very much." She was particularly aware that attending church "wasn't a pleasant thing" for James Jr.—"to sit there in church, not being able to pass the sacrament." After James married, he stopped attending the Mormon church. He refused to return to church activity after the priesthood revelation of 1978 and would not discuss Mormonism with Ethel. He did not join another church but retained enough interest in religion to borrow a Bible from her.[20]

Despite her son's obvious distress over Mormonism's policy of black priesthood denial, Ethel found peace by accepting the restriction as a "revelation." When she prayed to know why blacks could not hold the priesthood, "the only answer that I have ever gotten was if and when God sees fit this will happen." She expressed warm appreciation for white priesthood holders who gave her blessings when she requested them, often at some sacrifice. "I know without priesthood we wouldn't have anything to go on," she affirmed.[21]

The second Keys daughter to affiliate with Mormonism, Virginia Keys Wright, also remembered her mother's devotion to Mormon precepts. As a young woman living in New York City with Ethel, she studied Mormonism with her sister; but "I couldn't get into it at the time. I wanted to, but I was kind of half skeptical." Years later, her interest revived when she, a daughter, and a grandson were suffering from illness simultaneously. "I asked God to please show me what steps to take," she recalled. "Out of the clear blue sky 'Mormon' came into my mind." She telephoned the number listed for the LDS Church in Richmond, Virginia, and two priesthood holders came and gave her daughter and grandson blessings. When her daughter and grandson were healed, Virginia decided, "It's time for me to go to church." Her resolve quailed, however, before the fact that "it was just whites there." After another illness, she promised God: "You give me one more chance. I'm going to that Church. I don't care if nobody else is there but me. I'm going."[22]

At her request, white members picked her up, took her to services, and brought her home. "For about three years, I was the only black in there," she recalled, but "I wouldn't be going to church for somebody to speak to me. I would be going for all the other different reasons because it's something I want to do." She was baptized in July 1976, two years before the priesthood revelation. Virginia also recounted that she had seen blacks and whites leave the Mormon church because the special treatment they received while they were investigating the church had stopped after they joined.[23]

Virginia did not mention whether her daughter joined the LDS Church, although she did talk about a granddaughter who joined in 1983 and attended faithfully for awhile. At the time she was interviewed in 1986, Virginia had an eleven-year-old daughter from another marriage. The girl went to the Mormon church but was bored with the children's organization, the Primary. Virginia hoped, but was not sure, that she would continue to attend church.

The third Keys sibling, Raymond W. Keys, also joined the Mormon church as an adult. After growing up in rural Virginia, he moved to Washington, D.C., as a teenager to work. He fought in World War II. Raymond never married. In 1978, when he was sixty years old, he became ill and applied for retirement. A year later he "returned home" to Virginia, living in Hewlett (which became Ruther Glen). His sister Ethel gave his name to the Mormon missionaries, and an older missionary couple came to his home. "I agreed to listen to them," recalled Raymond, when Cherry interviewed him in 1986, "and enjoyed them very much. I then decided to join the Mormon Church." He was baptized in August 1981, at age sixty-three.[24] Although unable to attend meetings regularly because of illness, Raymond enjoyed reading the scriptures, being in contact with other Latter-day Saints, and welcoming LDS members to his home.

When asked how white Mormons accepted him, he explained, "I don't see a whole lot of difference because I carry myself in the right way. I love them all." Raymond did not state what office he held in the Mormon priesthood. But when asked about it, he responded enthusiastically: "[The priesthood is] beautiful. I know many things are possible through the priesthood. And I am a priesthood holder! I pray daily that I will always be worthy."[25]

The Redd Center has not been in contact with members of the Sargent-Keys family since 1986. At the time of the interviews, Virginia was fifty-four and unsure of her future as she went through a difficult divorce. Ethel was sixty-two, and her son was inactive in the church. Raymond was sixty-eight and had no children. Virginia and Ethel explained that their brothers and sisters, most of whom were Baptists, appreciated their mother's religion but none had joined.[26] As a result, it is questionable whether another generation would embrace Mormonism.

The Brown-Wright Family

The second case study also covered three generations, although over a shorter period of time than that of the first study. Hilda Brown and Wesley Jennings Brown, the latter a farmer, carpenter, and sawmill worker, raised their twelve children as Baptists near Baton Rouge, Louisiana. This case study focuses on the experiences reported by their two daughters, Katherine and Dorothy Mae, who became Mormons. Dorothy Mae's husband, Dunk Wright; three of their children, Betty, Michelle, and Van; and Van's wife, Shirley, also joined the LDS Church. Eventually, Hilda and Wesley also became Mormons.

The story begins with Katherine Brown Warren, the Browns' second child. She became a Baptist at age fifteen but "never was satisfied with that faith. I just could not get into that religion." She started reading the Bible on her own, even though "I was taught not to read the Bible because it will run you crazy." Her mother asked her not to read it aloud to her brothers and sisters for that reason.[27]

Katherine's uneasiness with the Baptist faith continued after she gave birth to a daughter and a son as a single mother. She describes herself as looking for a religion that would give her "another comforter," as mentioned in John 14:16. Her sister Dorothy had a neighbor who was a member of the Church of God in Christ. The neighbor told her, "The Lord wants you to receive the Holy Ghost." As a result, she visited churches. When her children were seven and six years old, she joined the Church of God in Christ in Mississippi. "They were really good people," she recalled in 1987. "They taught you to live the clean, moral life, and they helped my two children and I get an apartment."[28]

In 1961, Katherine left her children in Louisiana with her mother while she lived in Hartford, Connecticut, with an aunt. Katherine worked at a hospital caring for mentally ill patients. Three years later, she brought her children to Connecticut. In 1967, when her daughter was ten and her son nine, Mormon missionaries came by and gave Katherine a copy of the pamphlet *Joseph Smith's Testimony*. Katherine believed Smith's account of being called by God and Jesus Christ to restore the New Testament church. She told a friend that she wanted a Book of Mormon, and the friend just happened to have one. A garbage collector had fished it out of the trash because it looked like a Bible and had given it to the friend because he knew she was "a church-going lady." Katherine's immediate reaction was: "It was some good! Before I got the book, there [was] something in my heart. The Lord was leading me to search." The descriptions of baptism in the Book of Mormon led to a series of questions about various methods of baptism. At this point, she still had not met any Mormons, except for the brief encounter with the missionaries in 1967.[29]

In 1968, Katherine moved back to Baton Rouge and was pleased at the enthusiastic response when she suggested at a gathering of her extended family that they start a Bible class. This systematic Bible study was an anchor in her life over the next few years as she married her children's father and moved to New Orleans, returning to Baton Rouge for the weekly Bible class. "I kind of introduced the Book of Mormon little by little," she remembers with a laugh.

In New Orleans, she also found a telephone number for the LDS Church, located a ward, and began to attend meetings. "I had a time getting in the Church," she says ruefully. The first obstacle to overcome was the racial prejudice of the members. No one spoke to her, communicating clearly that "they didn't want any blacks." After three years of determined, stubborn attendance, she finally wrote to the church president, Spencer W. Kimball, and asked what she needed to do to join the Mormon church. "He sent my letter to a member of the ward. They sent the missionaries out to me with my letter." Even after she told them of her desire to be baptized, they discouraged her: "It's hard to become a member of this Church," they told her. "Have you heard [that] Joseph Smith said it wasn't time for the blacks as yet?" Grudgingly they continued, "[But] if the blacks come to us, we will receive them. We can't cast them out."[30]

Katherine began taking the missionary discussions in 1975. Following church procedure, she could not be baptized without her husband's permission, which he initially refused to grant. She resolutely continued attending church despite his discouragement. Finally, in late December 1976, her husband gave his permission, and Katherine was baptized on Christmas Day. Katherine was the only black attending the ward, although Freda Beaulieu, an elderly black woman who joined the Mormon church with her parents and her brothers and sisters as a child, was a ward member. After joining, Katherine was told by the bishop that white ward members were leaving because of her church activity. But he told her, "Don't feel bad because [white members] are leaving. The Lord is going to bless the Church through the blacks." Despite this encouragement, he and other ward members told her that blacks would never have the priesthood until "Jesus comes in his glory." Two weeks after such a discussion with her bishop came the June 1978 announcement of the revelation.[31]

Even nine years later, when Cherry interviewed Katherine, she reported that "very few" white Latter-day Saints "accept me." When asked why other blacks left the LDS Church, Katherine reported that many told her "it's because whites don't live the gospel. . . . They are respecters of persons. They treat you cold." She was able to persevere, however, because "I look over their errors and see the Lord."[32]

Katherine remained close to her children. When she married their father, he commented, "I have never seen anyone so close." Katherine's daughter, husband, and five children "are in the Church." In fact, her daughter and son-in-law were living in Germany and were baptized a year before she was. Katherine's husband insisted that he was "born a Baptist . . . and [would] die a Baptist" but he read the Book of Mormon, prayed with her, and attended church. Katherine did not mention her son's religion.[33]

The next baptisms in Katherine's family—two years and three months later—brought thirteen relatives into the LDS Church in the same service. These baptisms were clustered among Katherine's nieces and nephews. The second generation of baptisms began with Katherine's niece Betty Baunchand, the daughter of Katherine's sister Dorothy. Betty had been baptized a Baptist as a child, but as a twenty-eight-year-old married woman she joined some of her siblings in attending the Church of God in Christ for a year. They decided to be baptized, but reversed their decision when the minister refused to baptize one sister because she wore lipstick and fingernail polish. The family joined a Bethany Baptist Church in Baton Rouge, which had a racially mixed congregation of whites and blacks. Severia, Betty's husband, worked with LeGrand Jones, a white Utah Mormon, when both men were employed by the Exxon Oil Company in Baton Rouge. LeGrand "used to talk to my husband a little bit about the Church," recalled Betty. When he asked the Baunchands if the missionaries could visit them, they agreed. Reconstructing the chronology later, Betty realized that the invitation followed soon after the June 1978 priesthood revelation. Aunt Katherine had phoned her with the news, but "we really didn't understand it because I didn't know anything about the Church."[34]

Before the missionaries' first visit, Betty told a sister that the Mormons were coming and asked if she had questions. The sister joined the next discussion. Other relatives also joined in the teaching sessions until "the room was full of us being taught." When missionaries issued the baptismal challenge, they all accepted, even Betty, who was eight months pregnant. On January 21, 1979, she, Severia, and their ten-year-old daughter, Sharon, along with two sisters, a brother, two nieces, a cousin, and others, were baptized in Baton Rouge.[35]

Betty had no trouble accepting the previous ban against ordaining black men to the priesthood "because the Lord works on His own time clock. It wasn't time for the blacks to receive the priesthood. We may not understand everything now, but we are going to understand it better in the by and by." She concluded, "Who are we to question the Lord? I just believe the gospel. He said it, and that's good enough for me." She also felt that "we have been accepted graciously with open arms" by white members. But her daughter, Sharon, age seventeen at the time of the oral history, was not going to church. Betty lamented, "There was not one black guy that she could even go out with. . . . That could have pulled her away because the Church teaches you that you should have a courtship with someone within the Church." Betty did not seem to consider the possibility that her daughter might date white Mormon men. She reflected, "It's hard on the youngsters to get a testimony and realize what it is about the Church."[36]

Betty's younger sister, Michelle, was one of the thirteen baptized in January 1979. Although Michelle was only twelve at the time of her baptism, she had attended the various Baptist churches and the Church of God in Christ with her family, but these churches had not satisfied her quest for a fulfilling faith. In contrast, Michelle recalled, "We knew that the [LDS] Church was right, and that what we had been taught by the missionaries was of God." Like Betty, she was untroubled by the ban on priesthood ordination. She remembered hearing an announcement on a news program about the policy change in June 1978. She had asked her mother why blacks were just now being given the priesthood in the Mormon church. She did not remember receiving an explanation from her mother at the time and, when Cherry interviewed her in 1987, still had no answer except "that it wasn't time yet, and that the Lord had His plans."[37] She was aware of white members' mixed reactions to her family's baptism: "Some left the Church because we were joining . . . and some . . . still aren't in the Church. There are some that confessed that they were . . . opposed to letting blacks come in. Now they are some of our closest friends."[38] Michelle felt that "the Lord really blessed us because He knew that we were all searching for the gospel. Our whole family made the move."[39] As a result, she felt it had been easier to remain affiliated and ride out the rough spots.

Michelle participated fully in Young Women, the Mormon church's program for teenage girls. She enjoyed the church programs and made friends easily at church and at school, where she was a cheerleader and homecoming queen. "I blossomed in high school," she recalled. The teachers "adored me" and "a lot of the kids that I went to church with were in the same school. They looked up to me." She attended Southern University in Baton Rouge, continuing to read the scriptures, pray, attend church meetings, and focus on church teachings.[40]

Michelle and Betty's mother, Dorothy Mae Brown Wright, was Katherine's sister. Dorothy was the oldest of Hilda and Wesley Brown's twelve children. While Betty and the other relatives were taking the missionary discussions, the missionaries also started teaching Dorothy. "When I first heard" the gospel, recalled Dorothy, "I knew it was true because I knew there had to be something better than we had." Her husband, Dunk, "knew it was true, too," but he felt that his original baptism was acceptable in the sight of God and "couldn't accept a second baptism." Dunk admitted that he had a hard time leaving the Baptist Church. He and Dorothy were not baptized until May 31, 1979, four months after Betty, Michelle, and the other eleven relatives were baptized.[41]

The ripple effect of conversion next reached Dorothy and Katherine's parents, Wesley and Hilda Brown. Wesley had grown up a Methodist and had become a Baptist after marrying Hilda, but he became disillusioned—saying, "It got so rotten." He didn't explain the problem when he was interviewed in 1987. Wesley recalled that Dorothy enthusiastically had told her parents that Mormonism "was the true church, the church of Jesus Christ," and Wesley's perception of "the people" who were Mormons made it "a better church to join than the one I was in. . . . I wouldn't want to be in anything false." He and Hilda were baptized after Dorothy and Dunk.[42] Hilda died and was buried with a Mormon funeral. Her granddaughter Betty recalled that the gospel was a comfort: "Her death didn't hit as hard as I thought it would."[43]

Although several of Dorothy and Dunk's children were baptized in January 1979, at the same time as Betty and Michelle, one son, Van C. Wright Sr., did not join until later. He had attended his Aunt Katherine's family Bible group when he was "eight or ten" years old, and he affectionately remembered her zeal. "She was, like, on a mission that she should get the family members together to teach them." After Van's graduation from high school in 1968, he considered it "a miracle" that he was not drafted into the U.S. Army and sent to Vietnam. He met Shirley Walker, who enjoyed riding motorcycles and partying. They married in 1970, and their son, Van Jr., was born in 1975. But their marriage was a troubled one. Shirley settled down to family life, but Van continued to party. According to Van, "After Van Jr. was born, I rode a lot of times by myself. . . . I shift worked for Exxon, and then I rode my bike. I wasn't with my family like I should have been." Van had no interest in the religion that was absorbing his sisters (Betty and Michelle) and other relatives. In fact, he recalls that he and his father, Dunk, "used to gang up" on the newly baptized thirteen and challenge Mormon truth claims by asserting, 'You can serve God anywhere.' . . . I wasn't even in tune enough to come to my mother's baptism" in May 1979—which was also his father's baptism.[44]

At that point, his marriage was unraveling. Five months later, in October 1979, Shirley left him. It was a wakeup call. "I made a covenant with God that if I could have my family and have a second chance I would lead them back to Him," he vowed. He was baptized November 3, 1979. Although the divorce became final in 1980, Shirley was struck by the "change" that "come over him as far as his attitude about his family and his life." They were remarried in October 1981. Shirley was determined not to become a Mormon, at least partly because it was a white church. Her father had been killed by the Ku Klux Klan in Mississippi in 1964. However, after observing Mormonism's positive effects on her husband and in-laws, she agreed to listen to the missionaries. This experience led to a conviction of Mormonism's truth claims, and a month after their remarriage, Van baptized her.[45]

Interviewed separately in 1987, Van and Shirley Wright acknowledged making a conscious choice about how to deal with the now-defunct priest-hood restriction and with the coldness of some white members. Shirley felt frustrated that no one could provide an adequate explanation of the ordina-tion ban but decided not to let it "bog me down. I don't allow it to hinder me." Van constructed an explanation rooted in a larger social context: "At the time the Church was organized, the blacks didn't hold the priesthood because blacks didn't have their freedom. They were slaves." It took until the 1970s "for this world to even start accepting black people in places."[46]

Although Shirley felt that Mormons often avoided her because she was black, she went out of her way to talk to and hug those who avoided her and felt that they gradually came to accept her. Van also sensed negative feelings toward blacks from white Mormons but had, like Shirley, concentrated on building positive relationships with them. He concluded, "The whites in the Church have come to love us."[47] Van and Shirley had three sons: Van Jr., Ja-bar, and Bakari. In 1987 Van Jr. was eleven; Jabar, four; and Bakari, two and a half. At that time Van bragged that Van Jr. was doing well in football and school. "He likes the Church," Van said of his oldest son. He continued, "I guess all of my kids like to pray. They have learned to love the Lord. They don't mind bearing their testimony. I guess they like to talk in the mike."[48]

Michelle, the youngest of the Brown-Wright clan to be interviewed, spoke enthusiastically but also wistfully about the LDS Church's future influence in the world. She admitted that it had yet to overcome a history and image of prejudice, but she believed that things would change if more blacks served missions, if the Mormon church involved itself in black community activities, and if LDS Church leaders would make a statement to put the past policy in perspective. She admitted that such a statement was not likely to come since "the Church does not act like that."[49]

The Redd Center has not kept in touch with the members of the Brown-Wright family, and attempts to contact them in 2001 were not successful. But in 1987 when they were interviewed, those who had become Mormons expressed love for and faith in the LDS Church. They unanimously affirmed the importance of priesthood power. Dorothy commented, "I know that the priesthood has the authority to act in God's name. I really respect the priesthood, and the Lord works through the priesthood. The priesthood has power." Van agreed: "I know we don't even comprehend the great power . . . that we hold." Betty affirmed, "I have all the faith in the world in the priesthood and what it can do for you."[50] The family members diligently incorporated Mormon teachings in their lives. They held daily family prayers and scripture study, held weekly family home evenings, attended church meetings, and accepted church positions. In return, they felt that God accepted their efforts at righteousness and blessed them with peace. They felt that they had followed divine direction in becoming Mormons and that their course of life was pleasing to God.

Analysis

The conversion stories of the Sargent-Keys and Brown-Wright families span the period before and after black men were granted LDS priesthood. Interviewed eight or nine years after the lifting of the ban, these individuals had remained affiliated with Mormonism and had therefore found ways of accommodating the historic restriction and whatever lingering effects it had in exacerbating racist feelings of some Mormons, especially in Louisiana and Virginia.

As I suggested earlier, only a quantitative analysis could determine the percentage of black U.S. converts to Mormonism who later disaffiliated from the church and what fraction of that percentage was decisively affected by the now-obsolete priesthood ban and/or the perceived coldness of white church members. As noted earlier, because the LDS Church does not identify members by racial categories and because, even if it did, membership records are not open to researchers, it is currently not possible to determine the answers to these questions. Care must be taken, therefore, in generalizing the results of this qualitative study of two multigenerational families. However, as stated earlier, I have hypothesized three reasons for these families' affiliation with Mormonism. A discussion of these three reasons may also shed light on the situations of other African American converts in the United States.

One factor in the successful long-term affiliation of these African American converts to Mormonism seems to have been their high level of tolerance for ambiguity, manifest as a willingness to suspend demands for explanations on racial matters. The historical development of the priesthood ordination ban is a complex one. The earliest days of the Mormon church under Joseph Smith were marked by a far more liberal stance than the era of the second church president, Brigham Young, who imposed greater restraints. After the deaths of black men who were ordained to priesthood office during Joseph Smith's lifetime, ordination does not seem to have been offered to other African American men. Custom, tradition, various statements of a theological nature over the pulpit, and a certain amount of "folk" theology used to explain the de facto ban raised its status over the intervening generations. By 1978, what is commonly regarded as a revelation shared by all of the general authorities of the LDS Church was required to change the policy. The wording of the announcement of the change, canonized as Official Declaration No. 2 in Doctrine and Covenants, does not offer an explanation for the policy or for its change. Consequently, it is unlikely that even detailed historical, political, and/or sociological explanations would be satisfying to prospective members motivated primarily by intellectual or political interests. In short, it was primarily a willingness to accept the ambiguous status of the now-obsolete policy that enabled African American converts to minimize its dissonant effects in adjusting to Mormonism. Michelle Evette Wright expressed a typical resolution: "It wasn't time yet, and . . . the Lord had His plans."[51]

A second factor in the ability of these two families to maintain their affiliation with Mormonism was their focus on meeting spiritual needs, rather than social needs, at church. All of the interviewees reported incidents of aloofness on the part of white members, a reluctance or a refusal to shake hands with them or sit by them, and racist comments made to them. If feeling welcomed and accepted had been their primary motivation for seeking a new religious congregation, it seems likely that they would quickly have sought a black congregation or a denomination that had been more successful at integration. Katherine Brown Warren was amazingly persistent in attending Mormon services for three years when, by her report, no one would speak to her and when she had to write directly to the president of the LDS Church to find out how to be baptized. Obviously, acceptance by white members was not an important requirement, helpful and pleasant though it would have been. Instead, as she put it, "I look over their errors and see the Lord."[52]

In contrast with Katherine's experience, her two nieces, Betty and Michelle, were baptized on the same day with eleven other members of their family. Almost certainly they reinforced each other's commitment, provided perspective and support during difficult moments in the transition, minimized negative experiences through shared understanding, and maximized positive experiences by shared rejoicing. A unity of family belief and religious practice seems to have been especially important to the Brown-Wright family, since its members stressed in the interviews that they adopted such family-centered LDS practices as weekly family home evening, attending meetings as a family, scripture reading, and family prayer. Similarly, Nellie Sargent's decades of cheerful service to Mormon missionaries, her daughter Novella's faithfulness in Washington, D.C., and her daughter Mary's regularity in observing such Mormon customs as the monthly fast, even when she did it alone, influenced Mary's children, especially the three who joined the LDS Church. The younger generation was likewise impressed by the three women's dependency on the priesthood for blessings and their view of the Book of Mormon as a precious physical object.

Other sociological factors may also be at work. As Cardell Jacobson points out in his chapter in the present book, Wade Clark Roof, a sociologist, and William McKinney, a theologian, analyzed conversion from one religious tradition to another as fitting one of three main patterns: (1) "upward movement," in which conversion brings people to a higher socioeconomic level; (2) "conservative movement," which is motivated primarily by reaction to secular trends in society and the former religion, and (3) "movement away," in which primarily young people are disentangling themselves from church affiliation altogether.[53]

Both the Sargent-Keys and Brown-Wright families fit the "upward" and "conservative" movements. While Wesley Brown was a carpenter in rural Louisiana, his daughters married skilled workers in Baton Rouge. His granddaughter Michelle attended college; her brothers and sisters are middle class. The Brown-Wrights found appealing the conservative values espoused by the Baptist Church, the Church of God in Christ, and the LDS Church, but they drew back from the extreme of affiliating themselves with a denomination that forbade wearing nail polish and lipstick. Mormonism, itself a conservative religion, thus occupied a comfortable niche between the too-harsh strictures of one ultraconservative denomination and what Dunk Wright characterized as a "rotten" second denomination.

However, the dominant motivation of these individuals, both for the initial affiliation and for the successful maintenance of that affiliation, was a personal confirmation that God wanted them to be Mormon and that, in Mormonism, they had found the truth. This final reason—faith—remains mysterious, beyond rationality, and not susceptible to the quantification of social scientists.

Theologians and philosophers have struggled to define faith. For the Danish theologian Soren Kierkegaard, faith was a leap, explaining that the leap was the most difficult move for a dancer, especially to leap and then fall, all the while maintaining the same step. In Kierkegaard's search for the "knight of faith," he explained he could "imagine" him, although he had never met him. He wrote, "I can, I think, describe the movements of faith perfectly, but I can never perform them."[54] The author of the New Testament epistle to the Hebrews faced the same dilemmas when he defined faith as "the substance of things hoped for, the evidence of things not seen" (Heb. 11:1).

In the same way, the African Americans in this study believe that the Church of Jesus Christ of Latter-day Saints is the "true church" and their key to eternal salvation. Their faith gives them an emotional and spiritual resilience that enables them to overlook the puzzling history of Mormonism's exclusion of African American men from priesthood ordination and also to shrug off the hurtful incidents of insensitivity and prejudice on the part of white Mormons. The case studies in this article show the "movements of faith," but like Kierkegaard and Paul, I can explain only the effects. Shirley Walker Wright, who returned to her newly baptized husband with no intention of adopting his religion, put it this way: "Man cannot convert you. The Spirit has to. You have to allow the Spirit to come in and do His job."[55]

Notes

1. I use "black" and "African American" interchangeably throughout this study.

2. See Alan Cherry, *It's You and Me, Lord* (Provo, Utah: Trilogy Arts Press, 1970), and Mary Sturlaugson, *A Soul So Rebellious* (Salt Lake City: Deseret Book, 1980). The quote is from the latter, p. 28. Sturlaugson later wrote two more books, continuing the record of her experiences in Mormonism; see Mary Sturlaugson Eyer, *He Restoreth My Soul* (Salt Lake City: Deseret Book, 1982), and *Reflection of a Soul* (N.p.: privately published, 1985).

3. The Charles Redd Center for Western Studies was established in 1972 after Charles Redd and Annaley Naegle Redd donated funds to Brigham Young University. The Oral History Program was started in 1973 after the Redd Center sponsored a class in the techniques of collecting oral histories. Since then, the center has recorded hundreds of oral histories, which I have used in my publications. The transcripts are open to researchers in the L. Tom Perry Special Collections and Manuscripts Division, Harold B. Lee Library, Brigham Young University, Provo, Utah.

4. See my *Black Saints in a White Church: Contemporary African American Mormons* (Salt

Lake City: Signature Books, 1994). Nearly all the interviewees and survey respondents attended meetings and participated in Mormon activities.

5. Until October 2002, these interviews were conducted annually. Since that time, they have been conducted biannually. In temples, "eternal marriages" are solemnized for the living and, by proxy, for the dead, for whom are also performed proxy baptisms, ordinations to the priesthood (for males), and the "endowments," or a ritual sequence of instructions and covenants for righteous living. Because entrance to the temple requires priesthood ordination for males and because of the central value assigned to marriage and parent-child sealings, not only black men but also black women, whether married or single, were denied entrance to the temple before the June 1978 revelation.

6. Embry, *Black Saints in a White Church*, 95–180, 70.

7. For example, Rodney Stark and Charles Y. Glock define varieties of religious belief and quantify strata of "orthodox" and "unorthodox" believers but do not attempt to determine why people accept "traditional supernaturalism" (Stark and Glock, *American Piety: The Nature of Religious Commitment* [Berkeley: University of California Press, 1968], 57–58). Wade Clark Roof likewise affirmed that "the traditional religious world view rests on an assumption of a supernatural order [and] . . . posit[s] the mysterious forces of a sovereign Deity at work in everyday human affairs," again without attempting to explain why some individuals possess faith and others do not (Roof, *Community and Commitment: Religious Plausibility in a Liberal Protestant Church* [New York: Elsevier, 1978], 8).

8. The powerful but mysterious ability of faith to transcend logic is certainly not unique to African American Mormons. To take a broader example, no objective evidence exists for the foundation of all Christian religion, the divinity of Jesus Christ. See Vivette Porges, Joshua Simon, and Robert Sullivan, *Who Do You Say That I Am? Reflections on Jesus in Our World Today* (New York: Macmillan, 1996).

9. Jerri Allene Thornton Hale (later Harwell), interview by Alan Cherry, 1985, transcript, 16, LDS African American Oral History Project, Charles Redd Center for Western Studies, L. Tom Perry Special Collections and Manuscripts, Harold B. Lee Library, Brigham Young University, Provo, Utah. Unless otherwise noted, all of the oral histories cited are part of this collection.

10. In a departure from the usual scholarly convention of referring to historical persons by surname in second references, I attempt to steer the reader through the sometimes complicated relationships in the multigenerational examples by identifying each individual consistently by first name on second reference with, where relevant, the relationship spelled out.

11. Jessie L. Embry, "Without Purse or Scrip," *Dialogue: A Journal of Mormon Thought* 29 (Fall 1996): 77–93.

12. Information about the family's early history comes from Novella Sargent Gibson (the Sargents' daughter), interview by Chad Orton, 1985, transcript, Brigham Young University Oral History Project. This transcript is incomplete because of technical difficulties with the tape. The only copy of the partial transcript is in my possession. The pages are not numbered. All subsequent quotations from Novella Sargent Gibson in this chapter are from this source.

13. Virginia Keys Wright, interview by Alan Cherry, 1986, transcript, 19.

14. Ethel Ann Keys Kelley, interview by Alan Cherry, 1986, transcript, 3.

15. Ibid., 5, 3.

16. Ibid., 3–4; Virginia Wright interview, 11 (quote).

17. Kelley interview, 2, 4.

18. Ibid., 4, 6.

19. Ibid., 2, 6, 14.

20. Ibid., 4–5.

21. Ibid., 18–20.

22. Virginia Wright interview, 3, 6.

23. Ibid. 6, 16, 18.

24. Raymond W. Keys, interview by Alan Cherry, 1986, transcript, 1–2.

25. Ibid., 6.

26. Virginia Wright interview, 19–20; Kelley interview, 11.

27. Katherine Brown Warren, interview by Alan Cherry, 1987, transcript, 2.

28. Ibid., 3.

29. Ibid., 4–6.

30. Ibid., 6.

31. Ibid., 6–7, 11, 17–18.

32. Ibid., 16–17.

33. Ibid., 9–10.

34. Betty Wright Baunchand, interviewed by Alan Cherry, 1987, transcript, 3–5.

35. Ibid., 4–5. The names that Betty lists in the interviews do not add up to the thirteen. Her sister Michelle Evette also could not remember the exact people in the service. Not all the names are listed in the *Church News* article about the baptism, which focuses on Katherine Warren. The article said the thirteen members ranged in age from nine to forty-five and the youngest, Andrea Prophet, told the Joseph Smith story to the interviewer. See Elder Roger W. Carpenter, "Thirteen of Convert's Relatives Join Church," *Church News,* February 17, 1979, 13.

36. Baunchand interview, 6, 10.

37. Michelle Evette Wright, interview by Alan Cherry, 1987, transcript, 18.

38. Ibid., 7.

39. Ibid., 18.

40. Ibid., 16.

41. Dorothy Mae Brown Wright, interview by Alan Cherry, 1987, transcript, 4; Dunk Wright, interview by Alan Cherry, 1987, transcript, 6.

42. Wesley Jennings Brown, interview by Alan Cherry, 1987, transcript, 1, 4. None of the interviews lists the baptism dates of Wesley and Hilda.

43. Baunchand interview, 7. None of the interviews lists Hilda's death date.

44. Van C. Wright Sr., interview by Alan Cherry, 1987, transcript, 3–4, 7, 9 (quotes); Shirley Walker Wright, interview by Alan Cherry, 1987, transcript, 3–4.

45. Wright Sr. interview, 22; Shirley Wright interview, 10.

46. Shirley Wright interview, 10; Wright Sr. interview, 22.

47. Shirley Wright interview, 12–13; Wright Sr. interview, 20–21.

48. Wright Sr. interview, 13–14.

49. Michelle Wright interview, 18–19.

50. Dorothy Wright interview, 10; Wright Sr. interview, 25; Baunchand interview, 11.

51. Michelle Wright interview, 18.

52. Warren interview, 16.

53. Wade Clark Roof and William McKinney, *American Mainline Religion: Its Changing Shape and Future* (New Brunswick, N.J.: Rutgers University Press, 1987), 172–77.

54. Quoted in W. H. Auden, *The Living Thoughts of Kierkegaard* (Bloomington: Indiana University Press, 1971), 109–10.

55. Shirley Wright interview, 13.

5   Casting Off the "Curse of Cain": The Extent and Limits of Progress since 1978

ARMAND L. MAUSS

[The Lord] . . . by revelation has confirmed that all worthy male members of the Church may be ordained to the priesthood without regard for race or color.
—*LDS First Presidency*

[The 1978 revelation] continues to speak for itself. . . . I don't see anything further that we need to do.
—*Gordon B. Hinckley*

The anguished history of the black membership in the Church of Jesus Christ of Latter-day Saints is by now a well-told story, which does not need recounting here.[1] The story is rooted in three episodes in particular, each crucial in its own way, and each itself a culmination of a unique process: (1) Brigham Young's 1852 declaration of church policy denying blacks access to the lay priesthood; (2) a partial reconsideration, confirmation, and institutionalization of that policy in the 1880s; and (3) the 1978 revelation, which overturned the policy and extended the priesthood to "all worthy male members . . . without regard to race or color."[2]

As the twenty-first century arrived, a fourth process was underway with uncertain prospects: in particular, whether President Hinckley's quotation in the epigraph will continue to be the stated policy of the church. This process might be called the struggle to cast off the "curse of Cain," not only from the black peoples of the earth, on whom it was traditionally imposed, but indeed from the LDS Church itself, which continues to bear the burden of its own racist heritage. This essay deals mainly with that fourth struggle as it has unfolded since 1978. It is a struggle occurring on two levels. At the operational level, there is a conscientious outreach by the church toward black people everywhere.[3] Meanwhile, at the ideological level there is a less clear strategy for coping with the doctrinal residue of a discarded racial policy, especially in North America.[4]

Developments since 1978

The revelation and policy change of 1978, in a single administrative act, removed all formal restrictions on full participation in LDS church life by people of black African ancestry.[5] What has been much slower to change, however, has been almost two centuries of accumulated racial and religious folklore among white American Mormons. This folklore had been constructed over many years to defend and "explain" to Mormons and others the erstwhile policy of withholding the priesthood from a divinely disfavored lineage. Even though this policy itself has been overturned, the folklore for rationalizing it has lingered on at the grassroots, despite its manifest irrelevance to contemporary church life. In particular, the notion that blacks were descendants of Cain now seems ironically to have taken on a life of its own as a post hoc "explanation" for the historical origin of the obsolete priesthood restriction.[6] The general authorities of the church no longer offer such "explanations," but such rationales have continued to be circulated in conversation and in print through authoritative books written by earlier leaders and commentators.[7]

One of the great popular myths in traditional Mormonism, quite apart from racial questions, is that people can find in this religion all the "answers" they need. A consequence of this myth is people's manifest discomfort with quandaries that seem to have no ready explanations. Producing those explanations has always been a growth industry among the Mormon folk, as attested by a vast scholarly literature on folklore.[8] In the particular case at hand, the "explanation" has still been circulating that blacks are (as they always were) descendants of Cain, but that lately God has relented and removed the curse from that lineage so that black men could finally participate in the priesthood.

Since such ideas were not officially and explicitly repudiated in 1978 along with priesthood restriction, they have continued to be offered by well-meaning local members, leaders, and teachers whenever questions arise about why the restriction on priesthood had ever existed in the church.[9] In the apparent hope that with time all such vestiges of racism would eventually die a natural death, most church leaders have assumed a posture of benign neglect toward them, a matter that I shall consider more fully later in the essay. Meanwhile, the church has looked for ways of constructively engaging black people as current and future church members. In this endeavor, the church seems to have had less success in North America than elsewhere.

Mormon Missionary Outreach to Black Americans

It is difficult to ascertain just how successful the Mormon missionary program has been among black Americans since 1978. Ordinary church records do not keep track of race or ethnicity, leaving researchers dependent on unsystematic samples and anecdotal evidence. Certainly the church publications have given more exposure than ever before to stories of black conversion, the spiritual and social growth of new black members, and their inspiring encounters with divine influences. A sheer count of such stories would be misleading, however, since a large proportion of them deal with cases outside the United States. Newell Bringhurst made a study of how the *Church News* presented "the image of blacks as prime instruments of [church] growth and expansion" during the first decade after 1978.[10] He concluded that in strictly *geographic* terms the church had made great strides into large sections and populations of the world traditionally neglected by LDS missionaries, such as Africa. In numerical terms, however, Bringhurst found *Church News* claims of rapid black growth to be a little exaggerated in some of the countries. In the United States itself, growth was actually quite slow.

Despite the strained history of Mormon relationships with blacks and a studied avoidance of black proselytizing by the church before 1978, American blacks have occasionally joined the church from the very beginning, but especially since World War II. One informed Utah journalist estimated that the church had two thousand black members even before the priesthood policy was changed.[11] Most of these seem to have been attracted to the church through friendships with individual white Mormons encountered in the workplace or during military service. As noted earlier, such estimates can only be informed guesses, but whatever their actual number, these converts have been remarkable for their ability to look beyond all the trappings of racism to the Mormon spiritual core. A few of them have published accounts of their conversions.[12] These accounts reveal a variety of more or less successful efforts to deal with the cognitive dissonance and external black criticism involved in joining the Mormons. I will say more about this predicament later in this chapter.

Conversions of black Americans to the LDS Church seem to have waxed and waned with local conditions and initiatives, and by no means have missionary efforts been limited to blacks in Utah. A major drive during the early 1980s by the Mormon mission in North Carolina brought in some nine hundred black converts, but a few years later only a hundred remained active in the church.[13] The president of the California mission in Oakland during 1983–85 gave special proselytizing attention to the large black population in that area, and his missionaries succeeded in baptizing ninety-three new black members, constituting 5 percent of all the converts in the mission during that period.[14] Most of these lived in two Oakland wards (congregations) in particular, and they provided the nucleus for the organization of a northern California chapter of the Utah-based Genesis Group. This level of growth and enthusiasm did not long survive the normal change of mission presidents, but several black families went on to gain some prominence in local Mormon congregations.[15] The Watts area of southwest Los Angeles produced enough converts for a branch of some one hundred people in a little more than a year, almost all of whom were black.[16] Missionary successes with blacks have attracted attention in other important urban centers of the nation, including the South Bronx and East St. Louis.[17] Temporary surges in missionary success with black Americans elsewhere have often been reported anecdotally.

One important source of such reports is the collection of African American oral histories compiled by the Oral History Program of the Charles Redd Center for Western Studies at BYU.[18] This program is devoted to collecting oral histories from various ethnic and other groups in the Mormon orbit. For the LDS African American Oral History Project, 225 black Mormons (mostly recent converts) were interviewed during 1985–89 by Alan Cherry, a prominent black convert of many years. Although these interviews were conducted in various parts of the United States, they constituted essentially an "opportunity sample" of black Mormons, not a representative one. Particularly overlooked in the sample were members who had dropped out of church activity. Nevertheless, the oral history interviews were numerous enough to reveal a great range of social characteristics and life circumstances among the converts, as well as a variety of experiences with conversion, disillusionment, and acceptance in the Mormon community. The quality of these experiences has been captured in an important book based on the interviews,[19] and a number of articles have been published from the quantitative data these same interviews yielded.[20]

Taken altogether, this published work is qualitatively very rich. It indicates that those American blacks who joined the Mormon church and remained active in the decade after the change in priesthood policy were disproportionately young, well educated, upwardly mobile socially, and largely of southern origin and upbringing.[21] The converts claimed to have been especially attracted to Mormonism by its "plan of salvation" linking this life to the next, and by its emphasis on family life and values. In general, however, they seemed more attached to the general Christian teachings in the LDS Church than to the uniquely Mormon teachings. Members in the South, especially, credited the lay priesthood with keeping them involved in the activities of the church. Yet many who were still active offered accounts of others who had dropped by the wayside because of the insensitivity of white members, lapses in the church's retention efforts, or simply their own difficulties in trying to maintain the LDS way of life.

Through such reports from those still involved, it is possible to infer some of the reasons for an apparently large drop-out rate among black Mormons in the United States. These reasons included (in no particular order) discomfort over class and cultural differences with white Mormons in most congregations; feelings of being treated categorically as blacks instead of as individuals; exaggerated attention as "novelties" of some kind in their treatment by whites; continuing undercurrents of racism in such LDS popular beliefs as the curse of Cain; white resistance to intermarriage or even to interracial dating; and in general a level of white acceptance that was considered civil but not warm. At the same time, the black interviewees recognized that these difficulties were the kinds that tended to occur between blacks and whites in America generally, not just in LDS congregations.

In my interviews with Ruffin Bridgeforth in 1981 and 1985 and Darius Gray in 1999, both leaders of the Genesis Group, they acknowledged that they devoted much of their time to counseling black church members who had been offended by the traditional racial teachings in Mormonism.[22] In general, these black leaders were quite restrained and philosophical about their own disappointments with racial slights from white Mormons, but they clearly shared the indignation that had so often been "unloaded" on them by the black members who came to them for spiritual counseling, as well as by many others throughout the country who had reached them by mail or telephone for the same kind of help. A recurring source of irritation was the continuing circulation among ill-informed and credulous white Mormons of the old racial myths about Cain and Ham and other dubious doctrines, especially in Utah. This issue arose more than once in personal interviews that I conducted during the summer of 1985 with several black couples and individuals in southern California, who had joined the church in the recent past. One black couple in Riverside, California, reported that their children had dropped out of the church because of teasing by their white peers about their supposed descent from Cain.[23]

Some irritants came out of sheer insensitivity, such as the occasion reported by Marva Collins when her ward Relief Society sisters decided to raise funds through a "slave auction," in which members would perform household tasks for the highest bidders. The women were totally oblivious to the impact of such an idea on their only black member.[24] In short, my own few interviews with black Mormons in southern California and Salt Lake City produced reports very much like those in the Cherry and Embry oral history interviews.

While these accounts of life in the church for new black converts contained much that was reassuring and inspirational, the recurring problems with white ignorance and insensitivity were also readily apparent, even among those still active in the church. Indeed, the president of the Genesis Group was quoted in an interview with the *Salt Lake Tribune* as saying that the single most important reason for the attrition of black church members was the attitude of some white members.[25] Whatever the number of those offended enough to drop out, their departure would be understandable and presumably a source of great concern to church leaders from the top down. So far, however, this official concern has focused less on challenging the racist residue among white Mormons than on maintaining public relations outside the church.

Public Relations Outreach by the LDS Church

Besides the usual missionary and congregational programs, the LDS Church has also tried to cultivate warmer public relationships with its black members and with black America more generally. A recurrent effort has been to participate in the national celebration of Black History Month each February or at least to encourage the black Mormons to do so. One of the earliest of these initiatives was taken by the black LDS community in Salt Lake City itself, with the sponsorship of the church. The first annual Ebony Rose Black History Conference was held in the Twenty-first North Ward there on February 21–22, 1987, with a promise that the second annual one would be held in Washington, D.C. The 1987 conference included workshops on a variety of practical topics and on black history, especially black LDS history, plus a worship service. One featured speaker was Mary L. Bankhead, perhaps the oldest surviving black Mormon at that time and a descendant of one of the pioneer Utah black families. The official church auspices were indicated by the keynote speaker, Elder Yoshihiko Kikuchi of the Seventy, a Japanese national. Incongruous as that might seem in a black LDS American gathering, Elder Kikuchi's remarks were very well received as sensitive and supportive.[26]

In June 1988, at the tenth anniversary of the priesthood policy change, the church held a special all-day conference at BYU, the LDS Afro-American Symposium, after several weeks of advance publicity.[27] Black Mormons who had gained prominence in either religious or professional roles were brought in as featured speakers from as far away as Washington, D.C., Atlanta, and Chicago. Dallin H. Oaks, of the Quorum of the Twelve Apostles, gave a very upbeat keynote address, in which he emphasized the spiritual and scriptural basis for the church's outreach to black people, the faithfulness of black members, and the enormous growth of the church in Africa. The concluding speaker was James D. Walker, founding president of the Afro-American Historical and Genealogical Society in Washington, D.C. This conference and various other commemorative expressions by the church were duly covered by the national press in some fairly extensive newspaper and magazine articles. Most of this coverage was very favorable and forward-looking in tone, but it also acknowledged that vestiges of racism were still apparent in the church.[28]

As time went on, church-sponsored commemorations of important events in black history were no longer focused exclusively on black Mormons but also looked outward to the nation as a whole. In acknowledging the important contributions of black Americans, Mormon and non-Mormon, the church has served three important public relations purposes simultaneously: (1) focusing attention particularly upon the achievements of black Mormons, past and present; (2) legitimizing the celebration of black history; and (3) validating Mormon participation in that history. The commemorations have not been limited to sites and events in Utah. An example with great visibility was a large ecumenical religious service on Sunday, January 20, 1991, sponsored by the Interreligious Council of Oakland (California) but hosted by the LDS Church at its spacious Interstake Center on the grounds of the Oakland Temple. The theme of the service was "Martin's Dream and the Drug Crisis." It featured prayers, music, and a dozen speakers from different denominations, black and white, Protestant, Catholic, Jewish, and Mormon. Most of the several hundred in attendance were black. Afterward all were served refreshments in an adjacent hall by the women of the LDS Relief Society.[29]

Various religious organizations have used other large LDS buildings as the sites for commemorating Martin Luther King Day. For example, in January 1992, the San Fernando Valley Interfaith Council was offered use of the LDS Van Nuys Stake Center for a turnout of almost two thousand appreciative celebrants, including blacks and whites. LDS Church representatives in California have continued well into the new century to participate in the commemoration of Martin Luther King Day under the auspices of the Southern Christian Leadership Conference, the Interreligious Council of Southern California, and/or the National Conference for Community and Justice (NCCJ, formerly National Conference of Christians and Jews).[30]

Perhaps the single most remarkable illustration of the constructive public relations impact of Mormon outreach to the black population occurred in the wake of the Los Angeles riots in May 1992.[31] The riots had left much of South Central Los Angeles in shambles, with many of the inhabitants, whether black, white, Latino, or Asian, unable to get food, shelter, utilities, transportation, or work. Some churches in the neighborhood were doing what they could, with limited resources, to provide food and shelter. Two of these were particularly important in this effort, namely the Mount Zion Missionary Baptist Church and the First African Methodist Episcopal (AME) Church, both of which served mainly black congregations. A few leading Mormons in the immediate vicinity and nearby launched a local campaign to bring relief to the south-central inner city. The effort went forward under the auspices and initiative especially of the presidents in the Palos Verdes and the Los Angeles stakes. While much of the city was still smoldering, a series of Mormon car and truck caravans began delivering food and other supplies to the First AME and Mount Zion churches from Mormon congregations in neighboring stakes. The campaign went on for several days, including a Sunday when some of the LDS congregations even canceled their usual meetings in order to collect and distribute supplies.

The AME pastor, the Reverend Cecil Murray, had heard little about Mormons except their traditional racial doctrines; but he was apparently so gratified that he gave a public pronouncement encouraging people in the vicinity to talk with the local Mormon missionaries, who had theretofore been largely ignored or even threatened. This episode established an ongoing religious and social relationship between the First AME Church and the local LDS stakes that was still active at least a decade later, when a Latter-day Saint apostle was invited in December 2001 to attend a special AME service and to receive there, on behalf of the LDS Church president, this congregation's Lovejoy Award, in recognition of the outreach efforts by local Mormons during recent years.

Murray and other local black leaders apparently also intervened with Tom Bradley, then the black mayor of Los Angeles, to get his help in ending a six-year delay in the issuance of a building permit for a Mormon stake center in the area. The construction of the new stake center, in turn, pumped twelve million dollars worth of jobs and goods into the economy of South Central. Local Mormon leaders believe that the goodwill of black religious leaders such as Murray has also been responsible for protecting the new stake center against vandalism and for opening doors to Mormon missionaries. During Black History Month in February 2002, that same stake center served as the site of a large conference on genealogical research for black Americans, sponsored jointly by the LDS Church, the African American Heritage Society, and the California African American Genealogical Society. Under the title "Discover Your Roots," the conference featured the archivist Chris Haley, nephew of Alex Haley, as keynote speaker, and was attended by some four hundred enthusiastic black people of various religious persuasions. The new relationship between the LDS Church and the black community in southern California was obviously still thriving as the new century opened.[32]

During Black History Month in 1993, the church's *Deseret News* featured an article on BYU student teachers who were working with black inner-city high school students in Washington, D.C., and in the same month, the *New York Times* covered the growth of the church in Scarsdale, New York, where photographs showed a racially integrated congregation.[33] On February 5 and 12, 1994, the weekly *Church News* carried special articles on black LDS families and their activities in Roswell, Georgia; East St. Louis, Illinois; and Los Angeles, California. The BYU *Daily Universe* of February 13, 1995, was devoted in large part to the need for greater ethnic "diversity" on campus. As part of the commemoration of Black History Month in particular, the *Daily Universe* featured an article on black Mormon athletes and their needs at the university; another reported on the first three blacks in the twentieth century to serve full-time missions for the church.[34] These articles represent only a small sampling of the kinds of news coverage sought and received by the church during each Black History Month, especially in the 1990s. Nor was such coverage limited to February of each year; impressive news stories of a "human interest" kind about black Mormon converts could and did appear at any time of the year.

The twentieth anniversary of the priesthood policy change in 1998 was another occasion for commemorations. However, these celebrations were more limited than those of a decade earlier and largely overshadowed, both in Utah and on the national stage, by a widely circulated news story that the Mormon leadership was considering an official repudiation of the traditional racial doctrines. At issue here were the legends connecting Africans and their descendants with Cain and Ham, as well as some uniquely Mormon ideas about a divinely sanctioned hierarchy of lineages originating in premortal life. The news report about the impending repudiation first appeared in a *Los Angeles Times* article on May 18, 1998, and was carried around the world in various media.[35] However, when confronted by the press at a news conference, President Gordon B. Hinckley denied the report, saying that "the matter . . . has not been discussed by the First Presidency and the Quorum of the Twelve." True though that denial apparently was, the repudiation in question definitely was under discussion at lower organizational levels; and thereby hangs a tale.[36]

As recounted by Richard and Joan Ostling, the need for such a public repudiation had become apparent to Elder Marlin K. Jensen, a president of the third-ranked body of general authorities, the First Quorum of Seventy, and to some of the staff working under him in the church's Public Affairs Department.[37] The discussions at Jensen's level, however, had apparently not yet produced any specific proposal for consideration by the Twelve at the time of Hinckley's comments to the press. The main issue in question was the racist residue remaining in authoritative books written by prominent Mormon leaders of the past. These books (listed above earlier), some of them considered doctrinal "classics" among grassroots Mormons, had continued in print under church auspices long after the end of the priesthood restriction that they had ostensibly "explained." Yet to most white Mormons the "race problem" had been "solved" in 1978, simply by the change in priesthood policy.

Many black Mormons, however, if they joined the church much after that time, did so without being aware that the issue had ever existed until they read some of the books with the offending passages. Particularly in North America, where these books were readily available in church libraries and bookstores, black Mormons could learn about these old racial doctrines, sometimes from each other and sometimes even from non-Mormon black friends. When the black converts would understandably raise questions about these doctrines in church settings, they would be met, as often as not, with matter-of-fact affirmations of the doctrines by local Mormon leaders, who themselves tended to accept whatever they had read in "church books." The late Eugene England, a professor of English at Brigham Young University at the end of the twentieth century, reported that in surveys periodically administered to his classes, "a majority of bright, well-educated Mormon students" continued to express belief in the old racial folklore, claiming they had learned it from parents and teachers in the church and never questioned it.[38]

Some black converts, especially those who had gained a deep general appreciation for their new religion, were willing simply to swallow hard and dismiss all such ideas as carryovers from the past that eventually would disappear along with the rest of American racism. Others, however, took such offense that they soon dropped out altogether. Still others were willing to give the matter some time but were not prepared to remain quiet in the interim. It was one of these less docile black converts who, with the moral support of his white home teacher, began to remonstrate with church leaders by mail. In particular, however, it was through his home teacher's personal relationship with Marlin Jensen that an ad hoc committee was created by Jensen in mid-1997 to help draft a proposal to the other general authorities. The proposal was accompanied by examples from extant publications of demeaning references to blacks in LDS literature. It outlined the potential harm of such passages and recommended an official and public disavowal of the same as modern church doctrine.

The twentieth anniversary of the end of the priesthood restriction seemed an especially propitious time to expect an announcement of such a disavowal. However, when June 1998 approached with no indication that such a statement would be forthcoming, the black member of the ad hoc committee, who had initiated the process in the first place, became impatient. In the apparent belief that the process could be accelerated with a little encouragement from the press, he sought and received an interview with a reporter from the *Los Angeles Times* and explained what had transpired. The resulting press exposure had just the opposite of the desired effect, as church leaders refused to be prodded in their deliberations. The whole process was thereby aborted, and the "disavowal" that Hinckley finally issued turned out to be nothing more than a denial that he was considering any such disavowal.[39] The rest of the ad hoc committee was chagrined and irritated that one of its own members had leaked the story to the media, and Jensen presumably suffered some embarrassment at the raised eyebrows of some of his superiors.

Even if the proposal from Jensen had worked its way up to President Hinckley, it is by no means certain that the president would have supported the kind of public repudiation recommended. In his May 1998 demurral, he reiterated his belief that the twenty-year-old policy change "continues to speak for itself."[40] In a later interview with the *Los Angeles Times* reporter who wrote the first story, President Hinckley, who had recently returned from visiting LDS congregations in Africa, added, "I don't hear any complaint from our black brethren and sisters. I hear only appreciation and gratitude wherever I go. . . . I don't see anything further that we need to do."[41] The apparent assumption behind such comments by the president and his colleagues is that the abandonment of the restrictive racial *policy* in 1978 was meant implicitly to include an abandonment of the various traditional *doctrinal folklore* that had once been used to justify that policy. Such an assumption does little to neutralize the dubious and offending doctrinal myths that remain in older church literature, especially when they continue to appear in reprintings of that literature.

The manifest confidence of President Hinckley and perhaps of most other Mormons that there was no necessity for further disavowals of discarded doctrines could only have been strengthened by the remarkable invitation the president received to address the Western Region One Leadership Conference of the National Association for the Advancement of Colored People (NAACP). In the first address ever given by a Mormon president to the NAACP, on April 24, 1998, Hinckley was given a standing ovation and presented with a NAACP Distinguished Service Award by Julian Bond, chairman of the board of directors. Although the main theme of his address was the importance of strong fathers in maintaining stable families, the president also made a number of well-received comments about the need to improve relationships between the races. Conceding that he was "deeply concerned" about the prejudice remaining in America, he nevertheless expressed his typical optimism about the future. Already, he said, he was meeting "men and women of great distinction, tremendous capacity, [and even] brilliance in many professions [coming from] diverse ethnic and racial backgrounds." He concluded with the ringing declaration that "each of us is a child of God. It matters not the race. It matters not the slant of our eyes or the color of our skin. We are sons and daughters of the Almighty. . . . When a child comes to realize that there is something of divinity within him, then something great begins to happen."[42]

Another span in the lengthening Mormon bridge to the American black community was constructed during Black History Month in February 2001. A church genealogy researcher working in the National Archives had happened upon the records of the Freedman's Bank, a Reconstruction-era institution that had gone defunct in 1874 but had left behind the banking records of thousands of freed slaves. With the backing of the church and the labor of 550 family history "buffs" who were inmates at the Utah State Prison, these banking records were electronically compiled from microfilms and collated into family groups. The project took eleven years, but with the data in that form, it was possible to identify vital statistics and family connections for nearly half a million freed slaves and their ancestors going back into the eighteenth century. As many as ten million contemporary American blacks have ancestors identified in those records, which the church offered gratis on the Internet or at cost on compact disks. The project was hailed by prominent scholars and black spokespersons who were quoted in the media.[43]

The release of the new disks was announced during a highly publicized and well-attended press conference called by the church on February 26, 2001, in Salt Lake City. Predictably, one of the reporters in attendance asked whether this project and the attendant publicity were offered as part of a church gesture of conciliation to the nation's black people in light of traditional racist doctrines. The church public relations official in charge bridled at the question and offered a rather abrupt response. Fortunately for the Public Affairs Department, a skilled church authority was present from the Seventy and intervened with a much less defensive and more appreciative response to the reporter.[44] The point highlighted by this exchange is that, even as the church was getting some credit for its generous dealings with blacks, its unrenounced racist teachings about a "divinely cursed" lineage were still available to be cited again and to cloud an otherwise successful encounter.

The special commitment of the LDS Church to genealogical research, however, will likely prove a convenient and congenial meeting ground with black Americans in the future. As if in response to the LDS offering of the Freedman's Bank records in 2001, the National Museum of African-American History and Culture in Washington, D.C., opened Black History Month in

2002 by bringing much of its core collection to the LDS temple in Maryland for a two-month exhibit at the visitors' center on the temple grounds. The featured speaker there on the opening day was Frederick Douglass IV, and the next night was devoted to an inspirational "fireside" meeting under the auspices of the Genesis Group from Utah. Early in the month at the same location, the church also sponsored an all-day conference on African American family history, then offered to microfilm copies of all the materials brought for exhibit by the National Museum.[45] The LDS-sponsored conference "Discover Your Roots," held in Los Angeles during the same February, was already described above.

Of course, all of these forms of LDS outreach to blacks, Mormon and non-Mormon, are intended to convey the message that real changes have taken place in the ways in which the church looks upon black people and their aspirations. It is a sincere message, even if it is not always delivered skillfully and sensitively. Having dropped the ban against the priesthood for blacks a quarter century ago, most church leaders do not seem to see the necessity for adding a formal, official repudiation of offensive racial doctrines; these are expected to disappear naturally from the collective memory with the passage of time. Certainly these old doctrines have not appeared in official church discourse for at least two decades. They are mentioned in the *Encyclopedia of Mormonism* only in passing as relics of the past no longer relevant in the modern church.[46] However, as long as these doctrines continue to appear in successive reprintings of authoritative books and are freely circulated by mouth at the Mormon grassroots, they will continue to rankle many of the black Saints.

Changed Mormon Posture on Civil Rights

Meanwhile, is there any evidence that the church's recent outreach to blacks has been accompanied by changes in Mormon public opinion about civil rights for black citizens? That is, since my surveys of the late 1960s, have the political and social beliefs and attitudes of white Mormons become more favorable toward black people and their civil rights? Answers to these questions can be found in national survey data collected across three decades by the National Opinion Research Corporation as part of the annual General Social Survey (GSS).[47]

The tables that follow present comparisons between Mormon and non-Mormon subsamples drawn from the GSS. Taken altogether, the tables cover a period starting in 1972 and ending in 1996. The LDS subsample accumulated across those years amounts potentially to as many as 452. The national subsample used for comparison is a random selection of about every tenth case across the same time span, which potentially totals about 30,000 cases. However, the actual numbers involved rarely reach those limits and indeed vary a great deal because not all the questions in the surveys were used every year. The numbers for the Mormon subsample, in particular, are sometimes quite small, partly from attrition caused by skipping some questions in certain years and partly from my subdividing the data by decade. Insofar as the data permit, the tables have been divided into four sections: one for each of the three decades of the 1970s, 1980s, and 1990s and one for the total time period taken altogether (1972–96). In each section, the surviving Mormon subsample is compared to a corresponding (but much larger) general or national subsample (without Mormons). In table 5.1 we can see responses to a question about whether whites have a right to live in racially segregated neighborhoods if they wish to do so.

The first three columns of this table reveal that American approval of segregated communities declined slowly but steadily across the three decades. Mormon rates of approval for segregation were smaller than the national average across all three periods and declined as fast or faster than in the national data. There were enough Mormon cases, furthermore, to produce statistical significance. On this measure, at least, the Mormons joined the rest of the nation in giving up segregationist preferences and might even have moved a little faster in that direction after the church policy on priesthood was changed in 1978.

Table 5.1 Whites Have a Right to Segregated Neighborhoods

| | 1972–80 | | 1981–88 | |
	LDS (*n* = 53)	Other (*n* = 5,491)	LDS (*n* = 121)	Other (*n* = 7,542)
Agree strongly	13%	20%	5%	10%
Agree slightly	17	17	15	13
	30%	37%	20%	23%

| | 1989–96 | | Average | |
	LDS (*n* = 96)	Other (*n* = 6,869)	LDS (*n* = 270)	Other (*n* = 19,902)
Agree strongly	3%	6%	6%	11%
Agree slightly	7	11	13	13
	10%	17%	19%	24%

Note: The title of this table is an abbreviated version of the statement put to respondents (GSS Variable Label = RACSEG). The remaining response categories were "disagree slightly," "disagree strongly," and "don't know" or no response. Distribution in the total table was statistically significant (x^2 p = .008).

Another indicator in the GSS of segregationist thinking was a question asking whether it was better for black and white students to go to the same schools or to separate schools. By the 1990s, so few Americans favored separate schools that the question was dropped from the annual survey. However, we can still compare Mormons with others during the 1970s and 1980s. As we can see in table 5.2, even during the 1970s the LDS respondents were less inclined than the others to favor segregated schools, so in the 1980s the Mormons did not have as far to go as the rest of the country to reach virtual unanimity on unsegregated schools.

The GSS data also permit a consideration of differences between Mormons and others in the nation (on average) with regard to three additional questions on racial issues: (1) open housing policy; (2) willingness to have a person of the other race home for dinner; and (3) whether blacks should "push" so hard to achieve civil rights goals. In none of these three measures did the distributions prove statistically significant, probably because the Mormon numbers were too small.[48] However, some of the differences between Mormons and others might still be considered indicative.

For example, in the first of these untabled indicators (GSS Variable Label = RACOPEN), the question was whether the respondent would vote to let an owner decide who occupies his or her property or would vote to prevent the owner from discriminating on racial grounds. In the 1970s, the Mormons (68 percent) were more likely than the others (60 percent) to favor owner prerogatives, but by the 1990s both figures had dropped by half and no longer differed (34 percent for both Mormons and others).

On the second of these issues, having a person of the other race come for dinner (RACDIN), Mormons were less likely than others to express any objection even in the 1970s, but by the 1980s the gap (never large) had widened somewhat (88 percent of Mormons had no objection compared with 81 percent of others). The GSS did not collect corresponding data for the 1990s. Fi-

Table 5.2 Is It Better for White and Black Students to Go to the Same Schools or to Separate Schools?

	1972–80		1981–88		Average	
	LDS (n = 53)	Other (n = 6,057)	LDS (n = 56)	Other (n = 4,028)	LDS (n = 109)	Other (n = 10,085)
Same schools	93%	85%	95%	90%	94%	87%
Separate schools	6	12	5	7	6	11
Don't know/no response	2	2	0	2	1	3

Note: The title of the table is an abbreviated version of the question put to respondents (GSS Variable Label = RACSCHOL). Distribution in the total table was statistically significant (x^2 p = .007).

nally, on the question of whether blacks should "push" so hard for their rights (RACPUSH), Mormons were a little less likely than the national average to object to black "pushing." In the 1970s, 66 percent of the Mormons and 70 percent of the others agreed (strongly or slightly) that blacks shouldn't "push." By the 1990s, the corresponding figures were only 29 percent for Mormons and 40 percent for others. I reiterate that in none of these last three (untabled) comparisons could the distributions have reached statistical significance, given such small Mormon numbers, especially by decade.

However, all three of these comparisons, as well as those shown in tables 5-1 and 5-2, are consistent with the general finding that, by the 1990s, if not sooner, Mormons had equaled or exceeded the national averages in their support of various civil rights for black citizens.[49] These data are consistent with those presented by Roof and McKinney, who analyzed GSS surveys from an earlier decade.[50] Their graphic presentation even then showed Mormons among the more "liberal" of the various denominations in attitudes toward racial justice.[51] Given this obvious convergence between Mormons and others in secular, civil racial attitudes, we are back again to the question that was vexing Mormons in the 1960s: Why should anyone care about the Mormons' *religious* beliefs on racial matters?[52] The answer suggested in this chapter is twofold: First, even if Mormons are no longer as racist as most other Americans in secular or civil attitudes, their racism, *whatever* its magnitude, is partly rooted in traditional religious beliefs.[53] Second, those religious beliefs continue to circulate among white American Mormons to the detriment of relationships with black church members, even if there were no consequences for interracial relationships outside the church.

White Mormons, Black Mormons, and the Negotiation of Mormon Identity

Mormonism has its roots and trunk firmly planted in its Anglo-American origins. While the many new branches and grafts of the past two centuries have made the religion somewhat less generically American in its culture, its converts from other ethnic backgrounds will probably always find some strains in trying to negotiate their new identities as both Mormon and ethnic.[54] Few, if any, have had to struggle as much with this process as the black American converts. Most peoples of the earth find in Mormonism an affirmation of their identities as cherished children of God. The clashes they experience between their new religion and some of their cultural traditions might require certain modifications in their ethnic identities, but usually only around the edges.[55] In such cases, the negotiation process has no necessary implications for their

essential identities in the divine cosmic plan. Even if they cannot claim literal descent from the divinely favored lineage of Israel, they are assured of adoption or "grafting" into that lineage after baptism.

The traditional Mormon definition of black African lineage was something
more fundamental and essential. This lineage, so the explanation went, actually originated before mortality, when a certain segment of God's spirit
children was identified and set aside for its premortal sins or failings, which
presumably were very serious offenses but not very clearly delineated. These
"justly" stigmatized spirits were the ones sent into mortality through the lineage of Cain, the most monstrous counterfigure in Mormon scriptural lore,
second only to the devil himself (and, indeed, a collaborator with the devil).
The Mormon version of this lineage myth was but an elaboration upon a general European legend that had been increasingly applied to Africans, especially
as a useful justification for black slavery. The degradation of life under that
institution seemed only to confirm and reinforce the myth. By the time Mormonism came along, many generations of both black and white Americans
had been inculcated with this definition of black identity.[56]

It was, of course, never a meaningful myth to Africans themselves, virtually all of whom were black, and it was less salient even in other parts of the
Western Hemisphere, where (in some countries) the descendants of black
slaves came to be the dominant populations. In those situations, black people had some control over the kinds of images and identities about themselves
that were passed down the generations. Furthermore, white control over national myths and daily life gradually waned, so that the black populations,
especially in Africa, were not constantly reminded of their inferior and oppressed status. (South Africa was an exception, until recently). In the United
States, by contrast, the legacy of slavery remained for at least a century after
the Civil War and in some respects even into the twenty-first century. During all this time, the unequal opportunities and unequal treatment of the
black minority by white neighbors and institutions, even outside the South,
have continued to reinforce traditional religious and cultural myths about the
black identity. It is no wonder that a mutual wariness and suspicion can still
be found between blacks and whites in the United States, even more so than
in all-black nations.

How do American blacks—and black Mormons in particular—deal with
this predicament at the level of the individual self?[57] How does a black member of the LDS Church negotiate an identity that manages the cognitive dissonance between an ethnic or racial definition that he or she can't escape and
a demeaning religious tradition that he or she was once encouraged to accept
in the process of conversion? As we might expect, this negotiation yields dif-

ferent resolutions for different black Mormons.[58] In my own interviews and informal conversations with black Mormons, both in Utah and in California, I have encountered several different resolutions, but the richest source of data on this question is the African American Oral History Project conducted by Jessie L. Embry and Alan Cherry at Brigham Young University, described above. Those semi-structured interviews encouraged the black Mormon respondents to talk at some length about their experiences with the church and with other Mormons in various parts of the country. In particular, the respondents were invited to reflect upon the meaning of the traditional Mormon teachings and policies regarding black people.

With more than two hundred such interviews, it would be an enormous task to review, organize, and categorize all of these responses so that a general typology might be constructed. Fortunately this task was undertaken by two sociologists, O. Kendall White Jr. and Daryl White.[59] They studied the Embry-Cherry interview transcripts and abstracted five different modes of identity negotiation that emerged in those interviews, as the black Mormon respondents articulated the relationship between their racial and religious identities. The scholars enriched their analysis with illustrative quotations from the actual interviews. The five different modes seemed to arrange themselves along a conceptual continuum. At one end of the continuum were respondents who gave precedence to their newly found Mormon identity over their racial one, and at the other end were those who did the opposite. In between were different combinations of racial and religious explanations for the identities that black Mormons embraced in their relationship to God and to the church.

The first type of identity resolution embraced the truth-claims of Mormonism while recognizing the traditional racial ideology that seemed to go with it. The erstwhile denial of the priesthood for blacks was explained as a lack of historic or even moral readiness on the parts of blacks themselves and/or their supposed ancestors back to Cain or Ham rather than as any error in the church. This mode was especially common among black Mormons who had joined the church in earlier years, while the priesthood restriction was still in force. The second type of identity resolution also gave precedence to the Mormon religious identity, while explaining the traditional racial ideas and policies as simply a great quandary, one which all would understand some time in the hereafter but that should not be allowed in the meanwhile to keep anyone from the true faith. The third mode called for relegating all racial issues in the church to the past. Whether the traditional teachings had a divine or a human origin was no longer relevant, and nothing was to be gained by hashing it over. The main thing these black Mormons wanted to do was to assert their own new identities as members of the true church and look to the future rather than to the past. Black Mormons assuming this posture, such as the oral history interviewee Marva Collins, were, in effect, validating the public comments of church leaders, especially President Hinckley, about the need to forget the past.[60]

The fourth and fifth modes, while still embracing a Mormon identity, put the responsibility for the traditional racist teachings entirely on the whites. In the fourth mode, the explanation was that the church had simply allowed human error to influence church policy, because of political compromises (in Missouri or Utah) or because of the need to mollify a few slave-owning converts. Black Mormons taking this position, even if they had joined the church before the priesthood policy change, always looked upon the racist elements in Mormonism as imported from the outside, never part of the true gospel, and certain to be changed eventually. Interestingly enough, this was the posture taken, in the Embry-Cherry oral histories, by some of the most prominent black Mormons from the pre-1978 period. These included Ruffin Bridgeforth, founding leader of the Salt Lake City Genesis Group; Catherine M. Stokes, of Chicago; and Cleeretta Smiley, of Washington D.C. Smiley candidly characterized the traditional Mormon racial teachings as "damnable heresies."[61] Finally, the fifth mode reversed the moral positions of whites and blacks with the argument that blacks had been denied the priesthood all those years because God knew that *whites* were not morally and spiritually ready to accept black members in full fellowship. This position carried the implication that the blacks had demonstrated superior moral strength through their patience and forgiveness.[62] In transferring the burden of responsibility for racist teachings and policies to the whites, the fourth and fifth modes maintained a positive identity for blacks while still embracing completely the Mormon religion and identity.

Additional evidence of black Mormons' struggle with identity can be found in a few publications that they have produced. Earlier in this chapter I listed a number of autobiographies by black Mormons, some published well before the 1978 policy change, to tell the stories of their conversions and their struggles with identity in a "white church." Besides these books, at least three periodical newsletters have emerged from the small black Mormon community in Utah. Two survived only a few years each, despite temporary church grants to help them get started, probably because they each depended upon only one or two key individuals to keep them going. One of these, *Ebony Rose*, was edited and published during 1985 through 1988 by Marva Collins, assisted mainly by family members. Another, *Let's Talk* (later changed to *UpLift*), was edited and published in Utah during 1989–94 by the Latter-day Saints for Cultural Awareness (LDSCA), led by Joseph C. Smith and a few associates. The third,

Genesis, published by the Genesis Group, is still being published irregularly (beginning in December 2003, the newsletter became available only electronically, at <www.ldsgenesisgroup.org/news>), but the original publication date is uncertain. It labels itself in each issue as "a non-correlated publication of the Church," but its parent organization, the Genesis Group, is "officially sponsored" by the church, so both receive a certain amount of funding.

All three newsletters have explicitly promoted the mission and teachings of the Church of Jesus Christ of Latter-day Saints. Accordingly, they all cultivate a strong Mormon component in the black convert identity. All of them have received the public support and endorsement of general authorities. They have all promoted to some extent a black identity, as well, but they differ somewhat in tone and in the amount of emphasis given to the black heritage. *Ebony Rose* was perhaps the least "assimilationist" of the three. Taking a cue from the advice of church president Kimball against racial intermarriage, an *Ebony Rose* editorial called for the construction of a large network through which black Mormons could meet each other and, in some cases, marry.[63] An earlier editorial by Collins had observed that assimilation is not entirely a good thing if it means that black Mormons must forfeit their black culture entirely. This publication also cultivated a connection with African Latter-day Saints to the point that its "Letters" section came to be largely preoccupied with correspondence from African "pen pals."

Without taking a position on assimilation, *UpLift* (and its predecessor *Let's Talk*) devoted a large proportion of each issue to black history in general (not just black LDS history) and to various expressions of "cultural awareness," meaning mainly a celebration of various aspects of the black cultural heritage. Perhaps in an effort to distinguish itself from both of the other publications, *UpLift* explicitly declared that its parent organization, LDSCA, "is a non-profit educational corporation . . . not a support group. The goal is to educate in cultural awareness . . . (and also to motivate members) . . . to hang on to the gospel . . . and to realize that you don't have to give up your cultural identity to be a member of the Church."[64] To emphasize this function, LDSCA bestowed its Ammon Award each year upon persons judged to have been especially instrumental in promoting cultural awareness as faithful Latter-day Saints.[65] *UpLift* also carried articles from time to time on Africa or Africans, and the Church Public Affairs Department periodically enlisted LDSCA leaders to participate in receptions at church headquarters for visiting African dignitaries.[66]

The Genesis Group, organized in late 1971,[67] did not always have a special publication of its own or a mission of outreach to Africans, to American blacks, or to anyone else except the struggling band of black LDS members in Utah. Indeed, after the 1978 revelation extended the priesthood to black members, the raison d'être of the Genesis Group seemed increasingly in doubt. A decade later its active membership, only around fifty to start with, had diminished to half that number, and there were fears for its survival.[68] Since then, the group has benefited from increased acceptance and support in Utah and at church headquarters; a productive collaboration with the "younger generation" of black Mormons found in the LDSCA (while that organization lasted); and a concomitant infusion of new and younger members.[69] Its functions have expanded to fill a real and growing need for helping black Latter-day Saints throughout the country negotiate the conflicting claims on their identities from the church, on the one hand, and the black American community, on the other.[70]

Formally and informally, the Genesis Group has also acquired many important functions. One of these is missionary outreach. Especially in recent years, with the priesthood restriction a thing of the past, proselytizing of blacks by black Mormons has sometimes proved effective. Able speakers, musicians, and other performers from the Genesis Group also periodically are invited to appear at social and religious events in various wards and stakes. Lately an important outreach function for the Genesis Group has been the counseling and educating of new black members and investigators of the church, as they become aware of the Mormon racial history. Especially before 1978, when the priesthood restriction was still in force, it was a shock for some blacks during and after conversion to discover that black men would not be able to hold the priesthood along with every other man in the church. Obviously a few of them joined anyway, but often only after lengthy consultations by phone and by mail with Genesis Group leaders able to reassure them of the prospects for change. Even since 1978, with no formal racial distinctions any longer part of the church program, the history is still there, and so are remnants of the old folklore about divine marks and curses. When black converts discover this racist history and residue, usually only after joining the church, their disillusionment calls for the kind of social and spiritual nurturing that Genesis Group members are uniquely capable of offering.

Finally, the Genesis Group attempts to meet the special needs not only of black members themselves, but also of racially mixed couples and families, including those families in which parents of one race have adopted children of another. In their normal LDS wards, active black members and mixed families tend to stand out as anomalies.[71] In contrast, at the periodic Genesis Group meetings and social events, they are able to feel much more comfortable, for most of the members there share the same predicament. The celebration of the unifying rather than divisive potential of "racial mixing" is apparent to anyone attending recent meetings of the Genesis Group or reading its newsletter *Genesis*.

The functions of the Genesis Group have thus changed somewhat since its origin, but a main function still consists of helping black members cultivate strong and favorable identities as Mormons, despite the racist heritage that some of them remember all too vividly.[72] The mission of the group has expanded to meet the needs of multiracial families that have been formed or recombined through divorce (or widowhood) and remarriage. In these situations, children especially must learn to integrate into their identities not only their Mormonness but also their associations with parents, siblings, and church peers from a variety of racial or ethnic settings.[73] Meanwhile, in recognition of the potential for church growth among the large black population of southern California, the LDS public affairs office there in 2002 initiated a series of bimonthly regional "fireside" gatherings for black church members in the region. The retention and activity of black Latter-day Saints depends on the success of these organizational efforts, and there can be no room for invidious comparisons among lineages. In this sense, the Genesis Group and related groups in other cities might represent harbingers of future Mormon efforts to reach outside normal congregational boundaries to serve the needs of black, mixed, and other special populations.[74]

Indeed, certain events of 2002 and 2003 invite the inference that the Genesis Group has assumed yet another unique function as a kind of "intermediary" between the LDS Church as an institution and black Americans generally. This point requires a little explanation. I have already mentioned the rather ambivalent position of the church in public relations terms since 1978, a point that I will explore further in my conclusion. This ambivalence arises as the church tries simultaneously to support some of the political and cultural interests of African Americans, especially its own black members, and to live down its own racist past. In pursuit of that latter objective, in particular, the church has tried consistently to avoid public statements, events, or acts that would remind the world that it once withheld the priesthood and temple privileges from its black members.

At the same time, the church has tried in various ways to emphasize the positive and beneficial effects of its program in the lives of black people. Where this objective can be achieved without reminding anyone of earlier priesthood policies (e.g., in various outreach efforts through genealogy or humanitarian efforts in Africa), the church as an institution has sought to be identified as closely as possible with such efforts. On the other hand, wherever the embarrassing past is likely to be suggested in any celebration or commemoration, the church has generally preferred to see that these events take place under direction less closely connected to the church hierarchy. Tacit support has nevertheless often been given by sending a church official as an observer or speaker, but not to conduct the event. Such indirect forms of support can be seen in the conferences mentioned earlier, including the one commemorating the tenth anniversary of the priesthood policy change, which was held under BYU auspices but not sponsored by the church itself. Most subsequent anniversaries have received very little attention at the church level and little or no mention in church publications. In recent years, the church has found ways to join tacitly in the commemoration of Black History Month each February, usually with one or more well-publicized events emphasizing family history and genealogy.[75] Increasingly, however, as the Genesis Group has revived from its doldrums of the 1980s, it has become the preferred site for commemorations and celebrations of Martin Luther King Day, Black History Month, Black Mormon pioneers, and especially the major attention given in Utah during the twenty-fifth anniversary of the 1978 revelation that changed the priesthood policy. The Genesis Group has thus become, on many occasions, the face of the LDS Church to black America; and Darius A. Gray, scrupulously modest though he is about his own role as president of this group, has in turn become the face and personification of the Genesis Group.[76]

A climactic verification of this process could be seen in the three-day celebration of the twenty-fifth anniversary, held June 6–8, 2003. The Genesis Group was front and center in leading the celebration and also in the extensive press coverage of this celebration from both inside and outside the church.[77] The main event was held in the historic Mormon Tabernacle on Temple Square, with Gray conducting, and featuring the Mormon convert Gladys Knight and the Saints Unified Voices gospel choir from Las Vegas. One of the speakers was Elder Merrill J. Bateman of the Seventy, until recently president of BYU, who spoke movingly of his experiences with church members in Africa.[78] The weekend had also featured two performances of *I Am Jane,* a play about the life of the black Mormon pioneer Jane Manning James by Margaret Blair Young; a special session at the Salt Lake Temple for Genesis members; and a Genesis Group picnic on Saturday afternoon.

While this June weekend was probably the most extravagant celebration in the history of LDS blacks, certain earlier events also showed the preference of the church leadership to defer to others for commemorations that might include reminders of the earlier racism in the church.[79] One such event was the installation of a new headstone at the grave of Elijah Abel, with a short accompanying ceremony, at the Salt Lake City Cemetery in late September 2002. This headstone for the neglected grave of Mormonism's best-known black pioneer was not a church project at all, though an apostle was sent to give a dedicatory prayer. The project to fund and design the headstone came from the initiative of a non-Mormon history buff backed by the Missouri

Mormon Frontier Foundation with some support from the Genesis Group and others.[80] At a public relations level, then, and with the help of the Genesis Group and other "intermediaries," the church has had some success in reconstructing its image and its relationship with black Americans.[81] The traditional racial mythology, however, is taking somewhat longer to dissipate, especially at the grassroots level.[82]

Conclusion: Dealing with Discarded Doctrines

In this chapter I have considered a variety of data from secondary historical sources, large-scale surveys, in-depth interviews with black Mormons, and other documents bearing upon the relationships between black and white Mormons in the United States. The evidence suggests that many white Mormons as individuals and the LDS Church as an institution have sincerely tried to relegate to the past the earlier teachings and practices that complicated for so long their relationships with black Americans. This effort seems to have been more successful in secular, civil relationships in the society outside the church than in congregational life. There are a few racially mixed wards and branches and even some that are predominantly black in Los Angeles and other urban areas. However, the overwhelming majority of white Mormons rarely encounter blacks at church, so a certain discomfort and wariness tend to remain whenever they do. Mormon missionary work among American blacks has not generally been thriving, even after the 1978 change in priesthood policy.

We cannot be sure how much the lingering racial myths in the Mormon religious heritage affect either the missionary work or the congregational relationships between blacks and whites. Surveys of Mormons in the 1960s demonstrated clearly that the religious hostility implied in those old myths played an important part in generating anti-black prejudice and discrimination. Almost four decades later, both the hostile myths and their secular implications have apparently diminished, but there is no reason to believe that any change has occurred in the *relation between* hostile religious myths and secular prejudice. Therefore, even if myths about premortal failings, descent from Cain, and the like have diminished in the lore and collective memory of Mormons, any residue can be expected still to generate prejudicial and discriminatory outcomes in the behavior of white Mormons. Authoritative writings by earlier church leaders, as well as recurring anecdotes at the grassroots level, suggest that some of this residue remains and continues to encumber relationships within the church, even if its impact has diminished on the outside. It is for that reason, that President Hinckley's call for the issue simply to be relegated to the past, without some sort of explicit and official disavowal, seems unduly optimistic to many black members.

Perhaps all religious traditions based on claims of divine revelation find it difficult to deal with major discrepancies between the received doctrines and later scientific understandings. As a relatively new religious tradition, Mormonism at least has not yet had to grapple with anything so fundamental as the legacy of medieval religious opposition to modern science. Yet, even if relatively free of the heavy baggage of ancient theological disputes and scientifically untenable dogmas, Mormonism carries more recent baggage with a special weight of its own. Many Mormons of my generation grew up with grandparents who could remember hearing the teachings of the religion from the lips of some of the founders themselves. These teachings were often a mix of canon doctrine, conjecture, and sheer folklore, but they were undeniably venerable precisely because they were so close in time to the founding era of miracles.

To repudiate any of the cherished religious lore of their immediate ancestors seems to some Mormons, especially the older ones, almost like a repudiation of the grandparents themselves, to say nothing of *their* teachers, who might have walked with God. Thus is the accumulation of ecclesiastical precedent sanctified in a way by family bonds; and thus is the divestment of relatively recent traditions sometimes more difficult than overturning those established centuries ago. One need point only to the struggle in Utah even now over plural marriage. Despite the long arm of the law and the strenuous repudiation by the church of polygamous *practices,* the traditional *doctrines* underlying plural marriage still survive even in mainstream Mormonism. Why should traditional racial doctrines be any easier to set aside?

Beside the kinds of racial myths at issue here, every community, indeed every family, has its own cherished organizational myths. A couple of these general myths seem to have grown with time in the ecclesiastical governance of the LDS Church. These are not found explicitly in scripture, in policy handbooks, or even in church discourse. Yet it is reasonable to infer that these myths operate under the surface in the organizational life of the church. The first is what I call the myth of continuity, which sees the history of Mormonism in linear, progressive terms (perhaps a little like the classical American myth of progress). There are no zigs or zags, no turning back, no repudiation of the past in Mormon church life or lore. There are changes, to be sure, but these are the products of continuous revelation. Such a linear definition of revelation is implied in a passage from the Book of Mormon: "For behold thus saith the Lord God: I will give unto the children of men line upon line, precept upon precept, here a little and there a little . . . [and] unto him that re-

ceiveth I wi*ll* give more" (2 Ne. 28:30; see also Doctrine and Covenar.
Isa. 28:9–10). *E*ven though new revelation might make the church qu
ferent from the way it was earlier, these changes are seen simply as the lc
fulfillment of po*li*cies and teachings already anticipated by earlier prophe

Thus, when th*e* priesthood restriction policy was dropped in 1978, th.
change was not por*tr*ayed as an actual reversal, since several earlier church
leaders had predicted *th*at it would happen. (Of course, several others, including Brigham Young, ha*d* predicted that it would never happen.) Even with the
earlier abolition of polygamy, the practice was only "suspended" and could
be restored at any time, since the theological basis was left intact. This myth
of continuity has the important function of validating the traditional claim
of continuous revelation (wh*ich is* canonical) and protecting the church
against the charge of purely pragmatic and expedient changes.

The second cherished organizational myth is related to the first: the myth
of history as time-filtered—the organizational equivalent of the old adage that
"time heals all wounds"—and similarly dubious ideas. This myth is typically
accompanied by an organizational posture of benign and selective forgetful-
ness. Thus, if the church progresses in a continuous, linear path by divine
guidance, then contemporary realities and understandings replace those from
the past, which will eventually be forgotten. Obsolete ideas and practices simply don't count any more, even if they originated as divine revelations. Where
discrepancies appear between the present and the past, there is no point in
reminding ourselves about the past. Especially if an event in the past is embarrassing, then recalling it and dwelling on it, even if only to repudiate it,
merely confuses the matter. Such negative thinking has no place in the Lord's
kingdom. If harm has resulted from earlier ways of thinking, then everyone
involved should forgive everyone else and get on with constructing a better
future. Apologies or ringing declarations of disavowal should not be necessary,
since few peoples or individuals have histories free of offenses against others,
and thus few are in a position to demand apologies. With time, memories of
these offenses will fade automatically, and we will all be better for it. Meanwhile, if we have made the requisite changes, let's not stir up useless and uncomfortable old memories.

This myth of time-filtered history promotes organizational morale by
accelerating the erosion of painful collective memories. The myth is particularly useful in an organization with a constant influx of new members or converts, who are unaware of very much in the organization's past. Almost all
discrepant ideas and practices from the past can be expected to disappear from
the institutional memory within a couple of generations. Along with the myth
of continuity, time-filtered history means that at any given moment in Mor-

...anizational life, the main motif in the church will be positive, confi-
...and optimistic, a posture personified especially well by the current
...ch president, Gordon B. Hinckley. Such myths promote success at the
...anizational level but are less effective in the retention of disillusioned in-
...viduals. As President Hinckley, in his interviews and public statements,
appeals to all of us to leave the racist legacy of the church in the past and look
to the future, most members will be able to do that at no cost to their own
identities or self-esteem. Many black members, however, reading recurring
passages from that very legacy in recently reprinted church books, will find it
difficult to see themselves or their identities in those passages and correspond-
ingly difficult to remain identified with the church. It is in that sense that the
ancient "curse of Cain," until it is completely cast off, will continue to be a
burden for the church itself, and its mission, as well as for its black members
as individuals.

Notes

The first epigraph is from Official Declaration No. 2, June 8, 1978, *Doctrine and Covenants
of the Church of Jesus Christ of Latter-day Saints* (Salt Lake City, Utah: Church of Jesus
Christ of Latter-day Saints, 1981 edition). The second epigraph is quoted in Richard N.
Ostling and Joan K. Ostling, *Mormon America: The Power and the Promise* (San Francisco:
HarperCollins, 1999), 104–5.

This essay derives in part from a portion of my book *All Abraham's Children: Changing Mormon Conceptions of Race and Lineage* (Urbana: University of Illinois Press, 2003).

1. See Newell G. Bringhurst, *Saints, Slaves, and Blacks: The Changing Place of Black People within Mormonism* (Westport, Conn.: Greenwood Press, 1981); Lester E. Bush, "A
Commentary on Stephen G. Taggart's *Mormonism's Negro Policy*," *Dialogue: A Journal of
Mormon Thought* 4 (Winter 1969): 86–103; Lester E. Bush, "Mormonism's Negro Doctrine: An Historical Overview," *Dialogue: A Journal of Mormon Thought* 8 (Spring 1973):
11–68; Chester Lee Hawkins, "Selective Bibliography on African-Americans and Mormons, 1830–1990." *Dialogue: A Journal of Mormon Thought* 25 (Winter 1992): 113–31.

2. Lester E. Bush, "Writing 'Mormonism's Negro Doctrine: An Historical Overview'
(1973): Context and Reflections, 1998," *Journal of Mormon History* 25 (Spring 1999): 229–
71; Armand L. Mauss, "The Fading of the Pharoahs' Curse: The Decline and Fall of the
Priesthood Ban against Blacks in the Mormon Church," *Dialogue: A Journal of Mormon
Thought* 14 (Fall 1981): 10–45; O. Kendall White Jr. and Daryl White, "Negotiating Social and Cultural Contradictions: Interracial Dating and Marriage among African American Mormons," *Virginia Social Science Journal* 35 (2000): 85–98.

3. James B. Allen, "Would-Be Saints: West Africa before the 1978 Priesthood Revelation," *Journal of Mormon History* 17 (1991): 207–47; Newell G. Bringhurst, "Mormonism
in Black Africa: Changing Attitudes and Practices," *Sunstone*, May–June 1981, 15–21;
"Report of Africa Area Presidency," in News of the Church section, *Ensign,* September
1997, 79–80; Mark L. Grover, "Religious Accommodation in the Land of Racial Democ-
racy: Mormon Priesthood and Black Brazilians," *Dialogue: A Journal of Mormon Thought*

17 (Fall 1984): 23–34; Mark L. Grover, "The Mormon Priesthood Revelation and the Sao Paulo, Brazil, Temple," *Dialogue: A Journal of Mormon Thought* 23 (Spring 1990): 39–53; Marcus H. Martins, "The Oak Tree Revisited: Brazilian LDS Leaders' Insights on the Growth of the LDS Church in Brazil" (Ph.D. diss., Brigham Young University, 1996); E. Dale LeBaron, "Mormonism in Black Africa," in *Mormon Identities in Transition*, ed. Douglas J. Davies (London: Cassell, 1996), 80–86; Rendell N. Mabey and Gordon T. Allred, *Brother to Brother: The Story of the Latter-day Saint Missionaries Who Took the Gospel to Black Africa* (Salt Lake City: Bookcraft, 1984); Alexander B. Morrison, *The Dawning of a Brighter Day: The Church in Black Africa* (Salt Lake City: Deseret Book, 1990).

4. Lester E. Bush, "Whence the Negro Doctrine? A Review of Ten Years of Answers," in *Neither White nor Black: Scholars Confront the Race Issue in a Universal Church*, ed. Lester E. Bush and Armand L. Mauss (Salt Lake City: Signature Books, 1984), 193–220; Mauss, *All Abraham's Children.*

5. The smaller sister denomination from the Mormon movement, known historically as the Reorganized Church of Jesus Christ of Latter Day Saints (name changed in April 2002 to Community of Christ), never adopted any formal racial restrictions in ecclesiastical life; Robert Ben Madison, "Heirs According to the Promise: Observations on Ethnicity, Race, and Identity in the Two Factions of Nineteenth-Century Mormonism," *John Whitmer Historical Association Journal* 12 (1992): 66–82.

6. William A. Wilson and Richard C. Poulsen, "The Curse of Cain and Other Stories," *Sunstone*, November–December 1980, 9–13.

7. Alvin R. Dyer, *Who Am I?* (Salt Lake City: Deseret Book, 1966), 541; Harold B. Lee, *Youth and the Church* (Salt Lake City: Deseret Book, 1955), 170–72; Harold B. Lee, *Decisions for Successful Living* (Salt Lake City: Deseret Book, 1973), 167–68; Bruce R. McConkie, *Mormon Doctrine*, 2d ed. (Salt Lake City: Bookcraft, 1966), see, for example, "Negroes" and "Caste System"; Bruce R. McConkie, "New Revelation on Priesthood," in *Priesthood* (Salt Lake City: Deseret Book, 1981), 126–37; Bruce R. McConkie, *A New Witness for the Articles of Faith* (Salt Lake City: Deseret Book, 1985), 510–12; Joseph Fielding Smith, *The Way to Perfection* (1931; reprint, Salt Lake City: Deseret Book, 1951), 42, 48, 129–30, and chaps. 7, 15, 16.

8. Richley H. Crapo, "Grassroots Deviance from Official Doctrine: A Study of Latter-day Saint (Mormon) Folk Beliefs," *Journal for the Scientific Study of Religion* 26 (December 1987): 465–85; Austin E. Fife and Alta Fife, *Saints of Sage and Saddle: Folklore among the Mormons* (1956; reprint, Logan: Utah State University Press, 1980); William A. Wilson, "The Study of Mormon Folklore: An Uncertain Mirror for Truth," *Dialogue: A Journal of Mormon Thought* 22 (Winter 1989): 95–110; William A. Wilson, "Mormon Folklore: A Cut from the Marrow of Everyday Experience," *BYU Studies* 33, no. 3 (1993): 521–40.

9. Ostling and Ostling, *Mormon America*, 105–6; Peggy Fletcher Stack, "'Black Curse' Is Problematic LDS Legacy," *Salt Lake Tribune*, 6 June 1998, C-1.

10. Newell G. Bringhurst, "The Image of Blacks within Mormonism as Presented in the *Church News*, 1978–1988," *American Periodicals* 2 (Fall 1992): 113.

11. Heidi Swinton, "Without Regard to Race," *This People* 9 (Summer 1988): 20.

12. Carey C. Bowles, *A Negro Mormon Views the Church* (Maplewood, N.J.: privately published, 1968); Alan G. Cherry, *It's You and Me, Lord!* (Provo, Utah: Trilogy Arts, 1970); Wynetta Martin Clark, *I Am a Negro Mormon* (Ogden, Utah: privately published, 1970); Joseph Freeman, *In the Lord's Due Time* (Salt Lake City: Bookcraft, 1979); John Lamb, "My Responsibility," *Improvement Era*, January 1966, 36–37; Dennis L. Lythgoe, interview

with Lucille Bankhead, 1972, transcript in my files; Wynetta W. Martin, *Black Mormon Tells Her Story* (Salt Lake City: Hawkes Publications, 1972); David H. Oliver, *A Negro on Mormonism* (Salt Lake City: privately published, 1963); Peggy Olsen, "Ruffin Bridgeforth, Leader and Father to Mormon Blacks," *This People* 1 (Winter 1980): 11–17; Mary Frances Sturlaugson, *A Soul So Rebellious* (Salt Lake City: Deseret Book, 1980); Mary Frances Sturlaugson, *He Restoreth My Soul* (Salt Lake City: Deseret Book, 1982); Sally Wright, "The Mormon Issue: Plain as Black and White," two parts, *Concord (Calif.) Transcript,* March 11 and 12, 1970 (about black Mormon convert Paul Gill).

13. Swinton, "Without Regard to Race," 22.

14. O. Ken Earl, telephone interview by Armand L. Mauss, Fall 1985.

15. B. Falconer Newhall, "Black Family Comfortable with the Mormon Faith," *Contra Costa (Calif.) Times,* November 26, 1994, B-4.

16. Robert Lang, telephone interviews by Armand L. Mauss, June 19, 1981, May 21, 1985.

17. David Gonzales, "Spreading the Word in the South Bronx," *New York Times,* November 16, 1994, B-1, B-2; John L. Hart, "East St. Louis Branch Blossoms Again," *Church News,* February 5, 1994, 8–10.

18. Jessie L. Embry, "Speaking for Themselves: LDS Ethnic Groups Oral History Project," *Dialogue: A Journal of Mormon Thought* 25 (Winter 1992): 99–110.

19. Jessie L. Embry, *Black Saints in a White Church: Contemporary African American Mormons* (Salt Lake City: Signature Books, 1994).

20. Cardell K. Jacobson, "Black Mormons in the 1980s: Pioneers in a White Church," *Review of Religious Research* 33 (December 1991): 146–52; Cardell K. Jacobson, "Religiosity in a Black Community: An Examination of Secularization and Political Variables," *Review of Religious Research* 33 (March 1992): 215–28; Cardell K. Jacobson, Tim B. Heaton, E. Dale LeBaron, and Trina Louise Hope, "Black Mormon Converts in the United States and Africa: Social Characteristics and Perceived Acceptance," in *Contemporary Mormonism: Social Science Perspectives,* ed.Marie Cornwall, Tim B. Heaton, and Lawrence A. Young (Urbana: University of Illinois Press, 1994), 326–47; Daryl White and O. Kendall White, "African American Mormons in the South," in *African Americans in the South: Issues of Race, Class, and Gender,* ed. Hans A. Baer and Yvonne Jones (Athens: University of Georgia Press, 1992), 139–53.

21. See Jacobson, "Black Mormons in the 1980s"; White and White, "African American Mormons in the South."

22. Ruffin Bridgeforth, interviews by Armand L. Mauss, Salt Lake City, July 2, 1981, May 23, 1985; Darius A. Gray, telephone interview by Armand L. Mauss, May 15, 1999.

23. See my *All Abraham's Children,* 284, for the identity and more details on this family.

24. Marva Collins, interview Alan Cherry, 1985, LDS African American Oral History Project, Charles Redd Center for Western History, L. Tom Perry Special Collections and Manuscripts, Harold B. Lee Library, Brigham Young University, Provo, Utah.

25. Peggy Fletcher Stack, "Revelation of 20 Years Ago Cause for LDS Celebration," *Salt Lake Tribune,* June 6, 1998, C-1.

26. Marva Collins, *Ebony Rose,* issues 25–26 (1987). Collins was publisher, editor, and author of many articles in this periodical, 1985–88.

27. The printed program and publicity flyers are in the Perry Special Collections, Lee Library, Brigham Young University.

28. Russell Chandler, "Mormonism: A Challenge for Blacks," *Los Angeles Times,* August 12, 1988, I-1, 28–30; Alan G. Cherry, "Silent Songs We've Never Heard," *This People* 9 (Summer 1988): 24–27; Neil Chetnick, "Embracing the Black Mormon," *San Jose Mercury-News,* August 13, 1988, C-1, 14; S.E., "Church News" column, *Standard-Examiner* (Ogden, Utah), June 4, 1988; Swinton, "Without Regard to Race"; entire summer 1988 issue of *This People.*

29. I am grateful to the LDS poet Carol Lynn Pearson for providing me with a copy of this event's printed program and a moving account from her journal of her feelings while participating in the service; now in my files.

30. These and similar accounts about LDS outreach to the black community in southern California are from "Interfaith Relations in California," Special Report to the Area President, Los Angeles office, LDS Public Affairs Department, December 1999, photocopy in my files.

31. The following account is summarized from Memorandum to Elder Robert D. Hales, Los Angeles Office, LDS Public Affairs Department, December 6, 2001, photocopy in my files.

32. I received a first-hand account of this conference on February 16, 2002, from the local missionary couple, Steve and Judy Gilliland, who had organized and coordinated it under the auspices of the Los Angeles office of the LDS Church Public Affairs Department. The conference was held all morning on Saturday, February 9, at the stake center across the street from the University of Southern California campus, near the First AME Church. It featured workshops on several different family history and genealogy topics. A copy of the brochure announcing the conference is in my files. Similar conferences at about the same time of year and in the same place have become annual events since then.

33. Ari Goldman, "Mormon Tradition and Zeal Inspire Growth in the Northeast," *New York Times,* February 7, 1995, B-35, B-41; Thira Schmidl, "Y Student Teachers in D.C. Learn Tolerance, Love," *Daily Universe (BYU),* February 21, 1995, 1.

34. Jon Mano, "Black Athletes Must Adjust to Lack of Diversity." *Daily Universe* (BYU), February 13, 1995, 2; Shea Nuttall, "Activities to Promote Understanding," *Daily Universe* (BYU), February 13, 1995, 2.

35. Peggy Fletcher Stack, "Church Leaders Haven't Discussed Racial Issue," *Salt Lake Tribune,* May 19, 1998, A-1; Peggy Fletcher Stack, "'Black Curse' Is Problematic LDS Legacy," *Salt Lake Tribune,* June 6, 1998, C-1; Peggy Fletcher Stack, "Revelation of 20 Years Ago Cause for LDS Celebration," *Salt Lake Tribune,* June 6, 1998, C-1; Larry B. Stammer, "Mormons May Disavow Old View on Blacks," *Los Angeles Times,* May 18, 1998, A-1, 20–21; Larry B. Stammer, "Mormon Plan to Disavow Racist Teachings Jeopardized by Publicity," *Los Angeles Times,* May 24, 1998, A-1.

36. Stack, "Church Leaders Haven't Discussed Racial Issue."

37. Ostling and Ostling, *Mormon America,* 103–5. The Ostlings' account is an accurate description of the efforts of this committee, upon which I also served, and the eventual outcome. Copies of much of the committee's correspondence (1996–98) are in my files.

38. Ibid., 106; Stack, "'Black Curse' Is Problematic LDS Legacy."

39. Larry B. Stammer, "Mormon Plan to Disavow Racist Teachings Jeopardized by Publicity," *Los Angeles Times,* May 24, 1998, A-1.

40. Stack, "Church Leaders Haven't Discussed Racial Issue."

41. Larry B. Stammer, "Mormon Leader Defends Race Relations," *Los Angeles Times*, September 12, 1998, B-10, B-11.

42. Quoted in John L. Hart, "Fathers Needed as 'Pillars of Strength,'" *Church News*, May 2, 1998, 3, and in "NAACP Leadership Meeting" in News of the Church section, *Ensign*, July 1998, 74.

43. Cathleen Falsani, "CD-ROM to Aid Black Genealogists," *Chicago Sun-Times*, February 19, 2001, 10; LDS Church Public Affairs, "Freedman's Bank Records," News Release and Fact Sheet, February 26, 2001; Bob Mims, "Ex-Slave Files a Prize for History Buffs," *Salt Lake Tribune*, February 21, 2001, A-1. The LDS black community had known about the project for several years. *UpLift* 3, no. 1 (1993): 1–3. The LDSCA (Latter-day Saints for Cultural Awareness) published this newsletter (1989–94), originally named *Let's Talk*, but from 1991 called *UpLift*. Only rarely were its articles bylined.

44. The story was also covered at some length in two programs on National Public Radio: Shirley Jahad on *All Things Considered*, February 26, 2001, and Howard Berkes on *Morning Edition*, February 27, 2001.

45. *Genesis* newsletter, January–February 2002.

46. Jessie L. Embry, "Blacks," *Encyclopedia of Mormonism*, 4 vols. (New York: Macmillan, 1992), 1:125–27; Cassia C. Flores and Enoc Q. Flores, "Race, Racism," ibid., 3:1191–92.

47. Armand L. Mauss, *The Angel and the Beehive: The Mormon Struggle with Assimilation* (Urbana: University of Illinois Press, 1994), 226; James A. Davis and Tom W. Smith, *General Social Surveys, 1972–1996* (Chicago: National Opinion Research Corp., 1996). This annual codebook contains basic distributions and names for the variables in the surveys, along with other documentation.

48. The reader should note that "statistical significance" refers *not* to the substantive "importance" of a statistical association but only to the likelihood that the association could have occurred *by chance*. Thus, for example, "$p = .01$" means that there is only one such chance in 100, as calculated by a formula such as chi squared (x^2).

49. For comparisons between Mormons and others on these questions during the 1960s, see Mauss, *The Angel and the Beehive*, 52, and, more extensively, Armand L. Mauss, "Mormons and Secular Attitudes toward Negroes," *Pacific Sociological Review* (renamed *Sociological Perspectives*) 9 (Fall 1966): 91–99.

50. Wade Clark Roof and William McKinney, *American Mainline Religion: Its Changing Shape and Future* (New Brunswick, N.J.: Rutgers University Press, 1987), 200.

51. Mauss, *The Angel and the Beehive*, 153.

52. Armand L. Mauss, "Mormonism and the Negro: Faith, Folklore, and Civil Rights," *Dialogue: A Journal of Mormon Thought* 2 (Winter 1967): 19–39.

53. For survey data and discussion, see Mauss, "Mormons and Secular Attitudes," and, more definitively, Mauss, *All Abraham's Children*, chap. 8 and appendix C, figs. C.3 and C.4. N.B.: due to a printer's error, the drawing for figure C.4 appears as that for figure C.1.

54. Fredrik Barth, ed., *Ethnic Groups and Boundaries: The Social Organization of Cultural Difference* (Boston: Little, Brown, 1969); W. Peter Robinson, ed., *Social Groups and Identities: Developing the Legacy of Henri Tajfel* (Oxford: Butterworth-Heinemann, 1996); Henri Tajfel, *Human Groups and Social Categories* (Cambridge: Cambridge University Press, 1981).

55. Joane Nagel, "Constructing Ethnicity: Creating and Recreating Ethnic Identity

and Culture," *Social Problems* 41, no. 1 (1994): 152–76; Eugeen E. Roosens, *Creating Ethnicity: The Process of Ethnogenesis* (Newbury Park, Calif.: Sage Publications, 1989).

56. The perpetuation of such myths and legends even in major Protestant denominations down to recent days is the subject of a small but important book by Cain Hope Felder, *Race, Racism, and the Biblical Narratives* (Minneapolis: Fortress Press, 2002).

57. The pathos in this predicament is dealt with sensitively and authentically in a trilogy of historical novels, *Standing on the Promises*, by Margaret Blair Young and Darius Aidan Gray, published in Salt Lake City, Utah, by Bookcraft, now an imprint of Deseret Book: Vol. 1: *One More River to Cross* (2000); Vol. 2: *Bound for Canaan* (2002); Vol. 3: *The End of the Journey* (2003).

58. Anthony P. Cohen, *The Symbolic Construction of Community* (New York: Tavistock, 1985).

59. O. Kendall White Jr. and Daryl White, "Integrating Religious and Racial Identities: An Analysis of LDS African-American Explanations of the Priesthood Ban," *Review of Religious Research* 36 (March 1995): 295–311.

60. A panel of active black Mormons in the Washington, D.C., area also took this position in a public presentation during the annual conference of the Mormon History Association in May 1998. The conference program committee, upon which I served, had reason to believe, however, that the black panel members had been well coached by local LDS Church leaders. Bill Broadway, "Black Mormons Resist Apology Talk," *Washington Post,* May 30, 1998, B-9.

61. Ibid.

62. According to Paul Swenson, "Gladys and Thurl: The Changing Face of Mormon Diversity," *Sunstone,* July 2001, 14–16, this attitude appears to be implicitly reflected in the public comments and demeanor of black celebrity converts Thurl Bailey (Utah Jazz basketball player and musician) and Gladys Knight (Hall of Fame pop singer). Their comments might also partly reflect the fourth mode described here.

63. Collins, editorial, *Ebony Rose* 20 (1986).

64. Editorial, *UpLift* 3, no. 3 (1993): 6.

65. R. Scott Lloyd, "Group Seeks to Expand LDS Cultural Awareness," *Church News,* September 4, 1993, 11. In the Book of Mormon, Ammon is a courageous missionary who took the gospel to the hostile Lamanites (Alma 17).

66. See, for example, *Uplift* 1, no. 1 (1989): 1.

67. See Mauss, "The Fading of the Pharoahs' Curse," 23–24.

68. Bridgeforth, interviews by Mauss; Gray, interview by Mauss.

69. *Let's Talk* reported its "merger" with the Genesis Group (*Let's Talk* 1, no. 3 (1989): 1); and then, as if to renew that relationship, Ruffin Bridgeforth, president of the Genesis Group, was made chairman of LDSCA board of directors five years later (*UpLift* 4, no. 1 (1994): 1).

70. R. Scott Lloyd, "Genesis Group Notes Silver Anniversary," *Church News,* October 26, 1996, 6.

71. The religious motivations for black Mormons to seek interracial marriages, despite the social pressures against doing so, are poignantly detailed in the oral histories analyzed in White and White, "Negotiating Social and Cultural Contradictions."

72. Bridgeforth, interviews by Mauss; Gray, interview by Mauss. In 2003, the Genesis Group established a Web site (<www.ldsgenesisgroup.org>) where interested persons can keep abreast of its activities.

73. Cohen, *The Symbolic Construction of Community*.

74. See Jessie L. Embry, "Separate but Equal? American Ethnic Groups in the RLDS and LDS Churches—A Comparison," *John Whitmer Historical Asosciation Journal* 12 (1992): 83–100.

75. For discussion of recurring family history events sponsored or cosponsored by the LDS Church, especially during Black History Month, see Janet I. Tu and Leslie Fulbright, "Mormon Church Helping Blacks Search for History," *Seattle Times,* March 21, 2003, Internet edition, and Denise Brown, "African Americans Discover Their Roots," *Church News,* April 19, 2003, 7. Both report an event in the Seattle area cosponsored by the Urban League. See also John L. Hart, "Family Research by African Americans," *Church News,* March 1, 2003, 3–4, about a special open house for African Americans at the LDS Family History Library in Salt Lake City.

76. In 2003, Gray received the Martin Luther King Jr. Award from the Salt Lake City Chapter of the NAACP for the contributions he and the Genesis Group have made to civil rights in Utah. Diane Urbani, "Two Receive Civil Rights Awards," *Deseret News,* January 14, 2003, A1, A-15, and "LDS Man Opening Minds—and Hearts," *Deseret News,* January 29, 2003, A-1, A-16; Tim Sullivan, "Utah Observes King Day," *Salt Lake Tribune,* January 21, 2003, A-1, A-4. Late in 2003, Darius Gray was succeeded by Don Harwell as president of the Genesis Group (*Genesis* newsletter, December 2003, 1).

77. See, for example, in the *Salt Lake Tribune* (all from the newspaper's Web site, <www.sltrib.com>): Linda Fantin, "A Warm, Calm Spirituality" (black conversion story), June 8, 2003; Peggy Fletcher Stack, "Twenty-Five Years Ago," June 8, 2003; Stack, "Knight Rocks LDS Celebration," June 9, 2003; Tim Sullivan, "Faith, Color, and the LDS Priesthood," June 8, 2003. See also four stories by Carrie A. Moore in the *Deseret News:* (Part 1) "LDS Past Crucial to Blacks," June 7, 2003, A-1, A-11; (Part 2) "Stories of Triumph, Struggle and Faith," June 8, 2003, A-1, A-20; "Knight and Co. Put Zip in LDS Hymns," June 9, 2003, A-1; "Black Mormons Say Life Better since 1978," May 25, 2003. In addition, see Eric Gorski, "Mormons Mark '78 End of Ban on Black Priests," *Denver Post,* June 9, 2003, A-1; Debbie Hummel, "Racist Past Ignored, Members Say," *Los Angeles Times,* June 21, 2003, H-11. *Meridian Magazine,* a Mormon Internet publication, carried related several stories June 6–9, 2003, <www.meridianmagazine.com>.

78. Many (perhaps most) white Mormons and their leaders, in the context of the church's missionary and outreach efforts, see the black peoples of Africa and of America as essentially the same. Accordingly, when asked about LDS relationships with blacks, white Mormons will frequently cite church growth in Africa, apparently oblivious to its irrelevance to the church's relationship with American blacks.

79. Young and Gray permitted some surprisingly candid historical material to appear in their trilogy *Standing on the Promises*. Similarly, at this writing, a new documentary film on the recent history of LDS blacks, *The Eleventh Hour Laborers,* is being produced by Robert J. Foster, BYU's first black BYU student body president, and Wayne Lee. It is directed by Richard Dutcher, the well-known director, producer, and star of *God's Army,* and has a musical score by Michael Hicks, a BYU music professor. All these artists are active LDS Church members, committed to giving the film an upbeat tone. Nevertheless, the church itself declined to sponsor the film, so it is being produced privately. See Internet stories: Jody Tait, "Former BYUSA President Produces Documentary on Priesthood Extension," *BYUNET,* <www.byunews.byu.edu>, May 5, 2003, and "The Eleventh Hour," *Meridian Magazine,* June 6, 2003, <www.meridianmagazine.com>.

80. Tim Sullivan, "Rebuilding Memory of Elijah Abel," *Salt Lake Tribune,* September 28, 2002, C-1, C-8; Lynn Arave, "Monument in Salt Lake Erected in Honor of Black Pioneer," *Deseret News,* Internet edition, <www.desertnews.com>, September 29, 2003; "Monument Honors African American Pioneer," *Ensign,* January 2003, 79. Fundraising appeals appeared in the *Genesis* newsletter, for example, August–September 2002, 3; October 2002, 5; November–December 2002, 4–5. Interestingly enough, in writing about the policy change on the priesthood, the Genesis Group cites the case of Elijah Abel and then refers to 1978 as the time when God "gave the priesthood back" to blacks. See, for example, *Genesis* newsletter, August–September 2002, 8.

81. Another "intermediary" in this process is the Web site <www.blacklds.org>, set up privately by a group of Mormon apologists, black and white, to promote a positive image of the church among blacks.

82. *Sunstone* magazine addressed this issue in "'Speak the Truth and Shame the Devil': A Roundtable Discussion on Church, Race, Experience, and Testimony," May 2003, 28–39. See also Joy Smith, "Long Promised Day? Love Lessons Learned while Styling Hair," *Sunstone,* October 2002, 52–53; Carrie A. Moore, "Race Still Issue in Religion, Blacks in LDS Church Say," *Deseret News,* January 28, 2003, B-8.

6 African American Latter-day Saints: A Sociological Perspective

CARDELL K. JACOBSON

Although religious institutions are considered to be a conservative force in societies, and although religious leaders often emphasize the stability of their own organizations, religion in the United States has always been in a state of flux. One kind of change in religious organizations is their development and growth. The development of the LDS Church has been discussed widely, and I leave that topic to other authors. A second kind of change occurs in the membership of a religious organization. In 1978 the Church of Jesus Christ of Latter-day Saints changed its previous restriction and allowed African and African American men to become ordained members of the priesthood. In this chapter, I examine some of the changes in attitudes and racial composition that have occurred within the Church of Jesus Christ of Latter-day Saints since the priesthood revelation of 1978 allowed the ordination of these men.

Known more commonly as the LDS Church or the Mormon church, the Church of Jesus Christ of Latter-day Saints has been noted for its previous policy of restricting Africans and African Americans from holding the priesthood. Though the policy was lifted in 1978, it has had lingering effects as outlined by others in this volume. In this chapter I note the history of racially separate religious worship in the United States, but also how difficult the LDS practice was for the few members who were black. Next, I discuss the racial attitudes of white LDS members of the church. I then examine the characteristics of a sample of those African Americans who have joined the LDS Church despite the previous priesthood ban. Finally, I analyze some of the reported experiences of some African American members who have joined the LDS Church.

Early LDS Racial Membership

Although some African Americans were members of the LDS Church almost from the beginning,[1] few joined during much of the nineteenth and twentieth centuries. Several factors combined to produce low numbers: the priesthood ban, the policy of not proselytizing among African communities, and the geographical isolation in the intermountain West.

In some respects, the LDS Church's practices were only a more formal version of those implemented in other churches. While many American churches had African American members, they often confined them to separate congregations or separate services. The establishment of African American denominations was a reaction by blacks to being denied access to white denominations. As documented by George Rawick in 1972 and later by Eric Lincoln and Lawrence Mamiya, the African American church became the core of the African American community.[2] As Wade Clark Roof and William McKinney state, "The black church emerged as an important institution, second only to the family, as a symbol and embodiment of racial solidarity and the quest for freedom and justice."[3] Ironically, only in the decades since the civil rights movement has the African American church become less central. Lincoln and Mamiya note that middle-class African Americans eventually migrated to "elite" African American congregations or became commuter parishioners, driving from middle-class areas, often in the suburbs, to the inner-city churches they previously attended.[4]

Despite considerable desegregation of most societal institutions, Sunday mornings remained highly segregated, as they had been for decades. As recently as 1987, Roof and McKinney estimated that 85 percent of black Americans attended churches of black denominations, a figure not much different, they note, from the 88 percent they estimated for 1920.[5] Other minorities were often segregated as well. In brief, these developments allowed and encouraged the development of racially separate worship throughout the United States.

Several important conditions existed for the LDS Church, however. These were particularly difficult for most African American members, and troublesome to some white members. A central issue was the priesthood ban that precluded participation by teenage African American boys and men in priesthood functions. This was particularly galling since, as members, they were often invited to attend the priesthood meetings. Yet they could not function as priesthood leaders or perform priesthood functions. This included, among other things, passing and blessing the sacrament or holding offices in the priesthood quorums. As adults, they were further precluded from giving priesthood blessings, even to members of their own family, and were unable to hold important offices in the church. These were prerogatives that came almost automatically for white men and boys who were in good standing in the church. Further, African American women and men could not be sealed to each other in temple ordinances or perform these ordinances for others. While many white members may have empathized with African American members, most were likely unaware of the numerous difficulties these conditions caused for the African American members. As a result African American LDS members often struggled with a variety of problems never faced or even imagined by white members.

White LDS Attitudes about Race

Despite the relative isolation of the church and the low number of African American members, the attitudes of white LDS members historically have not been and are not today much different than those of whites nationally. Armand Mauss makes this point in his chapter in this volume and has done so in many other writings.

Data from the General Social Survey (GSS), a data set composed of nearly forty thousand individuals accumulated by social scientists over the last thirty years, yield much the same conclusion. The GSS data show that the Latter-day Saints are less likely than non-LDS to live in close proximity to other races (table 6.1). At the same time, white LDS members do not differ from non-LDS on most attitudinal issues about race, and when they do, the LDS are sometimes slightly more tolerant than the national sample. For example, they are less likely to say that "whites have a right to keep blacks out of their neighborhood," and they are less likely than others to "object to sending their child to a school where a few of the students are from another race."

The nation as a whole has become more tolerant on many attitudinal issues, but so have members of the LDS Church. One such issue, attitudes about interracial marriage, is presented in figure 6.1. Overall, Mormons are slightly more likely than the national sample to oppose laws against interracial marriage, but both the LDS and the national sample have become more tolerant over a period of twenty-six years.

Even when LDS/non-LDS differences are statistically significant, the differences disappear when more detailed statistical analysis is done that controls for education, age, and gender. (See table 6.1.) This suggests that the slightly more tolerant LDS attitudes reflect a higher education level and younger ages of the LDS sample compared to their national counterparts.

Another trend is of interest. Latter-day Saints are no different from the rest of the nation in allowing racist teachers to speak or have books in the library.

Table 6.1 White LDS and Non-LDS Experience and Attitudes about Racial Issues

	Percentage Agreeing		Probability		
	LDS	Non-LDS	w/o controls	w/ demo g var's	w/ all var's
Any people of opposite race living in neighborhood	40.1	50.8	.001	.001	.001
Any people of opposite race living close	57.1	71.8	.001	.001	.001
Same block	30.4	47.1	.001	.001	.001
1–3 blocks away	39.8	30.8	.001		
Attend church with someone of other race	41.0	41.9	ns	ns	ns
Favor law against interracial marriage	17.9	23.8	.01	ns	ns
Not object to child bringing opposite race home to dinner	79.7	74.4	ns	ns	.05
Has anyone brought a friend of opposite race home to dinner	28.6	30.0	ns	ns	ns
Agree blacks shouldn't push where they aren't wanted	55.0	57.2	ns	ns	ns
Agree that whites have a right to keep blacks out of neighborhood	18.5	24.6	.01	.001	.001
Favor laws that say homeowner cannot refuse to sell to someone because of race	50.0	50.7	ns	ns	ns
Would vote for black president if qualified	88.1	81.7	.01	ns	ns
In general, favor racial busing from one district to another	20.2	24.9	ns	ns	ns
Percent think whites and blacks should go to same schools	93.6	87.5	ns	ns	ns
Object where a few children are black	1.0	4.9	.01	.01	.05
Object where half children are black	13.8	16.9	ns	ns	.01
Object where most children are black	40.1	38.1	ns	ns	ns

Source: General Social Survey. Demographic control variables are gender, race, age, and highest year in school. For all control variables, political party identification and self-described political views as liberal or conservative are added.

However, an interesting interaction with age appears on one item about "not allowing racists to speak in a community" (figure 6.2). Older white members of the LDS sample, when compared with the national sample, were somewhat more willing to tolerate a racist speaker. However, Mormons in their twenties were both more likely than earlier generations of the LDS sample to oppose a

Figure 6.1 Oppose Laws against Intermarriage

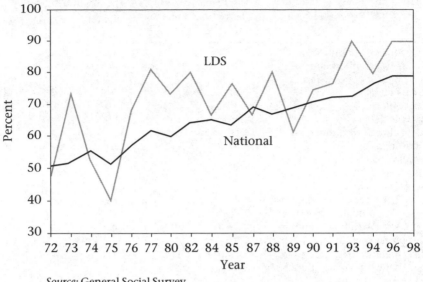

Source: General Social Survey

Figure 6.2 Opposed to Allowing Racist to Speak in a Community (Whites Only), by Age

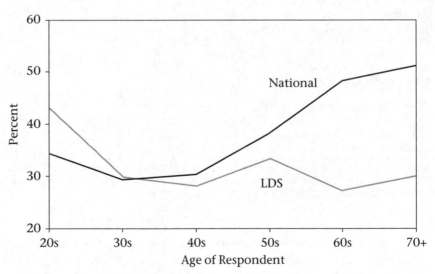

Source: General Social Survey

racist speaker and were slightly more likely to oppose a racist speaker than young members of the national sample. Though the trend for the young Latter-day Saints is likely not statistically significant, it is an interesting one. Further, I am optimistic that the trend is a well-established one.

One reason for my hopefulness derives from results of a survey I conducted of Brigham Young University students in the early 1990s. I found a positive relationship between religiosity and willingness to have close personal contact with members of other racial groups.[6] While the sample is small and discussions of causality are always suspect, I suggest that the increased contact LDS missionaries have with others groups under the positive conditions of missionary service improves attitudes about other races. A plethora of social science research suggests that intergroup relations are improved when contact occurs under favorable conditions.[7] Further, the effect likely generalizes to family members of the missionaries. These positive experiences, in which missionaries have contact with members of other groups and must represent the church positively, may compensate for the isolation of some white LDS from other cultures.

Being African American and Mormon

Since the June 1978 announcement, LDS missionary work has been directed to predominantly black nations where it had not been previously, and African Americans have been proselytized within the United States. Since the LDS Church does not keep membership records by race, the number of black converts to the LDS Church is unknown and is impossible to know. Nevertheless, the number is growing, and African American members are found in most LDS congregations located in large urban areas of the country. Little is known, however, about those African Americans who have joined this previously predominantly white church.

In the remainder of this chapter I present some data on African Americans who have joined the LDS Church and remained "active." This information has been garnered from two sources.[8] The first is a series of oral history interviews conducted primarily by Alan Cherry with the cooperation of Jessie L. Embry and the Charles Redd Center for Western Studies at Brigham Young University. All but one of the interviewees were converts to the LDS Church, and most joined after the 1978 change in priesthood policy. The oral histories conducted from 1985 to 1988 were obtained through a "snowball" technique in which the names of other black members were obtained through the first respondents. Cherry interviewed a diverse sample of converts, females (56 percent) as well as males (44 percent), and those who had been members for some time as well as new converts. Between thirty and forty interviews each were conducted in the Far West, the Northeast and Near South, the South, and the Midwest.

The interviews were conducted in the homes of the respondents or their friends and, in a few cases, in church buildings. Cherry followed a consistent but very general outline of topics to be covered. The interviews ranged from one to three hours and were tape-recorded. They were subsequently transcribed, and the transcriptions were sent to the interviewees for correction and/or clarification. The transcribed protocols range from ten to forty pages. Jessie Embry subsequently published *Black Saints in a White Church,* based in part on these oral histories.[9] My study of the oral histories is based on a content analysis of the transcripts, which I will refer to as the oral history sample, or the oral histories.

My second sample was a non-random sample comprised of sixty-six people who responded to a questionnaire also administered in several areas: Washington, D.C. (33 individuals); Atlanta, Georgia (10); Brigham Young University (14); New York City (5); and a few in other areas. Friends of mine in each of the areas distributed the survey to black members in their local wards in 2002. Slightly over half (58 percent) of the respondents in this sample were female. Unlike the oral history sample, where all but one were converts, 20 percent of the respondents in this sample had grown up as members of the church. Similar to the oral history sample, those who had converted to the LDS Church had all joined since the priesthood revelation of 1978—nearly half in the 1980s and half in the 1990s, with a few having joined since 2000.

The average age at which they had joined the church was thirty. Seven had joined during their teenage years, presumably when family members joined. The largest number had joined while in their twenties (18), with the next largest in their thirties (14), and the third group in their forties (10). Only a few had joined at later ages. I suspect that these age figures are typical of all who join the LDS Church; religious switchers of all denominations tend to be young.[10] The average age of the sample at the time of the survey was thirty-six. I refer to this sample as the survey sample, or the survey data.

Both samples have important limitations. They are primarily samples of active members who joined the church and stayed. In general, they do not reflect those who joined and later left, though the samples do include a few who attended only sporadically. The samples are also composed of volunteers, and social scientists know that volunteers are often more cooperative and positive than nonvolunteers.

Both samples are clearly religiously active. Where information could be ascertained, 78 percent of those in the oral histories had received a patriarchal blessing, and over 60 percent have been endowed in the LDS temple. Both activities are indicators of high levels of church activity. Over 95 percent of those in the oral histories reported reading the scriptures on a regular basis, and over 80 percent indicated that they have family prayer. Most tithed on a regular basis. No doubt those interviewed in the oral histories were likely to present themselves in a positive light. Nevertheless, the overall religiosity of the sample appears to be very high.

The survey data collected in 2002 are also based on opportunistic sampling. Those who filled out the questionnaire are also highly religious. Forty-nine of the sixty-six said they attended religious services nearly every week or more often. All but one said they felt somewhat or extremely close to God most of the time. And fifty-seven of the sixty-six said LDS Church activities and programs were an important part of their life.

Since both samples are opportunistic samples, any trends or changes can be presented only as suggestive. As a sociologist, however, I am interested in who, among African Americans, joins an essentially all-white church with a previous history of racial exclusivity on priesthood participation.

Both samples reveal some things about social class. The oral history sample included twenty-eight students and fourteen homemakers. The most common occupation was that of teacher or teacher's aide (22). Ten were nurses. Others managed fast-food restaurants, worked in retail stores, or pursued a variety of other middle- and lower-middle-class occupations. Among the employed, 72 percent were engaged in white-collar occupations and 28 percent in blue-collar occupations.

The General Social Survey (GSS) to which I referred earlier includes a prestige scale of occupations.[11] I used this scale to code the occupational prestige of the African American LDS sample. The average occupational prestige score of the LDS oral history sample, collected in the early 1980s, was substantially higher than that of the 1987 GSS sample of black Americans (46 compared to 32).

The oral history sample was also better educated than African Americans as a whole. This is shown in table 6.2, where data from the LDS sample are compared to the current population reports. Sixty-six percent of the oral history sample had attended or graduated from college, compared to 26.4 percent of the blacks in the current population reports. On the other hand, 36.5 percent of the national sample had less than a high school education, compared to less than 11 percent of the oral history sample.

The sample of blacks who joined the LDS Church not only had higher educational levels than members of the non-Mormon black community, they also had higher levels than the white LDS members in the 1980s (see table 6.2),

Table 6.2 Education Levels of the Black and White LDS Samples Compared to National Data

Education Level	Black LDS sample	U.S. Blacks sample	White LDS sample	U.S. Whites sample
Less than high school	1.1%	18.3%		12.0%
Some high school	9.3	18.2	15.9% or less	11.0
High school graduate	13.7	37.1	35.3	39.2
Vocational training	9.8		not given	
Some college	33.9	15.7	26.8	17.2
College graduate	32.2	10.7	22.1	20.5

Sources: White LDS sample data were collected in 1981 by Goodman and Heaton (1986). Black and White U.S. data are for 1987 and are from *Statistical Abstract of the United States 1989,* 109th ed. (Washington, D.C.: U.S. Bureau of Census, 1989), 131.

who in turn had slightly higher levels of education than whites nationally at the time.[12]

Similar patterns appear in the 2002 survey sample. All but thirteen of the sixty-six had some training beyond high school; more than two-thirds (47) had some college, with almost one-tenth (6) having graduate training. More than half had incomes equal to or above the national average, and twenty-six of the sixty-six indicated that they had professional occupations.

Impressionistic indications of upward mobility were also garnered from the oral history interviews. The coders estimated the social class of the LDS sample during childhood and at the time of the interviews. The ratings of the coders suggest that the respondents were somewhat upwardly mobile, with most of the mobility occurring from the working class to the lower middle class. Table 6.3 is a cross tabulation of the coders' ratings of social class of the respondents during childhood and at the time of the interviews. Forty-nine of the 108 who were judged to have grown up in the working class were rated by the coders as lower middle class when they were interviewed; nine were

Table 6.3 Coder Impressions of Social Class of the Oral History Respondents during Childhood and at the Time of the Interview

Social Class Growing Up	Respondents in Social Class at Time of Interview					
	Poverty	Working	Low-Middle	Up-Middle	Upper	Total
Upper Class				1		1
Upper Middle		1	4	5	1	11
Lower Middle		4	37	5		46
Working	2	48	49	8	1	108
In Poverty	2	11	4	1	1	19

$x^2 = 65.3$, df. $= 16$, p $< .01$

judged to be either upper class or upper middle class. Of the nineteen who grew up in poverty, two were thought to be still impoverished while eleven were thought to be working class, four were thought to be lower middle class, and two were judged as upper class or upper middle class. Most Americans have experienced some social mobility, however, so these results may not be atypical.

Educational mobility was also evident. In the oral history sample, thirty-three of the forty-three from lower-middle-class origins attended or graduated from college, as did sixty-one of the ninety-eight from working-class origins. Eight of the fourteen judged to have grown up in poverty also attended or graduated from college.

Among the 2002 survey sample respondents, the educational mobility is less prominent, especially when the education of the respondent is compared to that of the respondent's father. As shown in table 6.4, of the twenty-five respondents whose fathers had only a high school education, sixteen either went to college or graduated from college. Further, of the thirty-four respondents whose mothers had only a high school degree or less, twenty-six went to college themselves. On the other hand, some whose fathers or mothers had graduated from college had not graduated themselves. Overall, however, the numbers show some educational mobility.

In sum, the data suggest that those who joined the LDS Church and stayed are upwardly mobile both in terms of their education and their occupational status. The data are limited. Both samples are likely composed of middle-class African Americans who feel comfortable answering questionnaires and giving interviews. Nevertheless, the high measures of education and occupational status suggest that African Americans who join the LDS Church are, on average, doing better than African Americans in general.

Individuals in both samples appear to have more stable family lives than do those in the GSS sample. Most of the LDS oral history respondents were mar-

Table 6.4 Educational Attainment of the 2002 Sample Compared to Parents' Education

Respondent's Education	Mother's Education			Father's Education		
	High school	Some college	College grad	High school	Some college	College grad
High school grad or less	9	2	1	9	0	1
Some college	15	2	11	10	3	8
College grad or more	11	2	6	6	3	8
Totals	34	6	18	25	6	17

ried (49.5 percent) or remarried after being divorced (9.6 percent). Comparable figures for African Americans in the GSS sample were 32.4 percent and 22.4 percent, respectively. Seventeen percent of the LDS oral history sample were currently divorced or separated compared to 23.9 percent of the GSS sample.

As noted earlier, the LDS samples are relatively young. The average age of those in the oral history sample at the time of their conversion was thirty-four. Over three-quarters of them were under forty; one-third were under twenty-five. In the 2002 sample, the average age was even lower, thirty.

Finally, the African American converts appear to have had considerable experience with whites in other settings before joining the LDS Church. Measures of contact, especially contact under favorable conditions, are extremely difficult to obtain. Nevertheless, the oral histories indicate that fifty-three converts (nearly 25 percent of the sample) had some military service and at least sixteen grew up in military families. Furthermore, at least twenty-two individuals (10 percent) had been or were currently married to whites or Hispanics. In the 2002 sample, most had attended integrated schools, and nearly 60 percent indicated that three or more of their close friends were white.

Most of the respondents in the oral history sample had either some (17 percent) or frequent (53 percent) contact with whites while growing up, and contact with whites as adults was frequent. Obviously the frequent interracial contact would likely make African Americans comfortable about worshiping with whites. At the same time, however, the religious culture in the LDS Church is strikingly different than some African Americans would have experienced in previous churches. Thus, some Africans Americans are more likely than others to feel comfortable worshiping in a predominantly white LDS congregation.

The LDS Church as a Destination Church in Religious Switching

For the African American religious switchers who joined the LDS Church, the characteristics of the destination church may also be important factors. In this sense, membership in the LDS Church may convey several positive benefits that offset negative feelings about the church's previous (nearly) all-white composition and its past priesthood ban. First, it is now an integrated church. Local congregations are based on geographical areas so that integrated congregations are possible in some areas. In others, wards or congregations are often composed primarily of one race.

Second, the LDS Church has a middle-class core and lifestyle that may appeal to middle-class blacks or those who are socially mobile. Finally, the combination of doctrinal, biblical, and moral conservativeness with the middle-class composition of the LDS Church may attract middle-class blacks. The doctrines that seemed most appealing to the oral history interviewees were the "plan of salvation" and the emphasis on the family. Mentioned less frequently were the practice of baptism, the LDS view of the Godhead, the practice of baptism by immersion, the health code known as the Word of Wisdom, and having an unpaid, lay ministry.

An additional factor that distinguishes the LDS Church from mainline churches as the destination church is the proselytizing of the LDS Church. Because of the missionary activity throughout the United States, African Americans are more likely to encounter the LDS Church than other churches and to receive invitations to join. In the 2002 survey, forty-nine of the sixty-six respondents gave an account of how they came to join the LDS Church (the others grew up as members). Of the forty-nine, thirty-one indicated that they had joined the church because of direct or indirect contact from the missionaries. An additional six indicated that family members had previously joined the church, and six were introduced to the LDS Church through friends.

Sometimes the conversion experiences were quite spiritual. One respondent in the 2002 survey said that his prayers about being shown the right church had been answered in a dream in which he was shown two men. He visited a ward in Maine several years later and saw the men from his dream. Respondents in the oral history project reported similar experiences.

African American converts vary greatly in how they deal with the previous priesthood ban. Some are deeply troubled when they find out about the ban. About half (thirty of fifty-nine) of the respondents to the 2002 survey said they had known about the history of blacks and priesthood before joining the LDS Church. An additional nineteen had heard about it but did not know much about it. Only eleven said they did not know a lot about it. We have no data on those who have left the LDS Church or become inactive. Some may have left, at least in part, over the priesthood issue.

Some understand that other churches also discriminated in the past. For example, J. Joseph Faulkner stated in his oral history: "In other denominations, you could not only not hold the priesthood, but you could not attend the so-called white churches. . . . If you attempted to go, you would get lynched." He said further, "I was in the Baptist church for forty-five years and never did hold the office of deacon. . . . Within two months after I was baptized in the [LDS] Church, by my age . . . and being found worthy, I was ordained a deacon, teacher, and priest."[13] Faulkner was from the South, but Dan Mosley, who had similar feelings, grew up in Cleveland, Ohio. He reported:

"If a person would be clinical, every Christian denomination in America has discriminated against the blacks even for walking in the doors of the church, having a membership, being buried in the church."[14]

Still some respondents felt that problems continue to exist. As one person in the 2002 survey stated, "I have seen and heard of many race problems within the church in the South. Sometimes this keeps blacks in the South from joining the church. I see overall improvement though."

Black LDS Members' Perceptions of Acceptance in the United States

The degree to which African American converts feel accepted in LDS congregations also varies. I attempted to examine whether that acceptance varies according to sociodemographic characteristics. Four measures of acceptance can be ascertained from the oral histories: holding lay positions within the church, feeling excluded from church activities, having feelings about the previous priesthood ban, and experiencing feelings of tokenism.

Sixty-three percent of the oral history respondents held minor or medium-status lay positions within the congregations (e.g., Sunday school or primary teacher). Thirty-three percent held major positions within the congregation or held stake positions (e.g., stake Relief Society president). Four percent were full-time missionaries.

When asked whether they felt excluded from church activities, 62 percent of the respondents replied that they never felt excluded. Similarly, nearly 62 percent of the respondents reported no feelings of tokenism in the church. For example, just after Johnnie McKoy and his wife joined the church in Greensboro, North Carolina, the bishop called him to be the second counselor in the Sunday school and his wife to teach junior Sunday school. "We were still new in the Church, and there was some tension there," McKoy recalled. "My wife was beginning to be treated one way and I was beginning to be treated another. They respected me and admired me for coming to church, but they seemed to try to push my wife out. They were saying some nasty things to her." Eventually the Sunday school officers told Mrs. McKoy that "they were really giving her that calling because they were the worst kids in the Church."[15]

When negative events occurred, many converts believed they resulted from ignorance rather than from outright prejudice. Samuella Brown, for example, commented: "I've seen more ignorance than prejudice because Mormons, from what I've picked up and from what I learned . . . were always kind, caring, [and] considerate. . . . I perceive them as being a caring people, but just ignorant to certain things."[16]

Overall, the coded data indicate that most of the LDS African Americans experienced a reasonably high level of acceptance in the church. However, a significant proportion in this sample felt unaccepted, and this proportion would no doubt be higher if more "inactive" and disaffiliated members had been interviewed.

I also examined the social and demographic characteristics of LDS African Americans to see if socioeconomic class, gender, and/or marital status were associated with feelings of acceptance or tokenism. Few differences emerged.

Men were more likely than women to hold major church positions, but this is true among whites as well since several higher-level positions are restricted to male priesthood holders in the LDS Church. Females in the sample were more likely than men to experience feelings of tokenism. About half of the female respondents, compared to less than a third of the male respondents, reported such feelings. Single LDS African Americans seemed to feel less accepted than married members. White singles, however, have similar feelings in many LDS congregations because the focus of most LDS congregations is on families.

Surprisingly, the region of the country in which the respondents grew up was not a factor in perceived acceptance. Southern respondents in the oral history sample did not report significantly less acceptance than those from other areas of the country.

Those respondents with military experience, however, were more likely to hold higher lay positions in the church than those who had not served in the military. They were also less likely to report feelings of tokenism, and they were slightly less likely to feel excluded from church activities.

The general acceptance felt by most of the LDS African Americans in both samples can perhaps be exemplified by the comments of Delphine Garcia Young, a hospital worker and counselor in a bishopric:

> I have been truly well accepted by white Latter-day Saints. When you are around a white Latter-day Saint, it is just like going around your brothers and sisters. . . . They welcome you. They are not bigoted people where they will speak to you here and will not speak to you there. Every time they see you, you are Brother Young. No matter where you are, you are Brother Young. Whether you are in the street, whether you are in your home, whether you are in their home, you are Brother Young. . . . I have not met any that berate you; I have not met any that call you names; I have not met any who used racial discrimination; I have not met any that bring slanderous remarks toward you. I have not met any that are backstabbing where they say awful things about you. I have not met any that do all of those things.[17]

At the same time, some African American members have had negative experiences in the LDS Church. The harshest criticism in the 2002 survey was that, given the past history of the church, church leaders were not proactive in trying to change the lingering effects of its history. But most members surveyed in both samples felt accepted. Some expressed pride in the church's inclusiveness. They also enjoyed being in leadership positions. As one anonymous respondent wrote in the 2002 survey: "The gospel is now spreading to many black countries, Africa, Islands and black neighborhoods in the USA. If you are honest [in] the dealings [with] your fellowman, I believe no one can stop your chances. I believe my personality and my ability . . . [have been used] and I am moved into leadership positions."

Most of the 2002 survey respondents (thirty-four of fifty-nine) indicated that they think church leaders today avoid talking about the priesthood ban, but most also said they thought both white members and the leaders were attempting to improve race relations in the church. Some saw the improvement as consistent with changes in the nation as a whole. Still others saw improvement simply because African Americans continue to join the LDS Church.

Conclusion

Little is known publicly about the characteristics of African Americans who have joined the LDS Church. I have relied on two convenience samples to draw a few conclusions about who joins and about how these individuals feel they have been received in a church with "a past." To some observers it must seem ironic that a white church that previously excluded people of color from full participation now actively proselytizes African Americans in the United States and Africans worldwide. A further irony may be that many African Americans join and that, overall, those who stay often feel quite comfortable much of the time.

Although some strong self-selection occurs in the samples that I have relied on, I believe we may understand blacks' acceptance of the LDS Church by recognizing that the church combines biblical orthodoxy and traditional morality with middle-class values. The church also emphasizes the family. Thus, middle-class, upwardly mobile African Americans are attracted to the LDS Church.

Nevertheless, the data indicate that some African Americans struggle. And, unfortunately, some of their struggles are clearly imposed by white members' insensitivities, slights, ignorance, and sometimes outright racism. Most of the individuals in the samples examined here, however, feel comfortable. Many rejoice in their membership. Many would like both the membership and the leadership to be more active in ameliorating previous statements on race and in accepting African American members. Rather than hiding race, some want acknowledgment of it. But most of all, most just want to feel accepted and to succeed in their chosen church.

Notes

1. See Newell G. Bringhurst, *Saints, Slaves, and Blacks: The Changing Place of Black People within Mormonism* (Westport, Conn.: Greenwood Press, 1981).

2. See George P. Rawick, *From Sundown to Sunup: The Making of the Black Community* (Westport, Conn.: Greenwood Press, 1972); C. Eric Lincoln and Lawrence H. Mamiya, *The Black Church in the African American Experience* (Durham, N.C.: Duke University Press, 1990).

3. Wade Clark Roof and William McKinney, *American Mainline Religion: Its Changing Shape and Future* (New Brunswick, N.J.: Rutgers University Press, 1987), 90.

4. Lincoln and Mamiya, *Black Church.*

5. Roof and McKinney, *American Mainline Religion,* 138–44.

6. Cardell K. Jacobson, "Religiosity and Prejudice: An Update and Denominational Analysis," *Review of Religious Research* 39 (March 1998): 264–82.

7. For a summary of this literature, see David G. Myers, *Social Psychology,* 7th ed. (New York: McGraw-Hill, 2002), or any basic social psychology text.

8. What follows here draws in part from my "Black Mormons in the 1980s: Pioneers in a White Church," *Review of Religious Research* 33 (December 1991): 146–52.

9. See Jessie L. Embry, *Black Saints in a White Church: Contemporary African Americans* (Salt Lake City: Signature Books, 1994).

10. Roof and McKinney, *American Mainline Religion,* 172.

11. See James Allen Davis and Tom W. Smith, *General Social Surveys, 1972–1987: Cumulative Codebook* (Chicago: National Opinion Research Center, 1987).

12. See Kristen L. Goodman and Tim B. Heaton, "LDS Church Members in the U.S. and Canada: A Demographic Profile," *AMCAP Journal* 12 (1986): 88–107.

13. J. Joseph Faulkner, interview by Alan Cherry, 1987, transcript, 15–16, LDS African American Oral History Project, Charles Redd Center for Western Studies, L. Tom Perry Special Collections and Manuscripts, Harold B. Lee Library, Brigham Young University, Provo, Utah; hereafter cited as Oral History Project.

14. Dan Mosley, interview by Alan Cherry, 1985, transcript, 16–17, Oral History Project.

15. Johnnie McKoy, interview by Alan Cherry, 1986, transcript, 9–10, Oral History Project.

16. Samuella Brown, interview by Alan Cherry, 1988, transcript, 7, Oral History Project.

17. Delphine Garcia Young, interview by Alan Cherry, 1985, transcript, 24, Oral History Project.

"How Do Things Look on the Ground?"
The LDS African American Community
in Atlanta, Georgia

KEN DRIGGS

Atlanta, Georgia, is *not* Mormon Utah. It has a healthy Church of
Jesus Christ of Latter-day Saints community and one that is more racially,
culturally, and politically diverse. African American Mormons are an essential part of the mix. They are growing in numbers, in commitment, and in the
church leadership roles they fill.

Among the essential ingredients in the growth of this part of the Mormon
universe are veteran black members who serve as Relief Society presidents,
bishops, and stake high counselors, and in stake presidencies. They raise their
children to serve missions, they work regularly in the Atlanta Temple, and
they voice strong testimonies on the first Sunday of every month. African
Americans have laid a solid foundation there, and they are going to exert an
influence on the Mormon future.

On June 8, 1978, Spencer W. Kimball, president of the Church of Jesus Christ
of Latter-day Saints (Mormon), issued a statement extending the church's lay
priesthood to "all worthy male members." The following September the membership sustained this statement as a divine revelation, and it was placed in the
Doctrine and Covenants, one of the sacred texts of the LDS Church.

This step was necessary because, before 1978, the church had excluded
those of African American descent from holding the priesthood. Bruce R.
McConkie, a Mormon apostle, wrote in his semiofficial *Mormon Doctrine* that
African Americans "were less valiant in [the] pre-existence" and consequently "had certain spiritual restrictions imposed upon them during mortality."
Among those restrictions, McConkie wrote, "Negroes in this life are denied
the priesthood; under no circumstances can they hold this delegation of authority from the Almighty." In mortal life they were descended from Cain, the
Old Testament figure who slew Abel. "[Cain] became the father of Negroes,
and those spirits who are not worthy to receive the priesthood are born

through his lineage."[1] McConkie later distanced himself from some of these unfortunate views,[2] but those concerning Cain continue in current editions of his influential book.[3]

According to the 2000 census, the Atlanta metropolitan area includes 4,112,198 people, more than half of Georgia's population. Atlanta may have been the site of one of the decisive battles of the Civil War and the setting for much of *Gone with the Wind*, but today a majority of the city's center is black. It is the home of the Reverend Martin Luther King Jr. and the site of a national monument to his life. The King family and associates such as Congressman John Lewis and the former United Nations ambassador Andrew Young exert a powerful influence there. Former President Jimmy Carter, who broke down many barriers to black participation at the highest levels of government, built his influential Carter Center there. Besides being the home of Georgia Tech and Emory University it is also the home of the black Ivy League of Morehouse, Morris Brown, Spellman, and Atlanta Clark Universities. It is one of the most comfortable cities in the country for black professionals and business people. No institution is going to thrive in Atlanta if it does not make African Americans comfortable.[4]

One Mormon reference work reported 62,301 members of the LDS Church in Georgia in 2002, with over 24,000 members in Atlanta. They worshiped in ninety-six wards and another twenty-nine branches, as Mormon congregations are called. In 1983 the church dedicated a temple in the north Atlanta suburb of Sandy Springs.[5]

Since 1997 I have been a member of the Atlanta Ward, Atlanta Georgia Stake. The Atlanta Ward meets in a substantial new building at 1469 Lee Street, next to Fort McPherson and close to a MARTA terminal. The building was dedicated in 1995 by Casby Harrison Jr., then president of the Adams Park Branch.[6] When the Atlanta Stake was organized on June 26, 1996, the Atlanta Ward was created by combining the Adams Park, Perkerson Park, and Flat Shoals branches with about half of the old Druid Hills Ward. The stake boundaries are wide and include most of Atlanta's inner city.

According to the ward clerks, there are around 500 people carried on the rolls.[7] I often count those in attendance during sacrament meetings and find we average about 140 to 150 people; usually about half of the group is black and half is white. It is an interesting mix of Georgia Tech and Georgia State University students, inner-city families, some high-tech professionals, a few military families, recent immigrants from the Caribbean and Africa, and a few lawyers. It tends to be a younger congregation. Most of the teenagers are black and many attend a seminary program, or daytime program of religious education.

Understanding the Atlanta Ward

To understand the Atlanta Ward, it helps to understand someone who is rarely there, the former bishop and Atlanta native Fred ("Tony") Parker Jr. He is rarely there because in 2001 he was released as bishop and called as first counselor in the Atlanta Stake presidency. In 1977 Parker joined the U.S. Army as a seventeen-year-old looking for a career. The army brought him to Hawaii where he met an LDS Samoan woman whom he later married. His first contact with the church came at the visitors center of the LDS-operated Polynesian Cultural Center near Laie, Hawaii. The army transferred him back to the mainland, but his future wife and the church remained on his mind. He was baptized and married on the same day in February 1983, in Independence, Missouri, where her family had settled. Lina and Tony Parker became the parents of five children.

Parker's twenty-three-year army career took him to Fort McPherson, back home in Atlanta. He attended what was then the Adams Park Branch when Harrison was president. Harrison's successor was Daryl Blount, and the branch met in a little yellow house that area members still recall fondly.

Parker is an easy man to follow. He is always immaculately dressed and striking looking, with dark skin, a shaved head, and an athletic appearance. One stake high councilor jokes that he looks just like the Atlanta heavyweight boxer Evander Holyfield. Parker made a point of knowing everyone in his ward. Visitors and new members never escaped his heartfelt greetings. The bishopric was reorganized three times during his service, always with at least one African American counselor and sometimes two.

The night I really got to know him came in September 1999 when, under the guise of an elders' quorum social, he invited several young white men to his Jonesboro home south of Atlanta for tacos and a very exciting BYU-Washington football game on ESPN. (The Y won 35-28 on its way to one of LaVell Edwards's best seasons.) But besides football, the evening brought lots of happy talks with Parker and his family in their kitchen and family room.

Besides his boundless cordiality, Parker administered the ward with an obvious affection for all its members and a willingness to accept their sometimes differing dress, worship styles, and needs. What Mormons from the West may regard as "different" and slightly uncomfortable was often commonplace in the Atlanta Ward.

Worshiping with Friends in the Atlanta Ward

Two of my best friends in the Atlanta Ward are Kevin and M. J. Cheatham Butler. M. J. joined the LDS Church in 1989. She encountered missionaries at the home of a friend and in five months entered the waters of baptism. Previously she had attended Baptist, Jehovah's Witness, and Church of Christ churches. What she heard from the LDS missionaries was "very familiar," in particular their discussion about preexistence. She began attending an Atlanta area branch where, she told me, "I was the only splash of color" in the congregation. For the most part, she enjoyed her home branch; but she recalls tensions over the possibility of other African American Mormons joining the branch when two black women missionaries were assigned to the congregation. She briefly attended another Atlanta Ward, which was "[racially] uncomfortable, and it was intended to be that way."[8]

She had not heard of the priesthood ban until after she had joined. Her initial reaction was, "Oh, wait a minute, you guys too?" She prayed about the issue, felt she got an answer quickly, and has never looked back.

In 1996 she came to the Atlanta Ward. Her first thought was "This is neat. There are black people, how cool!" And she could not help but notice Bishop Parker. She recalled, "So I walk into this little 'white' Church of Jesus Christ of Latter-day Saints and I'm seeing this black guy, and he's not fair; his skin is really brown. That says it's okay." Cheatham, who is tall, ever smiling, and famous for her constantly changing hairstyles, quickly established herself as one of the more engaging members of the ward.

She met and married another convert, Kevin Butler. Earlier, after army service at Fort Hood, Butler had married a woman and settled in Austin, Texas, but found his seemingly comfortable life, with all the material trappings of success, unsatisfying. Two LDS missionaries knocked at his door, and their message immediately resonated. After his first marriage dissolved, he came to Atlanta to be near his daughter and found himself in the Atlanta Ward. Butler also was pleased to see an African American bishop, feeling his presence conveyed an important message and that the bishop became "a magnet."

One of the trademarks of the Atlanta Ward is that when speakers or testimony bearers greet the congregation they get a healthy "Good morning" in return. It is a variation on what is referred to as "call and response" in church meetings. One young priest who is fond of wearing short, stylish dreadlocks and shell necklaces, Jabari Ashe, will challenge the members from the podium to do better if the congregation's response is not vocal enough. Visiting stake officers invariably comment on their pleasure at this particular eccentricity of the Atlanta Ward.

One of my favorite experiences in the ward came when I was asked to help with the 2001 stake roadshow. Noelka Minter-Hill, whose husband, Lynn Hill, had served as a counselor in the bishopric, wrote and directed a skit called *Facing Your Weaknesses,* which began with an imaginary South African sequence, then moved to China and the United States. Our several rehearsals were often a bit like herding cats, with teenagers being teenagers, blown cues, and occasional rewrites; but it got done and everyone seemed to enjoy the experience. I certainly enjoyed the opportunity to get to know many African American members of my ward better.

Six wards and a branch gathered at the Brockett Ward building for the Atlanta Stake roadshows on October 27, 2001. I had not appreciated how diverse the stake was until I watched those roadshows. About half of the casts of two other ward roadshows seemed to be African American kids. The Brockett Ward youth had a particularly clever skit called *The Cat That Was Phat!* The Spanish-speaking Chamblee Branch presented a dazzling dance piece using elaborate Aztec costumes and sang songs in Spanish and Indian languages.

In typical Mormon fashion, everybody got some sort of prize, with the Atlanta Ward getting recognition for best music. I don't know that we were especially musical but our skit certainly had the most gospel and R&B flavor, right down to Lynn Hill's lip-synching to the gospel singer Kirk Franklin's "God Can." It almost seemed incongruous when the very "whitebread" Atlanta Ward bishop, Russ Shurtz, closed our skit by delivering a message about finding salvation in Jesus Christ.

God's Army, a movie by the LDS producer Richard Dutcher about the lives of Mormon missionaries serving in Southern California, made it to an Atlanta art theater. Clay Watson, a white Atlanta Ward youth leader and returned missionary, organized groups of teenagers to attend. Nearly all of the kids were black. I had seen the movie earlier and gave Watson a heads-up about the sequence where an earnest black missionary is blind-sided by an African American investigator couple who are incensed about the former priesthood ban. I was unaware of any reaction among the Atlanta audience members, but Jabari Ashe, who was near the age of eligibility to serve a proselytizing mission (nineteen), spoke about it at the next fast and testimony meeting. That was the first time I had heard the issue spoken of from the podium. Ashe said he was unaware of the issue until hearing about it in the movie but he spoke earnestly about how, over the years, many white people had come to the aid of his family in times of difficulty.

On another occasion I worked at the church's cannery in Atlanta and, for the first time, found myself in long conversations with two converts, Rob and Bertha Brunson. Rob would later be called to the bishopric. I had often noticed their three rambunctious young boys at church, always perfectly well groomed and wearing bow ties. Bertha is a doting and attentive mother. The LDS Church's emphasis on family values was and is paramount for them.

The Atlanta Ward has not experienced any racial tensions that I have observed, which makes Parker feel proud. The former bishop and those who served before him deserve much of the credit for that. Today Parker is well respected throughout the stake but is quick to credit these successes to his family.

Visitors to the Atlanta Ward

Atlanta is a major convention center, and the Atlanta Ward is the closest meetinghouse to the downtown hotels and convention centers. The city gets a steady stream of LDS visitors, often from the much "whiter" Mormon West. The 2002 NCAA Final Four, hosted by Atlanta, brought a number of visitors from the East and Midwest. It was interesting to watch their reactions. A few come knowing about the diversity of the ward; most were completely surprised. I remember the first time I looked up and noticed that all of the young men blessing and passing the sacrament were African Americans, some with Afros and corn rows. It was amusing to watch visitors look up with the same recognition.

Sometimes there are bumps in the road—indications that many Mormons still have some things to learn. I remember a visiting Nevada bishop who bore his testimony to the effect that he had always liked "the coloreds." Occasionally questions by visitors between meetings show a lack of tact or racial sensitivity.

While we see the occasional African American missionary serving in the ward, the overwhelming majority are young white men and women, frequently from small towns in the West where they have had little exposure to African Americans. Some have privately told me that the first extended conversations they have ever had with people of color have been in the Atlanta Ward. Yet I have never encountered a missionary who wasn't genuinely excited about serving in the Atlanta Ward and who did not thoroughly enjoy that exposure to this different community of Mormons. I suspect that those small-town Mormons return to their little Utah and Idaho communities to tell their families and home wards how wonderful it was to have this African American influence in the church.

One of the most visible African American Mormons today is the rhythm and blues singer Gladys Knight.[9] She once lived in Atlanta and still has business interests there, even after her move to Las Vegas. She is an occasional visitor to the Atlanta Ward and was asked to speak at the close of a 2001 sacrament meeting. It came on a day with a full attendance including some black investigators. There were fifteen minutes left in the regular meeting time when she stood up to speak; she spoke for perhaps forty-five minutes, and the congregation could have listened to her for another hour.

Knight is a dynamic, inspirational speaker. All her listeners, black or white, leaned forward in their seats toward her. It was the most direct discussion of race and the church's history in that area that I have ever heard in an LDS meeting hall. She told her own conversion story, about how she wrestled with the church's pre-1978 priesthood ban and why she emphatically rejected the idea that blacks should boycott the church because of it. "For generations white people would not let us vote," she said. "That doesn't mean we should refuse to vote today now that we have the right." She told the African American members that they were pioneers and urged them to make their own unique contributions to the church's development.

Knight also talked about how she missed the music of traditional African American worship and said it was a personal mission of hers to bring some life to Mormon music. Afterwards she posed for pictures with beaming white missionaries and had a long private talk in the parking lot with a young woman investigator who later joined the church. That woman, Cassandra Reed, is now the wife of a counselor in the bishopric, Anthony Reed, who served a proselytizing mission in Ogden, Utah.

It was after that sacrament meeting that I began having my first extended conversations with African American members about their thoughts on race and religion.

Visiting Other Units

I have tried to identify other congregations with substantial African American membership and to visit them as well. The Atlanta Stake is fortunate to have other wards with diverse membership. The thriving Twin Oaks Ward is about half white and half black and has a much-loved bishop, William Tucker. The Brocket Ward has a substantial black membership. I drove to Birmingham one weekend to visit the Ensly Ward in the Birmingham Stake and the Third Ward in the Bessemer Stake.[10] Members have told me of visiting similar congregations in Charlotte, Houston, Dallas, Chicago, and New York City.

The Twin Oaks Ward, located at 2083 Wesley Chapel Road, had been the East Lake Branch before the old Atlanta District was organized as the Atlanta Stake in 1995. I arrived a little late on the Sunday of my first visit, in the middle of a testimony by a courtly, soft-spoken gentleman in his sixties who turned out to be Bishop Tucker. He and his wife, Sadie, joined the LDS Church in 1988 after dedicated service to the Methodist Church. His wife was investigating the LDS Church, much to her husband's consternation, so he wanted to talk to the missionaries to stop this interference. As it turned out, he was baptized first. Bishop Tucker was a fixture in the Atlanta Temple as an ordinance worker before his call as bishop in 2001. By chance the Sunday I first visited was also Bishop Tucker's birthday, and the affection that both black and white ward members held for him was clearly evident.

Other striking testimonies I heard that day included those of Horatio McFarlane and his wife, Yaa; he was the Young Men's president and had served a mission in his native Jamaica. There was also a joyful and tearful testimony from a Ricks College student, Rodney Spradley, who had recently returned to Atlanta and had just received his mission call to Guatemala. I was so struck by Spradley's testimony that I asked around about him. I learned from several people that the young man had had a challenging life but greatly benefited from a circle of LDS friends who came together to support him. His mother had died of cancer when he was a child, and he was raised by non-LDS family members. By all appearances, the course of his life is now set in a direction that most members of the church would find exemplary.

Between meetings I talked to several African American members. The Twin Oaks Ward is wealthier and more middle-class than the Atlanta Ward. I encountered several black members who were successful businessmen and had been LDS for fifteen or twenty years. They were confident about their Mormonness and church leadership experience.

Darius Gray and the Genesis Group

The last weekend in February 2002 the Atlanta Ward had visitors from Utah, Darius A. Gray and Margaret Blair Young, authors of three historical novels about African American pioneers.[11] Perhaps more important to African American members, Gray was the first counselor in the original presidency of the Genesis Group. Genesis was created in 1971 under the direction of the First Presidency and Quorum of the Twelve Apostles, to provide support for black members of the church.[12] A very poised and polished speaker with a deep, resonating voice, Gray had wrestled with and answered for himself every difficult question Atlanta's black Mormons could toss at him.

Both Gray and Young attended the Atlanta Ward for sacrament meeting. I noticed that afternoon that, although it was not planned, three young black men prepared and blessed the sacrament while three of the five who passed were African Americans. During sacrament meeting I walked around the meeting hall counting the members and noting their races: seventy-two whites, seventy-four blacks, and an Asian woman, which was pretty representative for the Atlanta Ward.

First Young, then Gray, filled the sacrament meeting program with a combination of personal testimony and historical details about the lives of the black Mormon pioneers Elijah Abel and Jane Manning James. Gray told of his own conversion to the LDS Church thirty-seven years earlier in Colorado Springs, Colorado, at a time when he was told there were no more than three hundred African American Mormons in the world. It was the night before his baptism, during a final personal interview, that he learned he would not be allowed the priesthood. Gray left that interview angry, certain that he would not be baptized the next day.

But after receiving "personal revelation," he was baptized. On December 26, 1964, Darius Gray, a self-described "proud black man," decided to join a church that had a universal male lay priesthood except for him and others of African descent. But the Mormon world had changed a great deal since his baptism and he reveled in those changes. Gray told the Atlanta Ward: "Diversity is of God. God created our diversity. We can celebrate our diversity and not be separated by our differences."

That evening, Gray and Young spoke again at a multistake fireside in the Jonesboro Stake Center south of Atlanta. The meeting hall was packed with a crowd of 250 about evenly divided between blacks and whites. The meeting was opened by David Ingram, a white man, president of the Jonesboro Stake. Ingram described himself as "a child of the South" who went to high school in the early 1960s where he was taught "many things that were divisive." He left it to the congregation to conclude that he was speaking of race. He described his later conversion to the LDS Church and how racial tolerance was one of the things he began to learn. Then he introduced an African American stake high councilman, Darrell Campbell, whom he called one of the most spiritual men he had ever known.

Campbell joked that, earlier in the evening while sitting on the stand, he had looked for his wife. "It's not too often that I have trouble finding her." It took a few seconds for the congregation to get the joke, but loud laughter followed. A sincere speaker, Campbell went on to say, "I have spent twenty-one years preparing to give this talk." He mentioned his struggles joining a largely white church years earlier and how a home teacher brought him the book *Mormonism and the Negro,* which he found very helpful and answered many of his questions.[13]

He concluded, "You can count the seeds in an apple but not the apples in a seed." He called upon the congregation, especially the African Americans in the audience, to leave with their pockets full of seeds. Campbell believed that many more African Americans were ready to receive the Mormon gospel. "The scriptures say the field is *white* for the harvest, but we know the field is *black*. This is the South!"

Before Young and Gray were introduced as speakers, the stake presented a play about Elijah Abel drawn from their books. Members read the characters of Abel, his mother, the Prophet Joseph Smith, and Abel's missionary companion, all recounting his life as a Mormon. Young and Gray were both tearful during the presentation, and then they both spoke about their testimonies and historical research.

Gray again told his own conversion story, of his struggle over the priesthood ban, being part of a tiny minority in an overwhelmingly white church, and the formation of the Genesis Group as a dependent branch with national boundaries in 1971. He credited Joseph Fielding Smith, then president of the church, with making things happen by designating three apostles to work with and foster the group. After the death of Ruffin Bridgeforth Jr. in 1997, Gray was called as president of the Genesis Group. Gray recalled that the initial meeting with general authorities leading to the Genesis Group was on June 8, 1971. He felt it was no accident that the priesthood ban was lifted seven years to the day from that meeting.

He told the Atlanta congregation how pleased he was to see so many people of color in an LDS meetinghouse. "As Martin would say, 'I have seen the promised land and I am grateful.'" With that line Gray took questions, which proved to be one of the most interesting parts of the fireside. A tall, elegant young woman stood in the middle of the congregation to ask a question she evidently had thrown at him at an earlier reception: did he really believe that black folks' skin color was the biblical mark of Cain? There followed an intense discussion between Gray and several members of the congregation. Gray accepted some aspects of the lineage argument based on his own reading of the Bible but made it clear he did not regard his black skin as a curse.

One woman asked Gray, "Why did the priesthood rules change?" Behind me I heard another woman say softly, "I'm right with you, sister. I struggle with the same thing." Gray asked various people to tell the reasons they had been told about why blacks were not allowed the priesthood before 1978. No one mentioned McConkie or *Mormon Doctrine* by name, but all the reasons contained there were offered by black members of the audience. After hearing a half dozen explanations, Gray told the audience: "These reasons are all incorrect." He opened his Bible and read John 9:2–3 where Jesus told his disciples, in answer to their query about why a man had been born blind from birth: "Neither hath this man sinned, nor his parents: but that the works of

God should be made manifest in him." Gray suggested that blacks were not "cursed" but called to particular assignments just as all mortals are. How blacks and whites respond to one another is a crucible in which "the works of God [are] made manifest."

It took an hour after the closing prayer for the crowd to disperse. Young and Gray were besieged by members who asked them to autograph copies of their books and who wanted to continue the discussion one on one. Not everyone seemed satisfied with the answers, but everyone seemed stimulated by the discussion. I talked with several of my Atlanta Ward friends in attendance, and all felt especially energized.

Before leaving Atlanta, Gray made a presentation at the Auburn Avenue Research Library on African American Culture and History about the LDS Church's organization of the 1865 Freedman's Savings and Trust Company records of some seventy thousand former slaves' family records. He reported that it has been one of the most popular of all LDS genealogical research tools offered to the public.

What I Brought to This Experience

When I first considered writing about the Atlanta Ward, it was partly as a vehicle to discuss my own discomfort over the church's racial history. For me it had been a sort of primal sin, an injustice we had not confronted, a stain we were unable to wash out. I was born in 1948 and grew up in the segregated South, sometimes hearing overt racists in the little branches we attended and feeling that this was all very wrong. I recall my anger and discomfort at comments that the civil rights movement was really a front for dangerous communists and that the separation of the races was God's way. I still vividly recall a young rather unsophisticated black woman I worked with at a small Tallahassee, Florida, newspaper in the early 1970s who expressed surprise when she learned I was Mormon. All she knew about Mormons, she said, was that "you don't like black people." I did not have an adequate answer for her and felt ashamed.

I was afraid to discuss "it" with African American Mormon friends because I was ashamed of that part of our past. I know things have changed since 1978, and I suspected that many younger black Mormons might not know about that dark corner of our history. I didn't want to be the one to inform them so I tiptoed around the subject for my first couple years in the Atlanta Ward. I rarely heard it mentioned.

Then Larry Wright, a white freelance writer from Austin, Texas, contacted me during his research for a 2002 *New Yorker* magazine article about the

LDS Church.[14] Family business brought him to Atlanta, and we had a long face-to-face interview. It happened to be a Saturday when a couple from the ward married in the Atlanta Temple, with a wedding reception following at the meetinghouse. Terrence Smith, Pamela Ashe, and their families represent all that is positive about African American Mormons. I wanted Wright to see that. Writers covering Mormon life have a tendency to visit Utah to learn what they can without asking themselves if that really is representative of the LDS universe. That's a bit like going to Rome and assuming that what you see there is representative of all Catholics. So I persuaded Wright to come to the Atlanta Ward for the reception.

While photographing the reception, I would circle back to eavesdrop on his interviews with African American members. I was surprised that several of them brought up the priesthood ban, explaining to Wright how they got past that issue and were baptized. The first person he encountered was Ted Whiters, who went straight to the subject before Wright could bring it up. Whiters was one of the more engaging members of the ward, second counselor in the bishopric before his move to Auburn, Alabama. An able speaker and a passionately believing Mormon, he came to the church after a life of commitment to the Baptist faith. More important, he does not shy away from any issue when speaking of his own faith.

I was disappointed when the *New Yorker* piece came out without any mention of the Atlanta Ward or the growing racial diversity of the church. That was when I decided I had to write about this ward and its members.

A few months later a very bright member of the ward, Tanya Reed, asked in the Sunday school class if the old priesthood ban had been "inspired." Was it the prophet speaking as the Lord's mouthpiece? Both Reed and the teacher that day are twenty-something post-1978 members. For all of their adult lives, blacks had held the priesthood, so the question kind of stumped the teacher. I was in another class, but the discussion continued into the chapel hallways and found its way to me. Few Sundays have passed since then without my having some discussion with African American friends about how we are dealing with race as Mormons. Several have told me that we do not talk about matters of race and we need to.

So I entered discussions of the subject with a certain amount of concern, afraid I would encounter some unarticulated simmering resentment among African American members over our racial past. Had I been in their position I would have felt offended.

I did not find what I expected.

Most black members know something about the old priesthood ban. I have encountered only two African American Mormons who joined the church before 1978; one was Darius Gray. While the ban is still an irritant to a few people, for the most part they are much more concerned with what the church is anxious to offer them today. Some have dismissed it with an observation along the lines of "everybody else was segregated back then; why should we hold you to a higher standard?" Frankly, it bothers me that we did not meet a higher standard. I generally expect one from my religious leaders.

I was surprised at how many African Americans joined the church because the missionaries found them. I heard that over and over. They are attracted to the church because of its stress on family ties and on taking personal responsibility for your life, because of the detailed answers to eternal questions, because of the personal standards that are stressed, and because of the opportunities to serve. Larry Wright told me how impressed he had been with the church's institutional organization and ability to meet all the physical demands represented by clean, well-kept meetinghouses, teaching materials, and other necessities. Once African Americans join the church, perhaps no other factor is as important as fellowship—feeling included and wanted in a congregation.

Admittedly my sample may be skewed. I talked almost exclusively to active black members with strong testimonies, many of them in the church for years and a few of them second generation. These are the people who have overcome any misgivings about the old priesthood ban and focused on what are, for them, much more important priorities. Certainly there are lapsed black members or investigators who decided against joining and who might give me a different take. I thought perhaps my black Mormon friends were being polite and did not want to tackle the difficult topics. Frankly, however, I doubt that, because many of the people I interviewed have become good friends who have been candid with me.

What I found was a large number of people really trying to worship together as a community. Virtually everyone mentions the easy welcoming affection of the ward as a major reason for its appeal, the proverbial Mormon "good spirit." There is a complete lack of the backbiting, jealousy, and gossiping that generate tensions in any group. People try to see other members as brothers and sisters; they do not assume that the occasional insensitivity is a deliberate racial slight; and they do try to look out for each other. It is not perfect but it has been a surprisingly good start.

The Atlanta part of the Mormon universe has reason to anticipate a more diverse, multiracial future.

Some Conclusions

There has been a conscious effort at inclusion and recognition in the Atlanta Mormon community. It may be a bit uneven, but it is moving forward. This shows up when unit boundaries are drawn to allow for significant numbers of African Americans, creating a comfortable place to worship. It shows when African American members are given opportunities to serve at all levels in the ward and stake and when they are called to visible positions of true responsibility. I have observed the strongly positive reaction of African American members to high councilors, bishoprics, and stake presidencies of color. This validates the church's teaching that worthy members of any backgrounds will be called to administer the church.

Callings in the LDS Church have always been motivated by a number of factors. Not only do we search out the "best man" (or woman, in jobs that do not require priesthood) for the job, but we also try to give members a positive spiritual experience, to train people for more demanding callings in the future, and to send messages of inclusion.[15]

Once African Americans have been called to the administrative councils of the church, their voices are heard on issues large and small. This includes communicating that things such as religious musical tastes and emotional expression are not threats.[16]

Perhaps blacks and whites in the Deep South have so much shared history that they are more experienced in trying to make things work. The members of Utah's Mormon elite may not have had the opportunity for this real-world experience at building race relations. Sometimes they can be insensitive and clumsy no matter how well motivated. For me, a prime example of this is their inability to appreciate how offensive some of McConkie's *Mormon Doctrine* is to African Americans.

It is my opinion that, when the former priesthood ban comes up, there is still a clinging to the old justifications and almost no realization that, for many people, these rationalizations can be deeply hurtful. Missionaries are apparently not counseled in this area, and they sometimes contribute to the damage, however unintentionally. A few African American members have confidentially mentioned to me that the justifications offered by missionaries for the old priesthood ban have been very painful.

African American Mormons often have to defend their choice of religion to black friends outside the church. Some told me of friends who refused to believe that the LDS Church even allowed black members. We still have a pretty sorry reputation in some quarters and we can't hide from it. Efforts like the dispersal of the Freedman's Bank records are a constructive start.

But there is progress evident in Atlanta. Clearly a foundation has been laid there. Black Mormons find that many wards, though not all, present comfortable places to be. Their fellowship is appreciated, their talents will be called upon, and they are an important part of the LDS community.

Notes

1. Bruce R. McConkie, *Mormon Doctrine*, 2d ed. (Salt Lake City, Utah: Bookcraft, 1966), entries on "Negroes" (526–28), "Cain" (109), and "Ham" (343). McConkie was born in Michigan on July 29, 1915; was sustained to the First Council of the Seventy at age thirty-one, in 1946; and was ordained an apostle on October 12, 1972, by President Harold B. Lee. He served until his death on April 19, 1985, at age sixty-nine (*Deseret News 2004 Church Almanac* [Salt Lake City, Utah: Deseret News, 2004], 71). See also John L. Lund, *The Church and the Negro: A Discussion of Mormons, Negroes, and the Priesthood* (Salt Lake City: Paramount Publishers, 1967); John D. Hawkes, "Why Can't the Negro Hold the Priesthood," in Wynetta Willis Martin, *Black Mormon Tells Her Story* (Salt Lake City, Utah: Hawkes Publishing, 1972).

2. Lester Bush, "Introduction," *Dialogue: A Journal of Mormon Thought* 12 (Summer 1979): 9–12, esp. 11.

3. McConkie, *Mormon Doctrine*, "Cain" (108–9) and "Ham" (343): "Ham's descendants include the Negroes, who originally were barred from holding the priesthood but have been able to do so since June, 1978." "Negroes" (526–28) states: "In all past ages and until recent times in this dispensation, the Lord did not offer the priesthood to the Negroes. However, on 8 June, 1978, in the Salt Lake Temple, in the presence of the First Presidency and the Council of the Twelve, President Spencer W. Kimball received a revelation from the Lord directing that the gospel and the priesthood should now go to all men without reference to race or color." This statement appears in the edition designated "1966, 2nd printing, 1979."

4. Charles Whitaker, "Is Atlanta the New Black Mecca?" *Ebony*, March 2002, 148–50, 152, 154, 156, 158, 162.

5. *Deseret News 2004*, 447, 578; "Mormons Establishing Regional Office," *Atlanta Journal-Constitution*, September 5, 1998, F-1.

6. President Harrison, an African American, died in 2000. Unless otherwise noted, any individuals named in this chapter are African American.

7. Membership records in the LDS Church reflect baptisms and often include individuals who have not been active in years, many of whom may have moved to other affiliations. Those records should not be read as indicating active members.

8. These and all subsequent quotes from Mormons in the Atlanta area came in the course of interviews by the author.

9. Paul Swenson, "Gladys and Thurl: The Changing Face of Mormon Diversity," *Sunstone*, July 2001, 14–16.

10. On the Birmingham Stake see Greg Garrison, "Mormon Church Is Not Limited to Just Whites, Says Black Bishop," *Birmingham News*, May 8, 1992, E-1.

11. These three volumes are *One More River to Cross* (2000), *Bound for Canaan* (2002), and *The End of the Journey* (2003), all published by Bookcraft, now an imprint of the LDS Church–owned publishing company, Deseret Book, in Salt Lake City.

12. That first presidency was composed of Ruffin Bridgeforth Jr., Eugene Orr, and Gray. See Jessie L. Embry, *Black Saints in a White Church* (Salt Lake City: Signature Books, 1994), 182–85.

13. See John J. Stewart, *Mormonism and the Negro* (Logan, Utah: Bookmark Division of Community Press, 1960). For the most part this book sets out the same doctrinal explanations for denying the priesthood to African Americans that McConkie offers.

14. For the article, see Larry Wright, "A Reporter at Large: Lives of the Saints," *New Yorker,* January 21, 2002, 40–57.

15. There have been situations in church history when our failure to consider such factors have brought disastrous tensions with convert groups. See F. LaMond Tullis, *Mormons in Mexico: The Dynamics of Faith and Culture* (Logan: Utah State University Press, 1987), 137–68.

16. At the Jonesboro fireside, Gray spoke for many in attendance when he said that traditional African American gospel music was "part of our culture" and that white Mormons should not feel threatened when black members slipped off to listen to it. This didn't represent a lack of commitment; the black members were just enjoying their own musical heritage.

8   Unpacking Whiteness in Zion: Some Personal Reflections and General Observations

DARRON T. SMITH

Much of Western European history conditions us to see human differences in simplistic opposition to each other: dominant/subordinate, good/bad, up/down, superior/inferior.

—*Audre Lorde*

As an African American member of the Church of Jesus Christ of Latter-day Saints I was disturbed one otherwise enjoyable Sunday afternoon when I learned about an unpleasant incident that had occurred in my congregation earlier that day. This incident involved Joy Smith, who was teaching the lesson that day in the women's Relief Society meeting.[1] The lesson, from the manual provided by the church, was on "following the prophets," a popular topic that stresses the members' need to be obedient to higher authority. In an attempt to engage the class, she asked a hypothetical question: should all the teachings of Mormon prophets be obeyed—even teachings manifesting such racist thinking as the condemnation of interracial marriage? Before any meaningful discussion could take place, the Relief Society president abruptly interrupted and stated firmly to Smith that her discussion was "out of bounds" because it amounted to a criticism of church leaders, who are considered "the Lord's anointed." The teacher smiled, observed that probably many who shared the president's views would feel uncomfortable at the question, but that obedience could not be meaningful unless we had ways of processing contradictions between official statements and our personal views. She continued the lesson.

Each of the four teachers in Relief Society teaches once a month. Three weeks later, before Joy's next turn to teach, she was released from her calling and replaced by someone else—according to the president, for not following the manual. When Joy insisted on knowing more, the president announced stiffly: "Church is not the place for discussing these matters."

In short, Joy Smith, a white lifelong Mormon, had transgressed the boundaries of acceptability in her congregation. By identifying Mormonism's highest ecclesiastical leaders with a racist policy, she had dared to interrogate "whiteness," thereby creating an unsafe space for the white members of her ward's Relief Society, beginning with the group's president. Consequently, she had to be punished to communicate to the others that her behavior was inappropriate. Dreama Moon, a professor of communication, analyzes the purpose of "silencing dissenters." Thereby, "the tyranny of bourgeois decorum creates 'safe' spaces in which dominant ideologies go unchallenged, harmony is preserved, and the party line is maintained. Within these 'safe' spaces, dissenting voices are often punished by exclusion and ostracism by the white community."[2]

Joy Smith is my wife and the mother of our two beautiful biracial children, conceived in love in an interracial marriage. Our dilemma is thus public and visible, as was Joy's punishment. Even more humiliating than the public repudiation of Joy's ideas and, by extension, of the acceptability of our family was the fact that the Relief Society president felt compelled to ask a higher authority, the stake Relief Society president, to reteach the same lesson three weeks later in an effort to "make right" what Joy had disrupted. This communicated the president's official possessiveness about whiteness and, in that context, also communicated the attitude that she expected the rest of the women in the ward to share.

In addition to the pain I experienced personally and on behalf of my wife and our children, this incident resulted in a deeper spiritual disruption. As a socially conscious African American Latter-day Saint, I strongly believe that the church should serve as a forum to discuss—not simply approve of—matters of doctrine and also to explore in a thoughtful and spiritual manner related issues of controversy that have an impact on personal belief. The church cannot expect its members to be oblivious to or completely ignore crucial issues of race, gender, and sexuality, particularly given the central role these issues have played in the history of Mormonism from its earliest days. Ideally such ideas should generate intelligent and logical exploration, yielding deeper levels of understanding. As a consequence, silencing individuals who challenge white supremacist thinking in Mormon culture is a form of race evasiveness. Dreama Moon labels such individuals who challenge white supremacist thinking "truth tellers." My courageous, sometimes outspoken wife is a "truth teller" who suffered the repercussions of violating white silence.

My wife's ordeal resonated unpleasantly with an earlier conversation I had had with a high church official, a general authority, that demonstrated other aspects of the dynamics of race evasiveness in the LDS Church. I was urging consideration of a college-level course on race to be offered at the church's flagship institution, Brigham Young University. He questioned the need for such a class, further commenting that such a class would be divisive, dividing "us" rather than uniting "us." This "semantic evasion," as Christina Sleeter notes, personifies "racism making it (rather than ourselves) the subject of sentences. This allows us to say, for example, 'Racism causes poor education in inner-city schools.' *Who* is responsible for the quality of education in inner-city schools? The sentence does not suggest that anyone holds responsibility."[3] The church official, by his statement, probably without meaning to, thus denied any need for the church to address its own lack of racial awareness. He was unwilling to support an institutional intervention that would have permitted the exploration of race in the academy. The effect of his statement was to identify a course about racism as the *cause* of racism, rather than as a potential *solution* to racism.

Inevitably, such unwillingness on the part of church officials to engage in race discussions implicitly endorses and perpetuates the American myth that people of color are now meaningfully and productively engaged in the larger society and that racism is no longer a significant social problem. This belief, though comfortable and comforting, is false. The white pretense that blacks are upwardly mobile and economically solvent—in other words, no longer oppressed—assures the perpetuation of racism. What is needed instead is open and frank discussion or a strategy norm of "race talk." Race talk is an opportunity for important discussions, conversations, and dialogue that open the possibility of demystifying race and raising consciousness about the nature of white racism. It is not the aberration that most whites believe, but rather a fact of life central to the American experience.

Black slaves cleared American forests, drained American swamps, cultivated American land, and offered African medicinal remedies for their American oppressors, yet their contributions have historically gone largely unnoticed. According to James D. Anderson, discussions of race are usually channeled into politicized discussions of the Civil War, Reconstruction, the defense of slavery, and the civil rights movements of the 1960s and 1970s—all areas where race is impossible to ignore.[4] Yet outside these safely historical boundaries, discussing racial beliefs in U.S. society is often treated as a taboo that derails efforts to deal head-on with our past or present racism.

Alas, it has been my experience and observation that the LDS Church also participates to some extent in this national avoidance of race talk, a dynamic with the institutional potential to affect adversely missionary work, baptisms of African Americans, and the retention of African Americans. Its personal, spiritual, and community effects also have serious potential. Evading race talk is particularly problematic because most members of the church subscribe to the reassuring concept that African Americans converts, having found "the gospel," are satisfied and contented, that their lives improve dramatically, that they are just like white members, and that "all is well in Zion." This illusion is a way for whites to suppress the differential experiences that impact the lives of people of color.

To further clarify and problematize the central issues, in this essay I focus on two tenets of "whiteness theory," avoidance of race talk and color blindness. These concepts, in my estimation, offer substantial insights into understanding the prime cause for what I perceive as the continued marginalization of African Americans within the LDS Church. Whiteness theory is an analytical tool that specifically names and displaces whiteness as a monolithic power structure. It demonstrates the "normalization" of whiteness and white privilege at the center of knowledge production. Whiteness theory affirms that "white" is not a biological distinction, but rather a social construction that benefits whites and those passing as white. Among such benefits are "good schools and neighborhoods that provide better material advantages. Safety from toxic material or greater access to medical resources [are] among the material benefits of whiteness. Symbolic forms of privilege would include white conceptions of beauty and intelligence that are not only tied to whiteness but that implicitly exclude people of color."[5]

Whiteness is a cultural and social construction, a system of structural privileges that advantages whites in ways that people of color do not experience. Whiteness is not only limited to bodies and skin color but also to ideas, knowledge production, values, and beliefs that are held as the norm. The ways Americans come to appreciate history, art, literature, good health, and popular culture, for example, are a few advantages of the normalization of whiteness. People of color are rarely seen in movies except as villains or as sidekicks to the white protagonists. Books, greeting cards, children's toys, billboards, and popular magazines are overwhelmingly situated in whiteness. Is this an accident? Whiteness as a protected and often guarded entitlement goes unnoticed and, because unnoticed, also unchallenged. As a result, white people are either unable or unwilling to recognize how their elite position enables them in numerous and significant ways.

My use of whiteness theory in this essay provides an essential understanding of what Joyce King, a scholar of education, calls "dysconscious racism"— "a form of racism that tacitly accepts dominant white norms and privileges, and is not the absence of consciousness (that is, not unconsciousness) but an *impaired* consciousness or distorted way of thinking about race as compared to, for example, critical consciousness."[6] The sociologist David Wellman convincingly argued more than a quarter century ago that uncritical ways of thinking about racial inequity accept certain culturally sanctioned assumptions, myths, and beliefs that justify the social and economic advantages Anglo Americans have as a result of subordinating others.[7]

My motivation in writing this essay is the hope that church members and leaders will take a serious look at how whiteness is "normalized" and secured in American society—specifically, how the church engages in this process in both subtle and unsubtle ways. Although confessions of faith are unusual in a scholarly paper, I am disclosing my religious beliefs to situate my discourse with the reader as clearly and candidly as possible. I write from the position of a convert who chose Mormonism for the beauty of its doctrines, its commitment to healthy family life, and the empowerment inherent in its doctrines of eternal progression. As someone who has made covenants of consecration in Mormonism's most sacred space, I strongly feel that part of what I have to contribute to the community is my awareness of how racist practices and concepts can hamper the full realization of what Mormonism could potentially offer to African Americans. I consider it an integral part of my covenant to speak openly and honestly about the racist folklore I have observed in the church and the harmful social practices that stem from such beliefs. Like any institution that works with, for, and through human beings, the church is characterized by imperfections. Despite my recognition of those imperfections, I affirm my appreciation for and faith in Mormonism as providing answers to my deepest questions of faith and spirituality.

In the pages that follow, I first introduce procedures and enactments of whiteness within the church. I next analyze how whiteness functions as a mechanism for church callings and how spiritual "color blindness," attached to the commonly quoted Mormon scripture "All are alike unto God" (2 Ne. 26:33), is used to deflect attention from the concerns of African Americans and other people of color. I next suggest some ways in which avoidance of race talk functions in Mormonism. I conclude with some informal reflections on the function of the Genesis Group, an unusual church unit in Salt Lake City that is organized outside the normal ward congregational structure with a membership consisting primarily of African Americans. I see such a discussion as helpful in generating reflections about how a similar organization might facilitate restructured thinking about race among church leaders.

Enactments of Mormon Whiteness

Although Mormonism, as a Christian religion, contains strong messages about the inherent worth of each soul ("we are all children of God") and the equality of believers ("all worthy men are eligible to hold priesthood" and "the blessings of the temple are available to all worthy members"), it is also an authoritative institution, with clear levels of hierarchical authority and closely guarded boundaries of power. Although almost all adult members and many youth in any given congregation have "callings" that confer recognized privileges and responsibilities upon them, there is no confusion about how those callings are organized or who, in any given gathering of members, is in charge. This institutional structure extends upward from the congregation through successive levels of organization that are geographical in their boundaries but identical, within those boundaries, to the organizations of counterpart units. That is, several wards form a stake, presided over by a stake president with his counselors and a twelve-man high council. Above the stake presidency is a three-man area presidency; these area presidencies consist of members of the various Quorums of Seventy, the lowest-ranking general authorities. Above the Seventies is the Quorum of the Twelve Apostles, and above the apostles is the three-man First Presidency. The First Presidency and apostles are considered "prophets, seers, and revelators" with global, not regional, authority.

This tight supervisory structure means a high degree of congregational conformity. For instance, no congregation builds its own meetinghouse, selects its own officers, or sponsors its own programs or classes. The lesson manual that my wife used for her lesson was the same manual used worldwide, translated into the appropriate language. Furthermore, even though she was teaching a class consisting exclusively of women, this manual was actually the same as that being used to instruct the men, a (probably unconscious) reflection of the privileging of men over women that is implied by the fact that the hierarchical structure is formed around men.

As Joy also discovered in teaching her lesson on this assigned topic, maintaining silence is one way of preserving the privilege of whiteness. Rather than engaging in any dialogue that highlights racial privileging/discrimination and hence promotes growth in personal and social understanding, white people consciously suppress conflict (passive aggressiveness), not only because they wish to avoid the discomfort of confrontation but also because this avoidance enables them to maintain white hegemony. When white people say, for example, "Let's not be contentious," they eliminate opposition. Without opposition, whiteness always wins.

Unwittingly, the church then becomes a site where whiteness operates in opposition to people of color. Whiteness as a discursive concept looks at how language and symbolism are situated in whiteness as the "natural" state of being. Such ingrained cultural perceptions have historically and contemporarily been framed in dualisms. For example, the Book of Mormon, the book of scripture that gives the church its nickname, explicitly traces the history of two racial groups. One is "white and delightsome" (and righteous, except during periods of backsliding) while the other is "dark and loathsome" (and usually unrighteous).[8] More recently, Spencer W. Kimball, the church president who is credited with the revelation that permitted black men to be ordained to the priesthood, had manifested great concern for Native Americans during his long tenure as an apostle. Speaking in general conference in October 1960, he made a statement that was seen as powerful advocacy for this dispossessed minority but which also illustrates how language powerfully inscribes color consciousness:

> I saw a striking contrast in the progress of the Indian people today. . . . The day of the Lamanites is nigh. For years they have been growing delightsome, and they are now becoming white and delightsome, as they were promised. In this picture of the twenty Lamanite missionaries, fifteen of the twenty were as light as Anglos; five were darker but equally delightsome. The children in the home placement program in Utah are often lighter than their brothers and sisters in the hogans on the reservation.[9]

Such concepts are all functions of whiteness that privilege white "ways of knowing." These "ways of knowing" are invisible to most whites and become apparent (hypervisible) only when threatened. As the unmarked category, whiteness never has to speak its name or say anything racial. As Ruth Frankenburg observes, whiteness retains its space of "neutrality," allowing whites to view the "other" as deviant and inferior, as something to be viewed with fear and loathing, thus reinscribing established patterns of white supremacy. Whites frequently interpret the history of tension between whiteness and the "other" as a "people of color" problem. This explanation permits whites to distance themselves from the "other," while blaming blacks, Native Americans, Asian Americans, and Latinos for America's social problems.[10] The social construction of whiteness allows a discussion of racism without naming as racist anyone who explores how white people benefit from the reproduction of systemic racism.

Institutional Whiteness and Church Callings

A good example of whiteness as a "naturalized" condition in the LDS Church is the manner in which white maleness and leadership are intertwined. Mormon priesthood is an all-male institution that gives ordained men authority to speak in the Lord's name, preside and conduct meetings, administer the ordinances, receive revelations, and serve as called. The church revolves around, and is guided by, this lay priesthood. It would drift into oblivion without it. Church members rely on priesthood leaders to guide and direct institutional policy and to provide spiritual direction for church members.

Historically, however, the institutionalization of white male priesthood dominance has been the norm. Currently, the general leadership of the church continues its overrepresentation of whiteness, a condition that I see as problematic. Is it possible that the general church leadership, who are all white men, know "all ways of knowing" for each racial group, let alone the discourses of other countries and cultures? For many faithful members of the church, the operation of the Holy Ghost upon these inspired leaders compensates for any personal limitations. They feel, in fact, that race is irrelevant because the gospel and the priesthood are able to circumvent social barriers such as race and ethnicity. However, it is also true in Mormon theology that the absolute value placed on moral agency and free choice means that human beings must learn from experience, struggle to overcome failings and limitations, and strive mightily to hear and follow the whisperings of the Holy Spirit. Thus, the time- and culture-bound social and historic context in which Latter-day Saints of different epochs find themselves is as real as the gospel.

Still, this view may not be fully satisfying to others who see clear evidence, as in the Spencer W. Kimball example, that the interpretation of those who hold the most significant positions of authority in the church is also influenced by their Euro-American background. James Scheurich and Michelle Young convincingly argue that "influential people," which would, in my study, include general authorities, "and their 'world-making' or 'reality-making' activities or practices . . . are not separate from the social history within which they live: 'all knowledge is relative to the context in which it is generated.'" And, thus "when academics and public opinion leaders construct knowledge[,] . . . they are influenced by the ideas, assumptions, and norms of the culture and subsocieties in which they are socialized."[11] In other words, knowledge represents the social history of its framer. The position of faith, from which I speak, is that the gospel both includes and transcends social factors. Because of its divine origin, it can and does make truth claims that are absolute, not contingent, and hence transcends many relativistic limitations.

Before the 1978 lifting of the priesthood ban that had generated a century of grievous "race talk," no blacks appeared among the general authorities, confirming the normalized whiteness of the church. In addition, the numerous statements of past church presidents and other lecturers or spokesmen clearly articulated that blacks were ineligible for full membership in the church because they had failed to be "valiant" in the premortal life, language that clearly privileges white males. This explanation was given most directly by Joseph Fielding Smith, then an apostle, in his *The Way to Perfection*. According to Mormon beliefs, every human being existed in a pre-earth life. At one point, a premortal contest ensued between Jesus Christ and Lucifer (who would become Satan) over the conditions of salvation to which human beings would be subject. This contest, called "the war in heaven," required each individual to choose whether to follow Christ, who offered salvation on the basis of freely chosen obedience, or Satan, who would guarantee salvation but only by allowing mortals no free choice. Christ's plan was chosen, and Satan was expelled from this premortal realm along with those who chose to follow him, who became evil spirits to tempt human beings. According to Smith: "There were no neutrals in the war in heaven. All took sides either with Christ or with Satan. Every man (*sic*) had his agency there, and men receive rewards here based upon their actions there, just as they will receive rewards hereafter for deeds done in the body. The Negro, evidently, is receiving the reward he merits."[12] In short, according to Smith, who in 1970 became the tenth president of the church, black men, and hence their entire families, were responsible for their own exclusion from the priesthood. This explanation clearly shifts the blame for being excluded to black men themselves. (Women, of whatever color, have never been ordained to priesthood in Mormonism.)

Despite the lifting of the priesthood ban in 1978 by Smith's successor, only three men of African descent have become general authorities: Helvécio Martins, a Brazilian, who served in the Second Quorum of Seventy; Emmanuel Kissi, a Ghanaian, currently serving in the Third Quorum of the Seventy; and Emmanuel Opare, from Ghana, an Area Authority Seventy. Old stereotypes like the "valiancy" assertion have naturally diminished over time since the need for an explanation has diminished. Still, many church members do not recognize the racist overtones of the language of former church leaders, and anecdotal evidence indicates that white Mormons who grew up before 1978 still offer "non-valiancy" as an explanation when asked why the church once did not ordain black men to the priesthood. Consequently, the "naturalized" authoritative status of the white male discourse in the church is unquestioned, invisible, or confirmed as God's will. As a result, it seems normal to see white males call one another to important positions. Although these callings require sacrifice and are presented as opportunities for service, they also confer privilege and authority on those who hold them. Whites, both within and outside of the church, are seldom attuned to seeing people of color represented, valued, or empowered other than as entertainers, athletes, and other conveyers of pleasure for white audiences.

Although it is not possible to calculate the numbers of African Americans in the church today, observation and anecdotal reports suggest that the number is growing, especially in Africa. Hence, the absence of even one black face among the general authorities seated on the stand at each semiannual general conference seems problematic to concerned observers.[13] The ability to name these leading priesthood quorums as sites of whiteness is the beginning of awareness that can encourage deeper thought and eventual reform.

Color Blindness in LDS Discourse

In race discourse, color blindness means that people pretend not to notice or recognize race difference. It is a common idea in a variety of societal institutions, including the LDS Church. The Book of Mormon emphatically affirms: "For he [the Lord] inviteth them all to come unto him and partake of his goodness; and he denieth none that come unto him, black and white, bond and free, male and female; and he remembereth the heathen; and *all are alike unto God,* both Jew and Gentile" (2 Ne. 26:33; italics mine). This beautiful articulation of the ideal of human equality before God and the divine desire to bestow salvation on all holds up an unquenchable hope for all Latter-day Saints of whatever color.

While this scriptural verse is positive and hopeful, whiteness theory provides tools for observing that this particular verse has become operationalized as a way to maintain the modus operandi of differential socialization even among Mormons. Probably few would question that in the larger American society, white Americans are not neutral in associating with people of color, especially African Americans. Typically, they exert considerable effort to avoid them in schools, at work, and in other organizations, nor do they want to have the same kind of life experiences, even while they deny that they themselves have racist feelings. According to Christina Sleeter, whites live in largely white neighborhoods, socialize with other whites, use white media, vote for and sustain other whites, and so forth, and they are, for the most part, unconscious of the mechanism of selection that is at work in doing so.[14]

Color blindness, as Andrew Hacker notes in *Two Nations,* is a romantic notion that has yet to change the landscape of power and influence.[15] People of color remain at the margins with little influence in almost all organizations, including churches. Even so-called model minorities like some Asian Americans, who are more "accepted," are expected to be white-identified.

Another key fallacy of institutional color blindness is the common assumption that all Americans share a similar social experience. The language of color blindness hides racial oppression, making it harder to detect. In this way the language of color blindness deflects attention from those who are most oppressed in U.S. society while allowing whites to retain their racial privileges as the "normal" state of Americanness; whites can then absolve themselves of racism, congratulate themselves on not being prejudiced, and consequently further distance themselves from the "other." The discourse of color blindness, according to Ruth Frankenburg, "is good only insofar as their [people of color] 'coloredness' can be bracketed and ignored, and this bracketing is contingent on the ability or the decision—in fact, the virtue—of a 'noncolored'—or white—self. Color-blindness, despite the best intentions of its adherents, in this sense preserves the power structure inherent in essentialist racism."[16]

From my experience and observations, I have learned that LDS Church leaders at all levels, although well intentioned, have nothing psychologically equivalent to an affirmative action program. The candidate's worthiness and the leader's feelings of inspiration after prayer are the operative criteria in issuing callings. Again, the position of faith, to which I personally subscribe, is that the Holy Ghost communicates God's will to the leader, and many leaders tell how they are inspired to select someone who at first glance would seem to be an unlikely candidate.[17] However, the very strengths of these subjective procedures are also weaknesses. Because there is no way to evaluate this process objectively, it is at least possible that whiteness is still privileged in LDS wards and stakes and elsewhere and that white church leaders will feel most comfortable with individuals who reside in similar communities, have similar backgrounds, and "look like" them. When the white male leaders in a given unit make a mental list of who is worthy to serve in church callings or who the Lord needs for the job, it is possible that they may unconsciously exclude male African Americans and other men of color if the position to be filled requires ordination to the priesthood. These local leaders may have had little experience with people of color. Such forms of institutional whiteness are difficult to detect in Mormondom, I believe, because they are masked in authority, because white church leaders almost always reproduce similar white worldviews, and because members faithfully accept that such decisions are inspired without questioning them, let alone opposing them or proposing alternatives.

From my perspective, it would be very desirable to have more people of color given broader opportunities to serve in positions that can redirect and raise the consciousness of white church members. The lived experiences that members of color can present are often different from white ways of knowing. I believe that they can provide the church with a richer narration of how people of color appropriate and utilize gospel principles. I would be interested in encouraging efforts to identify and call African Americans, both men and women, to a broader range of opportunities to serve.

I am also interested in explicating and articulating the complex of sometimes unarticulated feelings that constitute a leader's position that a given individual is worthy and competent. It has been my experience that people of color who are white-identified (in other words, "safe") are more likely to receive callings to visible positions. As George Lipsitz, an ethnic studies professor, suggests, such individuals benefit from their "possessive investment" in vicarious whiteness.[18] For example, the same bishop of my ward who released my wife from her Relief Society calling informed me that I had been considered for a position associated with the bishopric as financial secretary but had been "passed over" because, in his words, the ward "needed someone who was good with numbers." He doubtless communicated this detail to assure me that I was not seen as unworthy, without realizing that it may have been no consolation to be seen as incompetent instead. While I am sure all bishops have their own reasons for calling men to the ward executive team, I was surprised to learn that mathematical ability was such a major criterion for this position. Normative Mormon discourse did not allow me to question his decision lest I seemed to be resisting his authority. Nor did the discourse allow me to suggest that I felt I had spiritual gifts and talents—including my racial sensitivities—that would have allowed me to contribute to the spiritual welfare of the ward members. Such an expression on my part might be seen as "aspiring" for a position and denying the bishop's inspiration. However, this example brought home to me the fact that the ostensible harmlessness in privileging subjective methods for issuing leadership callings has the unintended negative side effect of resecuring whiteness, anchoring it to the center at the expense of those who are forced to inhabit the margins. This repeated pattern can have a pernicious effect on the self-concept of Latter-day Saints of color and can permit church leaders to avoid race issues while insisting that they are color blind.

I witnessed another example of spiritual color blindness in the experience of Sister Fiki (pseudonym), a Maori member of the ward. Fiki expressed to me her concerns for her fifteen-year-old son, Lati. Despite his faithfulness in attending all church meetings and activities, he was frustrated because every other young man in his teachers' quorum had had the opportunity to serve for several months as president except him. When I brought Fiki's concern about her son's resentment to the bishop, he became quite defensive, insisting that "the time was not right" for Lati to become quorum president. In his conversation with me, there was no verbal recognition of Lati's talents and potential contributions. As far as he was concerned, the Lord decided such matters.

Although the bishop's action was taken unconsciously, by identifying the Lord's will as not only the ultimate source but the only source for callings, he denied any need to examine his own behavior and thoughts for possible bias.

To further justify his race-avoidance tactic, the bishop insisted that he was not prejudiced; after all, he had served the church in Africa and the Polynesian Islands as a missionary. This defensiveness demonstrates that color blindness is not necessarily overt racism but rather a distinctive discourse that avoids confronting the reality of discrimination while upholding the institutional whiteness of the church. His defensiveness also reveals the discomfort typical of most white men when race is addressed in such situations. The avoidance of race talk is similar to color blindness, but race avoidance is selective engagement of difference; color blindness avoids engagement altogether.

I am happy to report that, several months later, Lati was called as quorum president. I was thrilled at the announcement; however, I wished it could have happened before Lati developed feelings of restiveness and resentment—before, in short, he had to grapple with negative feelings stemming from treatment that he attributed to his color. I would like to encourage sensitivity training for church leaders regarding two critical aspects of racial socialization: (1) race shapes the lives of people of color in significant ways; and (2) white people need the skills and tools to identify racism as a very real social phenomenon before institutional change can occur. Despite the limitations of affirmative action, it had the effect of forcing white leaders to look—and look hard—for suitable candidates.

Evasion of Race Talk in Mormonism

The announcement lifting the priesthood ban on blacks in 1978 was clearly a turning point in Mormon race relations. Yet the refusal to engage in race talk persists even more than twenty-five years later. It has been my experience that white members of the church love to hear stories about people of color who have joined the church and made a transition to the LDS "way of life." Part of this reaction is the joy that any believer takes in hearing the faith journey of another who has found the same spiritual path; but in the case of people of color, white reactions seem to have two additional effects. First, white members who might feel discomfort and guilt about racism seem consoled and relieved by such stories. Second, as already mentioned, such conversion stories are usually processed in white consciousness as evidence that "all is well in Zion." Similar reactions greet news stories about topics such as the growth of the church in Africa and President Gordon B. Hinckley's history-making tour there. Unfortunately, such perceptions still avoid the social reality of racism that impacts the black experience both inside and outside of the church.

Most white members would not see the daily implications of whiteness, due in part to the invisibility of whiteness. Consequently, they perpetuate racist beliefs and practices. Dreama Moon notes, "The white enculturation process simultaneously depends on both the embracement and denial of whiteness. Thus, the 'trick' of white enculturation is racially to produce and reproduce white people through the creation of the illusion of a 'white' world, while simultaneously draining that 'whiteness' of any elements that would mark it as a specific structural and cultural location."[19] My wife's punishment for opposing whiteness and racial invisibility illustrates the institution's willingness to forbid confronting the controversial issue of interracial marriage. Rather than embrace race talk as a liberating discourse, the Relief Society president embraced her own whiteness as authoritative while refusing to see the potential harm in her actions. Both this woman and the bishop became adults after 1954, the year of the landmark U.S. Supreme Court decision in *Brown v. Board of Education,* ordering desegregation in education. Yet the generations that have followed have failed to dismantle the institutional structure of racism. It is not uncommon to hear young white people excuse their elders' racism by saying, "That's just how she was raised," once again evading race talk. Moreover, white Mormons of any age readily forgive manifestations of racial thinking or behavior among their leaders because of their good deeds and self-sacrifice. While the compassion that motivates such behavior is commendable, the results can be disturbing. A sanitized atmosphere envelopes racialized procedures and methods, repressing discussion about the life experiences of its members of color. The "one size fits all" policy is sobering or disconcerting, not only for African Americans but also globally among ethnic Latter-day Saints.

The Genesis Case Study

To encourage different models and approaches to rethinking race and allowing it to become visible in the white church, Mormonism might profitably look at the contributions of the black church.[20] This term is used in the literature to denote the worship space created by black Christians who were excluded from or marginalized within white churches. Rather than being a specific denomination, it refers to a self-created safe space within which black people could explore their faith and connect with Jesus Christ outside the boundedness of the rational, objective, detached method and modes of worship typical of white worship spaces. The tradition of shouting and emotional participation typical of worship in the black church is interpreted by many whites to be "primitive" or "immature," in opposition to "sophisticated" and "mature" manifestations in white spaces. Typical white hymns, for example, manifest more abstract ideas and stricter meter than Negro spirituals, which typically speak of a history of struggle coupled with an intensely personal relationship to Jesus.[21] The black church has traditionally offered a safe place for race talk. Its rich spiritual tradition is conceptually grounded in the life and mission of Jesus Christ but is behaviorally manifested in active community development and psychological and social support.[22] During the peak of the 1960s civil rights movement, for example, African Americans felt empowered by parallels between their struggle and the plight of the children of Israel as they sought to escape Egyptian bondage. The black church provided an opportunity for strategizing resistance to white hegemony and social injustices, thus significantly strengthening black resolve against the terror of whiteness.

Although Mormonism is not a traditional white church, it subscribes to the white conventions of correct worship. For example, even an emotional talk or testimony will elicit little or no audience response except an echoing "amen" when the talk concludes. Clearly, if African Americans who have actively participated in the black church become Mormon, they must abandon many of their traditional religious traditions and social practices and subscribe to a white style of worship or be considered transgressors of the church's cultural norms.

In this regard, the example of the Genesis Group is important. Neither a ward nor a branch—and hence completely outside the geographical norms of Mormon organization—this unit was organized on October 19, 1971, in Salt Lake City to meet some of the social and spiritual needs of marginalized members of color. The intent was to help black members in Utah feel included within white Mormon culture, while taking pride in their own racial background. The fact that it was organized by members of the First Presidency and Quorum of the Twelve (Joseph Fielding Smith, Nathan Eldon Tanner, and Harold B. Lee) provides it with the necessary authority to situate it within the church structure, even though it has to occupy a unique position. For instance, although the purpose of sacrament meeting, the most important Sunday meeting in every unit, is to partake of the emblems of Christ's crucifixion to renew the individual's baptismal covenant, this ordinance, which requires a priesthood-holding officiator, was not part of the Genesis meetings. Nor were such ordinances as the blessing and naming of infants, baptisms, and confirmations performed in Genesis. Rather, each person who attended Genesis meetings had his or her formal membership in a "mainstream" ward. There was a clear distinction between a "real" ward and Genesis's contingent and incomplete status.

No doubt many felt that the 1978 revelation allowing priesthood ordination for black men eliminated the need for the Genesis Group altogether, but its members still felt that it met needs that their geographic wards did not. The group's members still meet once a month on a Sunday evening for fellowship, music, and sharing their feelings about God. My wife and I have attended some of these meetings with our children and have enjoyed the fellowship and good spirit there. I respect and admire the selfless service of its officers and participants. The group is clearly meeting many of the genuine needs of its participants, and I have only the deepest respect for its achievements. It is particularly important in meeting the needs of white parents who have adopted black children and in giving those youngsters other black Mormons with whom they can relate. Darius Gray, the former president of Genesis, has articulated a vision of how Genesis must be more than the food, fun, and festivities that are often construed as multiculturalism. In an interview in 2001, he commented: "June of 1978 changed so many things and left unchanged too many things. We are far more tolerant of African-Americans in our presence, and while we are, the lack of comfort with ethnic and racial diversity affects the reception that blacks receive. While we've progressed greatly, we have yet a long way to go."[23]

Even though I recognize the important achievement and role of the Genesis Group, I must also confess to some disappointment and lack of personal satisfaction in the institutional identity that Genesis currently espouses. The brief comments that follow should not be taken as criticism of Genesis as it currently exists or recommendations that it change but rather as free-floating reflections on alternate identities and roles that could be assumed by an organization such as Genesis.

From the perspective of whiteness theory, an organization like Genesis provides blacks with a pseudo-safe space outside the traditional boundaries of the LDS ward while replicating, in every significant way, the established "whiteness" norm of Mormonism. Consequently, regardless of actual skin color, many of the black folks attending the Genesis Group have adopted many of the same mannerisms and behaviors that make them socially white.[24] As an institutional identity, the Genesis Group imposes LDS social and religious practices against a backdrop of blackness, but the framework is established by whiteness. From the perspective of whiteness theory, foregrounding whiteness as a norm requires that black members ignore the past and present racism within the church.

If a group like Genesis were to construct a different, more activist identity, it could strengthen Mormon voices of color by explicitly celebrating and articulating the diverse experiences of its members. It could build coalitions with the general church leadership to implement changes in the power structure. One of the most important functions it could serve would be as a site in which current church leaders could repudiate the Mormon history of discrimination against peoples of African descent and deconstruct the racist teachings that have continued to the present because such explicit dismantling has not occurred.

White and black members together must share the burden of creating change, interrogating how whiteness creates barriers for progress. It is not unusual to hear socially conscious black and white members counsel patience, saying, "Change is coming, but slowly." While I share their faith that the Lord has a timetable for change and that some of his purposes may be inscrutable to our limited mortal perceptions, I also am keenly aware that, from another perspective, the likelihood that white men occupying privileged positions can transcend race is small, especially when they are largely unconscious of their privilege and largely unaware that they have an investment in white supremacy that speaks through them, whether or not they perceive themselves as racist. Without conscious effort to become aware of racism and deliberate effort to dismantle it, change is not likely to occur.

Conclusion

In the years since 1776, the United States of America emerged from a welter of conflicting philosophies and energies, but among them unquestionably was an ideology of white supremacy. As history has taught us, it will take more than civil rights legislation to reverse the polarized psychological effects of racialized thinking. Whether whites admit it or not—in fact, *because* many whites cannot see it—they harbor racist thoughts that are embedded in organizational cultures. Lingering racism embedded in the organizational culture of the LDS Church, the 1978 priesthood revelation notwithstanding, is a significant case in point. This chapter used whiteness theory to explore the extent to which color blindness and avoidance of race talk hamper the LDS Church in realizing the ideal articulated in its scripture: that "all are alike unto God." It is my conviction that both of these tendencies inhibit progress toward true racial equality and that such progress begins by questioning "whiteness" and acknowledging that race matters.

Notes

The epigraph for this chapter comes from Audre Lorde, "Age, Race, Class, and Sex: Women Redefining Difference," in *Sister Outsider: Essays and Speeches* (Freedom, Calif.: Crossing Press, 1984), 114.

1. The Relief Society has weekly spiritual lessons, conducts a number of educational and charitable activities, and encourages the women to provide informal service to each other.

2. Dreama Moon, "White Enculturation and Bourgeois Ideology: The Discursive Production of 'Good (White) Girls,'" in *Whiteness: The Communication of Social Identity,* ed. Thomas K. Nakayama and Judith N. Martin (Thousand Oaks, Calif.: Sage, 1999), 183.

3. Christina Sleeter, "White Silence, White Solidarity," in *Race Traitor,* ed. Noel Ignatiev and John Garvey (New York: Routledge, 1996), 260.

4. James D. Anderson, "How We Learn about Race through History," in *Learning History in America: Schools, Culture, and Politics,* ed. Lloyd Kramer, Donald Reid, and William Barney (Minneapolis: University of Minnesota Press, 1994), 87–106.

5. Audrey Thompson, Summary of Whiteness Theory, <www.pauahtun.org/Whiteness-Summary-1.html>, accessed November 11, 2002.

6. Joyce King, "Dysconscious Racism: Ideology, Identity, and the Miseducation of Teachers," *Journal of Negro Education* 60, no. 2 (1991): 135.

7. David T. Wellman, *Portraits of White Racism,* 2d ed. (Cambridge: Cambridge University Press, 1977).

8. For example, the first (1830) edition of the Book of Mormon describes God's punishment of the Lamanites for their unrighteousness: "Wherefore, as they were white, and exceedingly fair and delightsome, that they might not be enticing unto my people the Lord God did cause a skin of blackness to come upon them . . . that they shall be loathsome unto thy people [the Nephites]." However, if they repent, "many generations shall not pass away among them, save they shall be a white and a delightsome people" (72–73, 117). The first edition is not divided into chapters and verses. In 1981 when the current edition was prepared, the editors left the first passage unchanged (2 Ne. 5:21–22) but changed the latter part of the second one to read: "save they shall be a pure and a delightsome people" (2 Ne. 30:6).

9. Spencer W. Kimball, "The Day of the Lamanites," *Improvement Era,* December 1960, 922–23. "Lamanite" is the Book of Mormon name for the "dark and loathsome" racial group whose members, in Mormon belief, are the ancestors of Native Americans.

10. Ruth Frankenburg, *White Women, Race Matters: The Social Construction of Whiteness* (Minneapolis: University of Minnesota Press, 1993).

11. James Scheurich and Michelle Young, "White Racism among White Faculty: From Critical Understanding to Anti-Racist Activity," in *The Racial Crisis in American Higher Education: Continuing Challenges for the Twenty-first Century,* ed. William A. Smith, Philip G. Altbach, and Kofi Lomotey, rev. ed. (New York: State University of New York Press, 2002), 230.

12. Joseph Fielding Smith, *The Way to Perfection* (Salt Lake City: Deseret Book, 1931), 67.

13. Only the First Presidency, Quorum of the Twelve, and First Quorum of Seventy are seated before the congregation in these conferences.

14. Sleeter, "White Silence, White Solidarity," 262.

15. Andrew Hacker, *Two Nations: Black and White, Separate, Hostile, Unequal* (New York: Scribners, 1992).

16. Frankenburg, *White Women, Race Matters,* 147.

17. For example, at the October 2002 general conference, Boyd K. Packer, acting president of the Quorum of the Twelve, related this experience when he was sent out to call a second patriarch to share the labors of the aging patriarch:

The stake president recommended a man with much leadership experience. However, I did not get the feeling that he should be the patriarch. I knew that the

First Presidency had said to stake presidents: "Because a man has filled with credit a presiding office and has attained a good age is no reason why he should or should not make a good patriarch; . . . [He should be one who has] developed within [him] the spirit of the patriarchs; in fact, this should be [his] leading characteristic, . . . [a man] of wisdom, possessed of the gift and spirit of blessing as well." As the evening meeting was about to begin, an older man came partway down the aisle and, unable to find a seat, went to the back of the chapel. He was not quite as well dressed as most of the others and obviously had spent much time out-of-doors. I whispered to the stake president, "Who is that man?"

Sensing what was on my mind, he said, "Oh, I don't think he could be our patriarch. He lives at the far edge of an outlying ward and has never held any leadership in a bishopric or high council." He was invited to give the opening prayer, and he had said but a few words when that confirmation came, as it does by revelation, "This is the patriarch." Boyd K. Packer, "The Stake Patriarch," *Ensign,* November 2002, 43.

Interestingly enough, the patriarch who was already serving had had exactly the same feeling when he saw the man enter the meeting hall.

18. George Lipsitz, *The Possessive Investment in Whiteness: How White People Profit from Identity Politics* (Philadelphia: Temple University Press, 1998).

19. Moon, "White Enculturation and Bourgeois Ideology," 179.

20. See C. Eric Lincoln and Lawrence H. Mamiya, *The Black Church in the African American Experience* (Durham, N.C.: Duke University Press, 1990).

21. See James Cone, *For My People: Black Theology and the Black Church* (Maryknoll, N.Y.: Orbis Books, 1984).

22. Beverly Daniel Tatum, *Why Are All the Black Kids Sitting Together in the Cafeteria? And Other Conversations about Race: A Psychologist Explains the Development of Racial Identity* (New York: Basic Books, 1997), 83.

23. Quoted in Carrie Moore, "LDS Blacks Seek Inclusion among Utahns," *Deseret News,* November 17, 2001, E-1.

24. I use the term "socially white" not as a pejorative but rather as a way to demonstrate the complexity of racial identification. Racial group identification is not a "fixed" construct. Race is an arbitrary, socially constructed human phenomenon that shifts depending on a number of factors. For example, geographical location, social class position, and occupational status are among a few variables that influence a person's so-called racial identification. The LDS Church is a mainstream, white, middle-class religious organization, so it should be no surprise that African Americans who join the faith tend to be middle class as opposed to working class. (For a more complete discussion, see Cardell Jacobson's chapter in the present book.) Just because someone is identified as phenotypically black doesn't necessarily mean that he or she identifies with the concerns of black people. Some blacks distance themselves from any semblance of "blackness" to find greater acceptance among whites. This phenomenon is known in the social science literature as internalized oppression or assimilation. In other words, middle-class African Americans who attend predominantly white churches become adept at reflecting the norms and values of the white middle class in a particular geographical and social space. With respect to black people in the Genesis group, many whom I have encountered maintain a positive black identity while others adopt a more social and middle-class white identity.

CONTRIBUTORS

ALMA ALLRED is the director of commuter services at the University of Utah and teaches LDS Church history at the University of Utah Institute of Religion.

NEWELL G. BRINGHURST is an instructor of history and political science at the College of the Sequoias in Visalia, California. He is the author of *Saints, Slaves, and Blacks: The Changing Place of Black People within Mormonism; Brigham Young and the Expanding American Frontier; Fawn McKay Brodie: A Biographer's Life;* and *Visalia's Fabulous Fox: A Theater Story.* He has edited a fourth book, *Reconsidering No Man Knows My History: Fawn M. Brodie and Joseph Smith in Retrospect,* and has written and contributed numerous essays to various dictionaries, anthologies, and other edited works.

RONALD G. COLEMAN is an associate professor in the Department of History and the Ethnic Studies Program at the University of Utah. He has been an educational consultant and has lectured at colleges and universities on African Americans in the American West. His publications include chapters and articles in *The Peoples of Utah, Utah Historical Quarterly,* and *The World Encyclopedia of Slavery.*

KEN DRIGGS is a sixth-generation member of the Church of Jesus Christ of Latter-day Saints and has attended the Atlanta Ward of the Atlanta Stake since 1997. He is a criminal defense lawyer, specializing in the death penalty, and a legal historian. Driggs has published extensively on Mormon history and on the death penalty. His first book is *Evil among Us: The Texas Mormon Missionary Murders.*

JESSIE L. EMBRY is the assistant director of the Charles Redd Center for Western Studies and an instructor of history at Brigham Young University. She is the author of seven books and over seventy articles, including *Black Saints in a White Church: Contemporary African American Mormons; "In His Own Language": Mormon Spanish-speaking Congregations in the United States;* and *Asian American Mormons: Bridging Cultures.*

DARIUS A. GRAY, a former journalist, was senior staff reporter and chief photographer at the CBS television affiliate in Salt Lake City. He also was an assistant on African affairs to a U.S. senator. He is an independent business consultant and a small business owner. Gray has presided over the Genesis Group, an official arm of the Church of Jesus Christ of Latter-day Saints organized in 1971 to support church members of African descent.

CARDELL K. JACOBSON is a professor of sociology at Brigham Young University where he does research and teaches classes on social psychology, race and ethnic relations, social problems, and sociology of religion. His recent publications have focused on denominational, racial, and ethnic differences in fatalism; factors predicting intergroup marriage; and persistent intentions to be childless. He has two books in process, an edited collection on experiences of minority members in the LDS Church and a monograph on intergroup marriage.

ARMAND L. MAUSS is professor emeritus of sociology and religious studies at Washington State University, now residing in Irvine, California. He is a past editor of the *Journal for the Scientific Study of Religion* and past president of the Mormon History Association. Mauss is the author of scores of articles and of two books on the Mormons: *The Angel and the Beehive: The Mormon Struggle with Assimilation* and *All Abraham's Children: Changing Mormon Conceptions of Race and Lineage*. With Lester E. Bush, he is coeditor and coauthor of *Neither White nor Black: Mormon Scholars Confront the Race Issue in a Universal Church*.

DARRON T. SMITH is a lecturer at Utah Valley State College and an adjunct faculty member at Brigham Young University. He practices as a physician assistant and is a doctoral candidate at the University of Utah in the Department of Education, Culture, and Society. He has written extensively in the area of race and serves as a column editor for *Sunstone* magazine.

INDEX

The University of Illinois Press
is a founding member of the
Association of American University Presses.

―――――――――――――

Composed in 9/13 ITC Stone Serif
with Stone Sans display
by Jim Proefrock
at the University of Illinois Press
Manufactured by Maple-Vail
Book Manufacturing Group

University of Illinois Press
1325 South Oak Street
Champaign, IL 61820-6903
www.press.uillinois.edu